FROM FANATICS TO FOLK

PATRICIA R. PESSAR ────────────────

FROM FANATICS TO FOLK

Brazilian Millenarianism and Popular Culture

DUKE UNIVERSITY PRESS   Durham and London   2004

© 2004 Duke University Press

All rights reserved

Printed in the United States of

America on acid-free paper ∞

Designed by Amy Ruth Buchanan

Typeset in Quadraat by Tseng

Information Systems, Inc.

Library of Congress Cataloging-

in-Publication data appear on the

last printed page of this book.

Frontis: Romeiros on a pilgrimage,

Juazeiro, 1974.

For two saintly women

and one wonderfully mortal man,

Maria das Dores dos Santos,

Irene Oberfield Pessar,

and Gil Joseph

CONTENTS

ILLUSTRATIONS

ACKNOWLEDGMENTS

At key moments in my life when I finally made the right decision or took the appropriate move, my father would playfully inquire, "What took you so long?" Were he alive today, my father might well pose this same question on the appearance of this book. The most professionally expedient step would have been to transform my 1976 dissertation on the Pedro Batista millenarian movement immediately into a book. At that time my research on popular religiosity in Brazil was arguably ahead of its day, but it failed to adequately explore the ways in which millenarianism was engaged with the state, church, and larger social forces. Realizing that I lacked the tools to move in these directions, I chose to publish several articles on millenarianism and defer the task of writing a more integrated and comparative study of the Pedro Batista movement. In the meantime I set my sights on a very different topic: international migration and refugee movements in the Americas.

During the long hiatus I continued to mull over solutions to the questions and challenges posed by my 1970s Brazilian research. The three people to whom I dedicate this book proved invaluable to this decades-long pursuit. Each in her or his own way has been an inspiration and advocate. Maria das Dores dos Santos (Dona Dodô) was the leader of the millenarian community of Santa Brígida when I first arrived in 1973. She is referred to by most of her followers as *madrinha* (godmother) Dodô. Certainly in her kindness, willingness to mentor, and unparalleled graciousness, she has been in every way a godmother to me and my project. This book documents and celebrates her remarkable life.

The second person who shepherded this project is my mother Irene Oberfield Pessar. She, along with my father, displayed nothing but support and enthusiasm as their twenty-four-year-old daughter headed off to a remote village in Northeast Brazil, a spot that most Brazilians dismissively labeled "*o fim do mundo*" (the end of the world). It was my mother who continuously reminded me that I was the guardian of a book that needed to be written. It is ironic that, early on, she urged me to write myself into the narrative and to bring a sense of intimacy and humanity to my tale. This was in the late 1970s when figures like Oscar Lewis were derided as popularists and the line between empirical ethnography and more humanistic prose was vigilantly guarded. I am deeply indebted to my mother who insisted I write *my* book. I also thank those pioneers who had the wisdom and courage to write more experimental ethnographies over the course of the 1980s and 1990s. I am the beneficiary of their example.

This book would never have become as thoroughly historicized nor have moved into matters of power and popular culture had it not been for Gil Joseph, my partner in debate, in wrestling with scholarly conundrums, and in a love for rural Latin America. More than any other scholar and friend, Gil has showered me with his characteristic enthusiasm and advocacy—never more appreciated than at those times when my own resolve has flagged. I had the good sense and fortune to marry this loving and inspiring man. This book has benefited immeasurably from long and far-ranging conversations with Gil about history and anthropology, power and resistance, hegemony and popular culture. I have also profited from our jointly taught graduate seminars on resistance and survival in rural Latin America, and from Gil's adept reading of multiple drafts of this book. We also are fortunate to share lives as parents. When I decided to return to Brazil in the summer of 1999 to conduct additional ethnographic and archival research, Gil seamlessly stepped into the role of sole parent. I thank him and our son, Matthew, for thriving while I basked in a long overdue return to Santa Brígida.

My interest in the topic of millenarianism dates back to my undergraduate days at Barnard College. I thank Mario Bick, Dennis Dalton, Marvin Harris, Abe Rossman, and Joan Vincent for kindling this interest and nurturing a youthful anthropologist in the making. In graduate school at the University of Chicago I focused on the study of symbolic anthropology and decided to pursue research in rural Brazil. Shepard Forman and Terry Turner guided my study of cultural production and social movements in Brazil. I am especially indebted to Shepard for having encouraged me to investigate the Pedro Batista movement. Victor Turner sparked my interest in religion, charisma, and the relationship between symbols and power. Moreover, he and Edie created a supportive and intellectually effervescent environment for all around them. I was also fortunate to enjoy the comradeship of spectacular peers in graduate school and in the field. They include Arjun Appadurai, Val Daniel, Steve Foldes, Riv-Ellen Prell, Leni Silverstein, Steve Soiffer, and Greg Urban.

Over the years that I have conducted research and published on Brazilian millenarianism, many scholars have graciously provided guidance and agreed to critique my work. They include Thales de Azevedo, Jan Brukman, John Butler, Kamari Clarke, Emilia Viotti da Costa, Roberto da Matta, Bela Bianco Feldman, Lou Goodman, Beth Jackson, Gil Joseph, Mary Ann Mahoney, Sérgio Muniz, Lidia Santos, Stuart Schwartz, Eric Van Young, Paul Vanderwood, and Barbara Weinstein. Paul and Barbara deserve special thanks for agreeing to read my manuscript on two occasions and for providing extraordinarily cogent suggestions. I am also grateful to those Yale graduate students in anthropology and history who over the years have helped me to hone ideas and refine my manuscript. In the last stage of my ethnographic and archival research I benefited immeasurably from the assistance and camaraderie of three young women. Amy Chazkel conducted archival research in Salvador and Rio in the summer and fall of 1998 and conducted interviews briefly in Santa Brígida. The following summer Vivian Flanzer and Heloisa Griggs accompanied me to Santa Brígida and proved to be the brightest and most dedicated research assistants an ethnographer could ever hope for. Heloisa returned to Santa Brígida and Salvador in the summer of 2000 to conduct interviews and gather additional archival material. She has also contributed to the transcription and translation of tapes and documents. Without Heloisa's assistance and good cheer, this book would have taken even longer and proved far less fun to write.

My project has benefited from the generosity of several funders. I received support in the mid-1970s from the Dougherty Foundation and the National Institutes of Mental Health. Faculty grants from both Yale University's Provost's Office and the Yale Center for International and Area Studies supported the research and writing I completed over the course of the late 1990s and early 2000s. I am especially grateful to Yale colleagues Abbas Amanat, K. David Jackson, Charles Long, Gus Ranis, Stuart Schwartz, and Bryan Wolf for their interest in my work and willingness to help me obtain funding from Yale University. For help in the preparation and production of this book, special thanks go to my incomparable editor Valerie Millholland and her staff at Duke University Press, and to my colleagues at Yale, Nancy Phillips, Kathy Sulkes, Cheryl Morrison, Beatriz Riefkohl, and Sarah Morrill.

There is of course another brand of generosity, and it is one of the spirit. This brand has kept me buoyed over the many years I have worked on this project. For this love and support I thank my parents, Hank and Irene Pessar; my sister, Linda Pessar Cowan, and her family; my grandmother, Lee Oberfield; my in-laws, Leonard and Norma Joseph; and most of all Gil and Matthew.

I have been a professional anthropologist for more than three decades, and my fieldwork has taken me to many places. Much like a first love, my heart and thoughts have always returned to Santa Brígida. Other stints of fieldwork have taught me that this is not only a matter of "firsts" but also a consequence of having been welcomed and accepted by an extraordinary group of individuals. The *romeiros* (pilgrims who settled in Santa Brígida) and *baianos* (original inhabitants) initially indulged me when my language and rural living skills were rudimentary. They have graciously allowed me to accompany their lives over several decades and have wholeheartedly encouraged me to share my observations with others. I have been blessed in countless ways for having maintained this association. I have learned the true meaning of faith and devotion and have been the recipient of countless acts of kindness. Many more inhabitants of Santa Brígida and Northeast Brazil have helped me over the years than I could hope to personally acknowledge and thank. Consequently, I apologize to those I do not mention by name. Several, however, require special recognition: Dona Maria das Dores dos Santos, Dona Cirilia Vieira and her entire beloved family, José Apóstolo da Silva, Mãe Ana, José Vigario, José Caetano, Joaquim Pedro Lucas and family, Dona Bilú, Dona Bahia, Dona Cícera, Dona Dina, Dona Pedrina, Dona Raimunda, Dom Elias, Raimundo Santana Gomes, Rosália Rodrigues França, Antônio França dos Santos and family, Lindoaldo Alves de Oliveira, José Rodrigues dos Santos, José and Julio Oliveira and family, Geraldo Domingos Neto, Apolinário Neto, the Ribeiro family, Antônio Bispo dos Santos and family, Eugênio dos Santos and family, the Paschoal family, João and Antônio Calunga, Zenor Pereira Teixeira, João Gonçalves de Cavalho Sá, Geraldo Portela, Monsenhor Francisco José de Oliveira, Padre Murilo de Sá Barreto, Padre Francisco Teles, Padre Rosevaldo, Marco Antônio Dantas de Almeida, Maria Rodrigues, Titus Riedl, and Paolo Marconi. To them and many others in Northeast Brazil who have shared their knowledge, deep convictions, and unstinting hospitality with me, I say, "*Deus lhe paguem.*"

INTRODUCTION

Iconic images of a communion wafer soaked in Christ's blood; a religious leader's severed head affixed to a spike and paraded through the streets of Salvador, Bahia; and nearly half of the entire Brazilian army pitted against a redoubt of starving yet determined rebels. It is little wonder that millenarian struggles have riveted the attention of everyday Brazilians and a host of international scholars and artists. For the most part people have been drawn to the large and dramatic turn-of-the-twentieth-century movements of Juazeiro, Canudos, and Contestado.[1] While I share this interest, I treat these three movements only secondarily and in the context of a smaller and less-known movement founded in the late 1930s by the penitent Pedro Batista.

The Pedro Batista Movement

After years of battling a mysterious and debilitating illness, Pedro Batista one day arose from his sickbed, drawn to the religious text *Missão Abreviada*. Glancing down at a drawing of Jesus praying at the foot of an angel, Batista experienced a sudden calling to return to his native Northeastern Brazil in order to preach about the impending apocalypse. Thus the middle-aged man who earlier had been a soldier, sailor, stevedore, and farmer now turned his hand to preaching.

In 1938 Batista headed on a penitential journey on foot from Southern Brazil northward where he crisscrossed the rugged Northeast backlands.[2] There he healed the sick and warned about the apocalypse; he also dispensed advice about attaining salvation: "He who drinks, stop drinking; he who smokes, stop smoking, practice acts of penitence, and cast off your life of sin; for the final Day of Judgment is drawing near." Batista also railed against ecclesiastical reforms, such as the elevation of the figure of Christ the King (Cristo Rei), seemingly above all other saints. Tapping into the anger and suspicion provoked by a long history of assaults on popular religious beliefs and practices, the thaumaturge blasphemed Cristo Rei as both satanic and a communist tool. Batista's prophetic teachings attracted several thousand devotees among poor backlanders from the states of Alagoas, Pernambuco, Sergipe, Ceará, and Bahia. At the same time his activities riled local state and church authorities, who branded him a fanatic and charlatan and who jailed him several times for vagrancy and disturbing the peace.

Seven years into his arduous mission, Batista decided to settle down. He chose the remote community of Santa Brígida in the northern reaches of the state of Bahia, drawn to it by a beacon of light. He was soon joined by some 2,000 followers, including another spiritual leader, Maria das Dores dos Santos (or Dona Dodô), whom some believed possessed the spirit of the Virgin Mary. The *romeiros* (pilgrims) built a holy city and prepared themselves and all humanity for the Kingdom of God on earth. They also established a prosperous farming community that by the 1950s had earned the political support and admiration of regional and national leaders alike.

Millenarian Movements

The popular mobilization organized around Pedro Batista belongs to that genre of social action classified as a millenarian movement. Such movements are distinguished by their followers' pursuit of a perfect age (symbolized in Judeo-Christian ideology as "salvation" and "the Kingdom of God"). This ideal existence is understood to be collective (i.e, enjoyed by the faithful as a group), this-worldly, imminent, total, part of a supernatural plan, and dependent on supernatural intercession (Cohn 1970). Millenarian beliefs and actions date back to biblical times (e.g., the Maccabean revolt circa 165 B.C.) and have been recorded since then among peoples scattered worldwide.[3]

Brazil has a long and enduring history of millenarian actions. They stretch in time from preconquest pilgrimages by the Tupi-Guarani in search of the mythical "land without evil," to later syncretic movements (combining native religions and Catholicism) among indigenous peoples protesting forced acculturation, through to today's followers of such urban-based movements as the Valley of the Dawn. These latter initiatives combine spiritist and Catholic or Protestant beliefs and practices (Holston 1999).

This study's treatment of the millenarian activities in Santa Brígida, Jua-

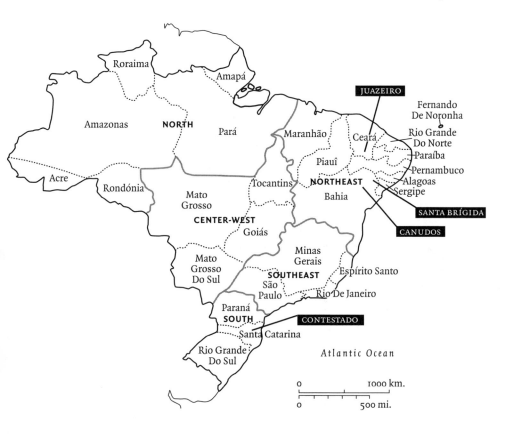

Brazil, including Santa Brígida, Juazeiro, Canudos, and Contestado.

zeiro, Canudos, and Contestado features a particular genre of backland millenarian activity characteristic of the mid-1800s and early 1900s. Leaders of such movements commonly began their careers as thaumaturges and settled their followers in holy cities. There they prepared themselves and wider Christendom for the Final Day of Judgment and the Kingdom of God on earth.

For well over a century social scientists and other observers have sought to explain why it is that periodically, and throughout much of the world, people have mobilized collectively in pursuit of divine intervention and a perfect age. In the case of the movements featured in this study, most scholars have pointed to the profound social changes and natural disasters occurring at the time. Backlanders were repeatedly plagued by devastating droughts, epidemics, and starvation. They also suffered from economic deprivation and social upheaval occasioned by increased capitalist penetration into the rural backlands and

Pedro Batista da Silva in 1967 shortly before his death. Photo by Sérgio Muniz.

the abandonment of time-honored patronage bonds. Moreover, at the turn of the century a newly emergent agrarian bourgeoisie and its republican backers had yet to develop a hegemonic ideology capable of reestablishing meaning, morality, and security to many poor backlanders.

While it is relatively easy to see how such trying historical conditions might support the development of the first three backland movements, it is far more difficult to do so in the case of the Pedro Batista movement. By the late 1930s, when Batista began his mission, the Brazilian state had made progress in consolidating its rule and legitimating its authority. Rural dwellers had also become far more habituated to capitalist discourses and relations. Thus in 1973, when I first embarked on ethnographic research in Santa Brígida, I questioned the utility of such popular theoretical writings on millenarianism as Eric Hobsbawm's *Primitive Rebels* and Peter Worsley's *A Trumpet Shall Sound*. Following the teleological logic of their arguments, advances in Brazilian state formation and economic development should have made millenarian forms of protest virtually obsolete in the Brazilian countryside by the 1930s and 1940s. Consequently, I was left to ponder why and how Pedro Batista had proven successful in initially convincing several thousand Northeasterners of the veracity of his apocalyptic message and the efficacy of his millennial mission. I also wondered what kept followers tied to the millenarian community in the mid-1970s, some years after Batista's death (in 1967) and in the context of a highly repressive military dictatorship bent on finally transforming Brazil into a superpower. I recognized that answers to these questions would clarify why and how a further instance of backland millenarianism had survived and continued to flourish long after at least one historian of the Brazilian countryside had relegated such popular mobilization to the dust bin of history (Pang 1981–1982). I also anticipated that a study of the Pedro Batista movement might reveal inadequacies in previous interpretations of millenarianism in general, as well as in the voluminous scholarship on Juazeiro, Canudos, and Contestado in particular.

Bringing Religion In

Over the quarter of a century in which I have studied the romeiros of Santa Brígida (1973–2000) I have come to an understanding that does not necessarily challenge earlier explanations of this movement and its predecessors. What it does do, however, is foreground the crucial elements of religious meanings, spiritual motivations, and ecclesiastical and folk Catholic institutions. These have too frequently been overlooked or marginalized in treatments of Brazilian millenarianism.

Many authors have chosen to feature the state and the capitalist economy as the central, elite protagonists in their narratives of millennial protest (e.g., Queiroz 1965b; Facó 1972; Diacon 1991). I follow the lead of scholars who insist that the Catholic Church merits equal billing (e.g., Della Cava 1968; Della Cava 1970; Oliveira 1985; Levine 1992; Hoornaert 1997). This latter group of researchers has taken up the important task of locating the turn-of-the-twentieth-century movements amid the struggles pitting church leaders and republican politicians. Although I build on this important scholarship, analysis should properly extend back several more decades. This permits a consideration of the ways in which humble backlanders interpreted and reacted to mid-1800 ultramontane church reforms and to the Brazilian emperor's efforts to desanctify his own authority.[4] Both moves were accompanied by modernizing initiatives in the countryside to root out discourses and practices of mystical enchantment (Monteiro 1974)—including folk Catholicism. In the wake of ultramontanism and republicanism many backlanders came to doubt their leaders' abilities both to maintain institutions and practices amenable to the attainment of individual salvation and to keep at bay the earthly evils associated with the coming apocalypse. These concerns represented not only a crisis of faith but also a breach of hegemonic understandings regarding power, order, responsibility, and destiny—understandings that had been forged among and between dominant and subaltern classes over the centuries. Pedro Batista and the leaders of the earlier backland movements affirmed popular fears and anger over the elites' abandonment of spiritual and secular obligations. These leaders also celebrated the common people's folk Catholic beliefs and practices as efficacious vehicles to reestablish material well-being and to ensure personal and collective salvation prior to the impending apocalypse.

The claim that religious beliefs are central to millenarian movements may seem like a virtual oxymoron. Unfortunately, many scholars of millenarianism in Brazil and elsewhere have neglected to describe and analyze millenarians' religious beliefs and spiritual motivations adequately.[5] This is likely an artifact of how Enlightenment thought became embedded in the social sciences. One of its enduring legacies is a discomfort with matters of religious belief and spiritual motivation.

The heyday of millenarian studies (and related scholarship on nativistic and revitalization movements) occurred in the 1950s and 1960s when social scientists and historians were seeking to understand "modernization" and "social change." Within that epistemological universe, religious meanings and motives were declared to be of secondary importance, if not epiphenomenal. In the hands of social functionalists, religion was the antidote for the social anomie modernity unleashed (e.g., Wallace 1956; Queiroz 1965b). In the hands of Marxist scholars, it was a vehicle for prepolitical mobilization or a mask for authentic class struggle (Hobsbawm 1959; Facó 1972). Either way religion was understood to be a stand-in for more pressing matters, and it was these latter social and political-economic issues that historians and social scientists sought to elucidate. Such marginalization of religion elides the crucial fact that in rural Brazil religious symbols and norms provided conceptual and ethical guides with which rural folk forged social and material lives. Moreover, these symbols and norms were repeatedly called on as backlanders evaluated the worth of those patrons, politicians, and clergy charged with protecting their dependents against the ravages of political unrest, economic downturn, and divine punishment.

Millenarianism as Popular Culture

Brazilian millenarianism is understood here to be a form of popular culture. Consequently, "issues of power and problems of politics" among and between members of the elite and the subaltern become central concerns (Joseph and Nugent 1994, 15). This approach rejects earlier renderings of millenarianism

that have portrayed it as originating from within backward, rural social forma-
tions and as largely autonomous from more dynamic national processes and
structures (e.g., Queiroz 1965a; Queiroz 1965b). Indeed, contrary to much of
what has been written, millenarianism is clearly not a primordial set of beliefs guarded zealously by marginalized Brazilians and grossly unsuited to the
"modern" world. Rather, at the turn-of-the-twentieth century and for many of
the decades that followed, millenarianism facilitated the creation of an alternative form of modernity. In Brazil, millenarian communities, like Canudos
and Santa Brígida, represented one of a variety of *"modern tracks toward the traditional* [through which] the (combined and uneven) development of the modern
world has created worlds of social, economic, and cultural difference" (O'Brien
and Roseberry 1991, 11). The construct of alternative modernity has helped me
to grapple not only with the origins of the Pedro Batista movement in the 1930s
but also with its ability to accommodate and endure over the course of nearly
seventy years of dramatic political, economic, and social change in Brazil.

More Than a Case Study

From one vantage point this book may be read as a case study of the Pedro
Batista movement. Yet it is a case study that insists on presenting a "deep background," one that situates the Pedro Batista movement within a relatively long
historical sweep and within that genre of related millenarian movements. If
this is read as a case study, it is an intentionally transgressive example. *From
Fanatics to Folk* aims to unsettle that very practice that equates millenarianism
with the construct of a discrete social movement. The case-study method—so
prevalent in studies of millenarianism in Brazil and elsewhere—serves to con-
stitute and legitimate our understandings of millenarianism as embodied in
distinct social movements. Such movements are envisioned as both emanating
out of conditions firmly rooted in fixed locations and possessing precise chronologies, usually beginning with the appearance of a messianic figure and ending with his death or the destruction of his holy city. This same spirit of spatial
and temporal boundedness informs, and often limits, the analysts' selection
of those social actors and institutions featured in a given case study.

   I challenge this standard approach to millenarianism in three important
ways. First, I insist on envisioning and studying millenarianism in historical
and spatial motion; thus my analysis of any particular episode of millenarian
activity is informed by an appreciation for Brazilian millenarianism as a long-
enduring yet ever-changing set of cultural meanings and social practices regarding power, identity, and destiny. I inquire why, how, and by whom mille-

narian symbols are drawn on at particular historical junctures. I also explore how the dialectic of changing social contexts and changing social actors contributes to modifications in millenarian discourses and practices.

What has been overlooked in many accounts is that millenarianism originated in Portugal as a foundational state narrative and technology of colonial rule (Myscofski 1988; Cohen 1998). Yet, several centuries later, it was transformed into a popular culture of resistance among those Brazilian backlanders who decried church reforms, the commodification of land and labor, and the intrusive actions of a centralizing state. In insisting that the brand of millenarianism championed by subaltern groups be understood as contributing to a "culture (or cultures) of resistance," I ally myself with those scholars who generally subscribe to Marxist understandings of political economy yet seek to decenter notions of power and struggle. In doing so they, and I, stake a claim for culture as a strategic site for contestation between dominant and popular classes (e.g., Foucault 1990; Bourdieu 1977; Williams 1977). Thus in the hands of the rural poor, millenarian symbols, practices, and communities have long produced alternative and often militantly transgressive subjects, who have challenged the dominant classes' moves toward a more homogenous and secular Brazilian citizenry. In the context of contemporary Santa Brígida, however, I question whether that strand of Brazilian millenarianism that links the four movements featured in this study and that has long fueled popular resistance can manage to retain its oppositional thrust. I raise this concern in light of the dominant reinvention of Santa Brígida and its cognate movements as sites of revered national folklore and faith. Consequently, millenarian communities that were once decried as backward and fanatical are now marketed as centers of religious and historical tourism.

Second, this study further complicates conventional understandings of millenarianism by blurring the temporal and spatial divides erected by social scientists and historians around specific movements. Instead, it charts the travels of millenarian discourses and practices across movements. It also interrogates the ways in which elite perceptions and management of older movements influenced the fates of newer ones. This revision occasions a much-needed exploration of the many ways in which particular episodes of popular millenarianism live on in the social imaginaries, cultural productions, and struggles of other social actors and their institutions—a process I refer to as "intertextuality" among movements.

Third, once most millenarian movements come to be appreciated not as finite events but as ongoing social and cultural productions, one is called on to analyze the full complement of social actors engaged in these productions. To this end, I consider groups that have yet to be adequately brought into millenarian studies, exploring, for example, their particular roles in representing the millenarian Other. These social actors include scholars, journalists, filmmakers, and museum curators.

New analytical frameworks and narrative structures are demanded once one conceptualizes Brazilian millenarianism as a traveling cultural formation in historical motion and ongoing social production. *From Fanatics to Folk* is a hybrid text that combines cultural history, comparative/intertextual case studies (of the Canudos, Contestado, Juazeiro, and Santa Brígida movements), and ethnography. What results is an account of changing millenarian discourses and practices that combines the sweep of the *longue durée* with the detail and intimacy of ethnographic fieldwork.

This book complements in two ways the substantial body of literature that reconstructs past movements through archival research. First, most scholars have been left to glean information on the consciousness and motivations of millenarians from what Eric Van Young colorfully describes as archival "fragments" that must be "expanded" and "rehydrated" by the historian (1999, 225). Important work on the cultural history of Brazilian millenarianism has been authored by such scholars as Duglas Teixeira Monteiro (1974), Pedro Antônio Ribeiro de Oliveira (1985), Alexandre Otten (1990), and Robert Levine (1992); I have benefited greatly from these pioneering efforts.[6] Although mindful of the dangers of upstreaming, I endeavor here to "expand" and "rehydrate" several archival fragments presented in these and other historical works by interpreting them in the light of information I have gleaned over the years while conducting ethnographic research in Santa Brígida.[7] Second, as an ethnographer I am in the enviable position of employing interview techniques, participant observation, and archival research to describe in great detail the creation and maintenance of an ongoing millenarian community. In short, a triangulated methodology—combining archival research, ethnographic fieldwork, and the reinterpretation of secondary source materials—undergirds this study. Archival and field research were conducted during the following periods: August 1973–December 1974; April–August 1977; and the summers of 1998–2000.[8]

An Overview of the Book

Chapter 1 sets out to answer this question: how is it that millenarian symbols, once employed effectively by Portuguese conquerors and missionaries to legitimate their rule, came to be transformed centuries later into a popular discourse of resistance inspiring the insurgents of Juazeiro, Canudos, and Contestado?

To answer this question it is necessary to review instances of accommodation and struggle over the centuries between hegemonic processes of rule, such as the patronage pact, and popular forms of culture, such as folk Catholicism. The latter is understood to be a constellation of beliefs and practices that developed among nonelite Brazilians in dialogue with, and sometimes in opposition to, the official tenets of the Catholic Church.[9] Chapter 1 also reviews the unsettling political, economic, and ecclesiastical transformations occurring over the second half of the 1800s, and it provides an interpretation of why thousands of backlanders found in millenarian symbols both a meaningful explanation of their times and guides for remediation.

Chapter 2 treats those cultural conventions and symbolic operations through which backlanders socially produced their charismatic leaders—the "sacralizing process," as I call it. Most scholars begin with a famous—or infamous—millenarian figure (depending on the rhetorical tropes in play) already in place. In their decision to do so, we are reminded of Karl Marx's critique of scholars who see the individual "not as historic result but as history's point of departure" (1973, 83). By contrast, my study carefully situates Santa Brígida's Pedro Batista, Juazeiro's Padre Cícero, Canudos's Antônio Conselheiro, and Contestado's João Maria and José Maria within that historical context of millenarian resistance that fostered and facilitated their emergence as popular leaders. Chapter 2 also examines how their charisma was conferred; in no small measure it was forged out of cultural struggles that pitted humble backlanders against power holders in local government, the church, and the press.

Ever since the last half of the nineteenth century, agents of the Brazilian state and church have attempted to retake—or at the very least discipline—those spaces that folk Catholicism and millenarianism afford, lest they foster the development of alternative identities, leadership, discourses, and practices. Yet as chapters 3 and 4 document, the romeiros' home communities remained strongholds of resistance, managing to keep alive outlawed religious beliefs and practices that were tapped and elaborated once the romeiros settled in Santa Brígida. Chapter 4 describes how the romeiros drew on popular culture to convert Santa Brígida into a "New Juazeiro/Jerusalem"—complete with its Garden of Eden, Calvary, and site of the future Kingdom of God.

Beginning in chapter 3 the book examines the tensions and negotiations within Santa Brígida, as well as between Santa Brígida and dominant institutions, over the appropriate relationship between folk Catholicism/popular millenarianism and processes of economic modernization and political centralization. As chapter 4 documents, in order to settle in Santa Brígida, Pedro Batista struck a bargain with a powerful regional political boss. The pact was predicated on the exchange of romeiro votes for political protection. In short order, the boss and other agents ensured that the state came to enjoy a clear and growing presence in the millenarian community.

What is fascinating about this phase in the history of the romaria (community of pilgrims) is that it clearly challenges dichotomous notions that pit power holders against the popular classes and religion against modernity, and allow for little play across these categories. Chapter 4 documents that within the romaria's spiritual vision there was a place for agents of the state and development technocrats. For their part, these outsiders were willing to do a fair share of "colluding." They did so, for example, by failing to register in official documents instances of millenarian beliefs and practices that they would have otherwise labeled "fanatical" and "subversive." Instead they elected to define and treat the messianic leader as if he were the equal of any conventional backland boss. He in turn returned the favor by often concealing his own and his romeiros' transgressive popular practices from public view and by welcoming in state institutions and agents.

Ultimately, though, there was a price to pay for collaboration with the state, as chapters 5 and 6 reveal. The state's success in inscribing itself within Santa Brígida came gradually to compromise Pedro Batista's stature as a charismatic leader among his romeiro followers. Moreover, the continued viability of that community as one in "a series of dispersed sites . . . where popular subjects might be formed" became imperiled (Rowe and Schelling 1991, 10). This was especially so as agents of the state managed to win over youthful romeiros who, in turn, abandoned the group's stringent penitential norms to embrace cultural patterns favored by the dominant classes. These chapters vividly illustrate both the allure and the fragility of charismatic authority.

As chapter 7 presents, in the latest phase of the engagement between Santa Brígida's romaria and agents of the church and state, one finds a reversal of sorts in the usual direction of the collaboration. As national Catholic Church leaders find their parishioners turning in ever increasing numbers to evangelical Protestantism and perceive their long undisputed position as defenders of the nation's morality and faith to be challenged (Birman and Pereira Leite 2000), they seek ways to retain their members and to infuse their rituals and theology with new excitement and passion. In this new historical conjuncture, clerics have come to reclaim popular charismatic leaders like Juazeiro's Padre Cícero and Santa Brígida's Pedro Batista and to revalue elements of folk Catholicism.

Moreover, amid fears of mass culture and globalization, nationalist elites of many countries, Brazil included, look to appropriate and revalue that which has been labeled primordial and authentic. It is within this context, and after decades of relative obscurity, that Santa Brígida has come to the attention of official culture brokers and agents of the state (such as the ministry of culture and tourism). As chapter 7 documents, once more asserting their power to affix meaning, these representatives of dominant culture now dub Santa Brígida's millenarian discourse and folk Catholic practices as "folklore." In this way they defang these popular manifestations and remove from public view their histories of resistance and struggle.

In these officials' rhetoric and interventions one finds a romance with the folk and folklore, as if they somehow contain a form of primordial solidarity that modernity has all but stripped from the rest of Brazil. Some also raise concerns that mass media and globalization may eventually destroy all that is authentic in national culture. The crusade for "cultural preservation/rescue" (resgate cultural) in "remote" places like Santa Brígida is one response. Yet as chapter 7 insists, the "folk" is neither unitary nor solidary, a point illustrated by the diverse reactions and struggles within the community of Santa Brígida over their appropriation by representatives of the church, state, and media. Moreover, although some romeiros are more than eager to engage the state in its newfound embrace, others worry about what this partnership may mean for their continuing ability to maintain heterodox religious beliefs and practices that contradict dominant secular and ecclesiastical precepts.

A Rejection of Grand Narratives

Since the earliest days in the formation of Brazilian social sciences, researchers have been intrigued by the phenomena of millenarianism. Whether they viewed it through the lens of Darwinian positivism (da Cunha 1944), social functionalism (Queiroz 1965b; Monteiro 1974) or materialism (Facó 1963; Moniz 1978), most authors used the example of millenarian activity to make universalizing statements about both human behavior and the future of Brazil. In most cases, rural folk and their brand of religion were deemed to be either an obstacle or wholly peripheral to the march into modernity. This study joins rank with that small yet growing body of literature that challenges such binary and totalizing thinking. In this spirit, I place folk Catholicism and rural millenarians among all other coeval entities, such as the state, church, and market, which together, and simultaneously, configure Brazilian modernity (Holston 1999). And, in doing so, I showcase millenarian subjects' competing histories and alternative dispositions to modernity.

Equally problematic is that Brazilian millenarian movements are generally portrayed as exceptional, anomalous, and pyrrhic. In contrast, my account features millenarianism over the long sweep of Brazilian history and shows it to have been both dominant discourse and popular culture—at different times the inspiration for colonial conquest, ravaged holy cities, and thriving pilgrimage centers. I argue for a revisionism that substitutes notions of millenarianism as "othered," "traditional," and sporadic with an appreciation of its integral, dynamic, and enduring qualities.[10] Indeed, it is this very centrality of millenarian discourse that leads a contemporary historian and social critic to write, "The drama of the country rests on this contrast between dream and reality, aspiration and achievement. Paradise is destroyed, and the peaceful empire does not materialize. . . . The people do not trust their leaders and institutions but do little to make the former more responsible to public needs and to change the latter, taking destiny into their own hands. . . . Hence a feeling of frustration, of disappointment with government and institutions, and the persistence of a vague hope that a messiah may eventually bring the solution to all problems" (Carvalho 2000, 77–78).

THE WORLD TURNED UPSIDE DOWN

The Origins of the Canudos, Contestado, and Juazeiro Movements

As one of the earliest Jesuit leaders in the colonial capital of Salvador da Bahia, Antônio Vieira must have felt the weight of destiny upon him as he composed the following sermon.

> The Portuguese reign was founded on July 25, 1139, when King Afonso I Henriques conquered the Moors in Turkey. God had said to the King at the dawn of this victory: "I want you and your descendants to establish my kingdom [the words of God to Gideon in the Old Testament]. . . . All the kings are of God, but the other kings are God's produced by men: *the king of Portugal is of God and created by God, and thus more rightly His.*"
>
> . . . The history of Portugal is truly a sacred history, a history of salvation. . . . Portugal is the seminary of faith to be propagated through the entire world. . . . The Portuguese are the angels of God sent to the pagans who have long awaited them (Isaiah 18:2–7). Soldiers and missionaries are united in a glorious mission. . . . For this mission, the union between the spiritual and temporal powers is necessary. (Hoornaert 1974, 35; emphasis added)

How very different this mid-seventeenth-century sermon, so rich in millennial expectations and providential bravado, sounds from this late-nineteenth-century verse, which was left behind in the carnage of the millenarian community of Canudos.

Backed by the law
Those evil ones abound,
We keep the law of God,
They keep the law of the hound [devil]
The Anti-Christ was born
That he might govern Brazil,
But here is our Counselor,
To save us from this ill! (da Cunha 1944, 164–65)

How and why did millenarianism, which entered Brazil in the early colonial period as an elite discourse and instrument of rule, later transform into
a popular set of symbols with which poor backlanders came to criticize their
superiors and mobilize mass resistance?[1] In tracing this transformation one is
reminded of Emilia Viotti da Costa's trenchant observation that "the religious
message is eminently symbolic, and its symbols will be decoded with reference
to people's experiences as a whole. When oppressed men and women, imbued
with notions that make them see the world as a battlefield where God's soldier
struggles against Satan and his followers, get together, no one can tell where
the struggle will end. . . . They may follow anyone who claims to be a savior—as
often happens in millenarian movements—but they can also come to question
the legitimacy of their rulers" (1994, 8). Both outcomes came to characterize
the struggles of poor backlanders at the turn of the twentieth century.

Millenarianism and Portugal's Prophetic Destiny

Sixteenth-century Jesuits like Manuel da Nóbrega, José de Anchieta, and Antônio Vieira proved worthy spokesmen for the early Portuguese colonizers whom
Eduardo Hoornaert aptly dubs "messianic warriors" (1974, 32).[2] These clergymen laid the foundation for the belief—or, at the very least, the assertion—that
terrestrial authority was sanctified and the human actions of the colonizers
wholly providential.[3] The Jesuit mission in Brazil was also explicitly eschatological. Instructors simplified Christian doctrine to "the singular but dramatic
issues of salvation and damnation," introduced elaborate penitential practices,
and proclaimed the imminent end of the world (Myscofski 1991, 84). These
teachings were also embraced and further disseminated by lay religious figures
like the thaumaturge Francisco Mendonça Mar. He is said to have undergone
conversion on hearing Vieira preach, and shortly afterward he dedicated himself to spreading the Jesuit's message by traveling on foot across the Rio São
Francisco region (Levine 1992, 274). Mar may indeed have pioneered the more

popular brand of millenarian thought that has inspired generations of back-land prophets, including Pedro Batista.

As the colonial period progressed, leaders benefited from ecclesiastical teachings and monarchical/patrimonial rituals of rule—into which millenari-anism was embedded (Oliveira 1985; de Groot 1996; Schultz 2001). In Brazil (as elsewhere) the attempt to construct hegemony represented an attempt to lessen the need for coercion and force directed against subordinated groups. It did not result in "a shared ideology but a common material and meaning-ful framework for living through, talking about, and acting upon social orders characterized by domination" (Roseberry 1994, 361). As Max Weber (1963) theorized, in colonial Brazil large landholders and officials of the monarchy and church recognized the utility of incorporating popular belief systems within this framework in order to better control their subordinates. Thus, rituals of rule ranged from royal coronations and the processions of religious brother-hoods to sermons delivered on sugar estates (Freyre 1946; Hoornaert 1974) and humble backlanders' petitions or promises (*promessas*) to favored patron saints.[4]

Powerholders hoped that over time these rituals might help to construct subjects who came to view hierarchy, order, and paternalistic authority as so-cially inviolate and divinely preordained (Otten 1994; de Groot 1996). To up the ante, church fathers in concert with secular rulers added the promise of sal-vation for those who obeyed these precepts and eternal damnation for those who failed to do so. Of course, even if none of these cultural constructions succeeded in converting unequal power relations into something that was at best sanctified and routine or at the least enacted as such through subaltern actors' begrudging participation in high rituals and everyday performances of deference, other forms of force could be quite effectively mobilized (Scott 1990; Sayer 1994); in the absence of either version of consent, the master's whip and the planter's monopoly over their sharecroppers' means of livelihood were often brought to bear (Costa 1985). When and if the terms of moral absolut-ism contained in the project of hegemonic rule were adopted—whether with conviction or through expedient complicity (i.e., James Scotts's "thin" hege-mony [1990])—they became elements in a normative pact or "moral economy" obligating patron and dependent alike (Thompson 1971; Scott 1976).

A Crisis of Catholic Conscience, Ultramontanism, and the Deterioration of State-Church Relations

Referring to the latter half of the eighteenth century, religious historian Rio-lando Azzi writes, "After three centuries in which Catholic faith was unshak-ably implanted throughout Brazil and maintained rigidly through the institu-tion of the inquisition, for the first time symptoms appeared of a progressive sundering of the bases of this monolithically constructed edifice" (1976, 133). The trends that contributed to what Azzi calls a "crisis of Catholic conscience" (ibid.) include urbanization and the substitution of secular forms of socializing and entertainment for religious ones; the introduction of European discourses about "culture" and "civilization" that were often antireligious and anticleri-cal; the expulsion of diverse religious orders from Brazil (linked to the Pomba-line reforms); the related demise of lay religious brother/sisterhoods; and the arrival of Protestants and spiritists who diversified religious choice and repre-sented a break with the highly hierarchical and authoritarian (official) Catholic tradition. Predictably, Brazilian church leaders reacted defensively and some-times defiantly to these challenges to the Catholic Church's previous influence (indeed, its proclaimed monopoly) over modes of authority and social control, spirituality, knowledge, and education.

To exacerbate matters, by the mid-1800s there was a marked decline in the symbolic displays and institutional demonstrations of the unity and shared mission of the church and the state.[5] Thus, despite the wording of the Consti-tution of 1824, which called the emperor "inviolable and sacred," Brazilian lib-erals had come to reject as retrograde and superstitious ideas about the sacred origins of the state and divine predestination.[6] Exemplifying this seculariz-ing trend, Brazil's Emperor Pedro II (who reigned from 1840–1889) returned in 1872 from a trip to the "enlightened" capitals of Europe and proceeded to formally abolish the practice of the royal handkiss—a remnant of Portuguese absolutism viewed as analogous to the kissing of the pope's foot or hand.

This decree was perfectly in keeping with the emperor's liberal politics and with his membership in the masons. His contemporary, statesman Joaquim Nabuco, described Pedro II as "not exactly anti-clerical—he saw no real danger in the existence of the clergy. Instead, he found the religious vocation unat-tractive. To him, a tireless student of the sciences, the soldier and the priest were two social phenomena with no future, two temporary necessities which he would like to put to better use" (cited in Bruneau 1974, 23). Although, in prin-ciple, Pedro II may have lacked much interest in religion, the Catholic Church increasingly demanded his attention as the Vatican embraced ultramontanism and drew many influential members of the Brazilian Catholic Church into the fold. Rome's ultramontane initiatives included Pope Pius IX's 1864 Syllabus of Errors, which denounced national churches, masonry, and the dominance of civil law over canon law. This was followed by the First Vatican Council's declaration of papal infallibility in 1870—that is, institutional centralization of the Universal Church in the papacy.

These measures had two highly significant, and contrasting, effects on Brazil (Bruneau 1974). On the one hand, they inclined Brazilian government officials to attribute even the mildest assertion of church independence to the pernicious influence of ultramontanism and, thus, to consider it a threat to national sovereignty. In this spirit, in 1847 the emperor refused the prestigious offer of a cardinalate in Brazil, the first in Latin America. On the other hand, encouraged by Rome's increasing efforts to gain control over the Brazilian church, to repudiate masonry, and to develop more acceptable pastoral practices, a small group of clergy proceeded to assert their autonomy vis-à-vis the Brazilian state (ibid.; Mainwaring 1986).

The test over who controlled the Brazilian church—the ultramontane forces and Rome or the Brazilian state that had always held the balance of power in church-state relations—came to a head over an incident known as the Religious Question.[7] In 1872 the staunchly ultramontane bishop of Olinda, Dom Vital, ordered the religious brotherhoods in his diocese to expel their masonic members. The bishop of Pará, Dom Macedo Costa, soon followed suit. Having received encouragement from Rome, Dom Vital stated in a letter addressed to an imperial minister, "Your Excellency understands that this question is one of life or death for the Brazilian church; it behooves me to support [it] with the greatest sacrifices" (Thorton 1948, 261).[8] The masons, in turn, appealed to the crown, whose council of state decided in their favor and ordered the bishops to lift their bans. In characterizing the prevailing mood when the bishops refused to obey and were temporarily imprisoned, C. G. de Groot writes, "Never had the chasm between the will of the imperial state—and thus the 'sacred and inviolable' emperor—and the will of God been so visible" (1996, 61).[9]

Such a political climate heightened the belief that the church was under siege. Zealous ultramontane clergy reacted to the challenge by attempting to reform and shore up the Brazilian church, discipline its parishioners, and tie them far closer to clerics than to their lay religious leaders. In assessing the thrust of this crusade and why rural practitioners were specifically targeted, Riolando Azzi's distinction between "traditional" and "reform" (*renovado*) Catholicism is apposite. The former was brought to Brazil by the early missionaries and is "Luso-Brazilian, lay, medieval, social, and familial" (Azzi 1977, 9).

The latter, dating back to sixteenth-century church reforms, tends to be "romanist, clerical, tridentine, individualistic, and sacramentalist" (ibid).

Although folk Catholicism contains features of both genres, traditional Catholicism—with its emphasis on such elements as lay brotherhoods/sisterhoods (*irmandades*), religious processions, pilgrimage sites, miracles, promessas, and ex-votos—left a far greater imprint on the religiosity of humble rural Brazilians.[10] In no small measure, traditional Catholicism won out because reform-minded church leaders were long stymied by state authorities who sought to limit ecclesiastical power by keeping the number and quality of priests low.[11] Not surprisingly, at the beginning of the eighteenth century, the archbishop of Bahia lamented the dismal results of this administrative neglect: penance, communion, and extreme unction (e.g., sacramental rites associated with reform Catholicism) were unavailable for most parishioners (de Groot 1996, 15). The absence of clergy provided fertile ground for the maintenance of traditional Catholic beliefs and practices—as well as syncretic, folk Portuguese, indigenous, and African elements—which were passed on orally and were managed by local irmandades and lay ritual specialists. Folk Catholicism emerged, then, as a site of cultural creativity and hybridity. It has also been a site in which, from the time of conquest to this day, subaltern actors (indigenous peoples, Afro-Brazilians, and poor mestiço sertanejos) have struggled against elite state and church projects intent on eradicating alternative and often highly localized understandings of identity, place, belonging, power, and destiny.

Ultramontanism Moves into the Countryside

The imperial era was marked by confrontations between proponents of traditional and reform Catholicism. It also witnessed moves by the church and state authorities to significantly reduce, if not obliterate, those social and cultural spaces in which alternative subjectivities might be created and "unorthodox" practices pursued. Backlanders confronted foot soldiers of a centralizing Roman Catholic Church determined to discipline parishioners to regard it as the exemplary moral foundation for all social life. In this spirit ultramontane clerics set out "to separate the sacred from the profane, the religious from the festive, and the spiritual from the social" (Azzi 1977, 11). They accordingly denounced such social and ludic dimensions of popular festivals and pilgrimage sites as games, dances, and the sale of food and goods.[12] Moreover, in the move toward orthodoxy, local religious customs, such as the Dance of São Gonçalo and penitential rituals, were decried as "abominable superstitious practice" (de Groot 1996, 84). Indeed, one bishop declared, "Such dances do not belong to

São Gonçalo but to the Devil; and as such they are intended to pervert customs and make us lose eternal salvation, launching us into the abyss of sin" (quoted in Azzi 1977, 32). In this repressive climate, visiting missionaries routinely imposed penalties on those who dared to engage in popular religious practices (de Groot 1996, 84).

The bishops proceeded to insist that religious ceremonies be physically removed from secular settings. And in the same reformist spirit, church leaders ordered the destruction of humble makeshift "chapels," which one bishop stationed in São Paulo state denounced as having been erected by devotees without ecclesiastical authorization or consecration. "These are not chapels," he wrote dismissively, "these are little cottages or huts" (ibid.).

The outcome was somewhat different in those few major pilgrimage sites like Bahia's Bom Jesus da Lapa and Ceará's São Francisco das Chagas de Canindé. There, devotion was so well established and the quantity of charitable contributions to church coffers so great that the bishops elected to either remove or greatly subordinate the lay officials who had previously administered these sites and place the pilgrimage centers under the jurisdiction of European religious orders. The aim was to convert these spiritual centers into sites of official ecclesiastical teaching. Unfortunately, the result was a catechism largely devoid of the type of eschatological themes and instructions for attaining salvation that the popular classes had come to anticipate and seek (Azzi 1977).[13]

Finally as ultramontane priests staked claims to exclusive rights both to mediate between humanity and the supernatural and to oversee their parishioners' pursuit of salvation, they branded as backward and fanatical such lay competitors as thaumaturges, healers, and spiritists. The same denigration and disrepute befell those clerics whom the popular classes dared to elevate for their profound spirituality and miraculous powers.

Padre Ibiapina: Hero of the Poor and Scapegoat of the Church

In the intriguing career of Padre José Antônio Maria de Ibiapina (1807–1883) is a clear demonstration of the church's attempts to impose its controversial reforms and of how these initiatives were received by Brazilian backlanders. Furthermore, the teachings and actions of this native-born missionary had a profound impact on the careers of Padre Cícero, Antônio Conselheiro, Pedro Batista, and Maria das Dores.

Padre Ibiapina is best known for two things. First, beginning in the 1860s he founded a religious congregation of women in the Northeast of Brazil. Twenty-two such charity houses, or *casas de caridade*, were built throughout the sertão. These served simultaneously as schools for the daughters of wealthy landowners and merchants, as orphanages for poor children, as centers for the manufacture of cheap textiles, and, in line with Ibiapina's personal ambition, as convents for his own lay congregation of nuns (popularly referred to as beatas).[14] Second, the priest was renown for his missionary efforts dedicated to encouraging his followers to make material improvements within their backland communities. Many of Ibiapina's most devoted laborers also elected to become beatos, dedicating themselves to lives of mendicancy, itinerancy, and penitence. Such beatos journeyed throughout the Northeast, where they repaired run-down churches and cemeteries, built makeshift chapels, and constructed new dams, open wells, and roads.

Ibiapina posed a multitude of problems for his ultramontane superiors. With his casas de caridade he had founded what amounted to an order of nuns. Church officials frowned on the fact that, without permission from Rome or any Brazilian bishop, he required the beatas to wear the habit and to make a profession of vows just as if their calling and religious congregation had been canonically approved. The bishops soon reacted against such deviation from orthodoxy, and by 1872 Ibiapina was forced to relinquish control of the charity houses. Apparently, before he left the region he prophesied that as long as one charity house survived, God would do no harm to his people (Della Cava 1970, 22, 28). Some three-quarters of a century after Padre Ibiapina delivered his prophetic warning, the romeiros' spiritual leader Maria das Dores—who had spent much of her youth in a charity house in her hometown of Água Branca, Alagoas—established her own lay order of beatas in Santa Brígida, likely with Padre Ibiapina's caution in mind.[15]

Not only did Padre Ibiapina engage in practices that contradicted the spirit of ultramontane reform, but he also inadvertently provoked backlanders' resistance to the church's new project, his good works, counsel, and healings having encouraged common folk to venerate him as a living saint (santo). For example, after having provided advice to an ailing woman who was subsequently cured, the missionary was hailed by the rural folk as a "miracle worker." Much to the chagrin of church officials, grateful backlanders erected an unauthorized chapel at the site where the woman had been cured; moreover, pilgrimages to both this and other sites where similar cures attributed to Ibiapina were alleged to have occurred became commonplace. The last straw for the church came when a journalist from Ceará wrote a series for the newspaper A Voz da Religião no Cariri (The Voice of Religion in the Cariri) in which he enthusiastically publicized the missionary's "miraculous" cures.

Five months after the articles appeared (in July 1869) the bishop of Ceará ordered all of Ibiapina's missionary work in the interior to cease (Della Cava 1970, 21).[16] While this generally unpopular move naturally pitted the bishop and Rome against the long-esteemed charismatic healer of the backlands, it was perfectly in keeping with the reformist church's firm commitment to scientific medicine. As clerics came to see it, when science regulated humanity's dealings with the body, the church could regulate those dealings with the soul. Or as one priest stated, "The doctor and the priest are the creatures chosen by God to alleviate the suffering of their fellow-men, and both have the same 'secret of the confessional': the doctor for things that concern the body, the priest for things that concern the soul" (de Groot 1996, 89).

Unfortunately for both the church and infirm backlanders, official medicine was not available for the majority of the Brazilian population (Costa 1985).[17] Consequently, despite the fact that the state and church had actually joined forces—with the former criminalizing folk healing in 1890 and the bishops of Northern Brazil issuing their 1915 Collective Pastoral Letter against spiritism—rural healers continued to attract large and devout followings (de Groot 1996). As such, these popular figures continued to frustrate attempts at exclusive ecclesiastical control over the spiritual order and state control over the citizenry's health (Borges 2001).

Economic and Political Transitions

Brazilians experienced profound challenges to their beliefs and practices not only in the religious sphere but also in their economic and political lives. These multiple assaults encouraged the formation of millenarian movements among poor backlanders over the course of the late nineteenth and early twentieth centuries.

In the mid-1800s, the locus of economic dynamism began to shift from the Northeast to Brazil's Central-South corridor. Many Northeastern oligarchs either resisted or could not afford to make the transition to more capital-intensive forms of production. By contrast, the coffee planters of the Central-South corridor introduced new technologies, demanded policies favorable to immigration, and instituted innovative marketing and financing schemes.

As the national economy expanded and became more diverse, agriculture was no longer viewed as the only, or even the most viable, sector for capital investment. New competitors included railroads, industry, urban facilities, and credit institutions. New groups (such as industrialists and bankers) emerged within the more diverse and complex national economy, and the expanded urban middle and working classes slowly began to consolidate. These pivotal sectors began to militate for the overthrow of the monarchy, with disgruntled members of these groups arguing that economic progress was hampered by imperial centralization and the hegemony exercised by the traditional landed oligarchy of the Northeast. With its greater autonomy and flexibility, republican federalism seemed to be the answer (Costa 1985; Pang 1981–1982).

As the republicans gained strength, Dom Pedro II found his power base shrinking. By the late 1800s many agrarian oligarchs who had earlier supported him faced economic decline, which led in turn to a reduction in their national political standing. Abolition (instituted in 1888) and internal migration further sapped their labor supply and their estates stagnated due to undercapitalization and inefficient forms of technology and transportation. Consequently, only token resistance followed when members of the military (who had come to view it as their duty to improve the nation's social and political organization) forced Dom Pedro II into exile in 1889 (Costa 1985).

Impact in the Backlands

These nineteenth-century economic and political transformations had grave effects in the Brazilian backlands. There, small-scale farmers and ranchers, tenants, and sharecroppers had long struggled to eke out a living and to defend a partially autonomous way of life (Chandler 1972; Forman 1975; Meznar 1986; Andrade 1980). Among the most unsettling innovations was the Land Law of 1850, which commodified land and sought to eradicate the practice of squatting on unused public land. At the same time the emperor bowed to international pressure and placed a ban on the further importation of African slaves. Both labor shortages and a highly competitive internal market for slaves ensued. Northeastern sugar planters and cotton farmers pursued short-term profits by selling their slaves at elevated prices to coffee growers. Then, in a desperate attempt to reverse their decline, Northeastern oligarchs increased their demands on their dependents by elevating rents and contributions of unpaid labor. Soon after, backlanders were subjected to the expanded reach of the state in the form of higher taxes, more state vigilance and controls, and a military draft. Rural dwellers protested the ever-increasing encroachments on their ability to meet basic needs and to control their own labor. For example, in 1874 and 1875 violent riots—the so-called Quebra Quilo (Smash-the-Kilo-Scales) movement—affected at least seventy-eight markets in the backlands of Pernambuco, Rio Grande do Norte, Alagoas, and Paraíba (Barman 1977). Robert Levine observes, "Backland participants in these riots, of course, were portrayed as primitives terrified of modern scientific innovations; yet one could

also praise them for figuring out that uniform scales and measures would in-
evitably lead to a higher tax burden. Examination of the tax records in the affected municípios, in fact, reveals that between 1870 and 1875 new taxes were created or raised in two out of every three municípios after standardized weights
were introduced" (1992, 90). Patronage that had long buffered the rural poor
against extreme deprivation proved to be far less dependable by the mid-1800s.
In some cases owners of sugar mills and underfinanced cattle ranchers found
that their own economic struggles made it increasingly difficult for them to
fulfill time-honored obligations to their dependents. In other cases more prosperous landowners were able to finance the purchase of yet larger tracts of
land and labor-saving technologies. They elected to expel squatters and cancel
tenancy arrangements since, despite increasing their holdings, mechanization
allowed for the reduction of the workforce (Pang 1981–1982).

While industrial capitalists, bankers, and large commercial farmers praised
the railroads for their capacity to integrate national markets and unify the nation, poor backlanders expressed far less confidence and enthusiasm. In fact,
the sense of dread many backlanders harbored—with some opining that the
belching steam engines were Satan's work and signs of the end of the world
(Otten 1990)—was not ill-founded. For example, in Southern Brazil, where the
Contestado movement would later unfold, the building of the railroad led to
the speculation and extreme concentration of land, the mass expulsion of small
subsistence farmers (posseiros) from their properties, and the introduction of
enclosures and trespassing laws.

Adding to the blow, many local patrons actually collaborated with newly arrived railroad officials. They did so, for example, when they served as labor brokers forcing their previous clients into manual labor for the railroads. Writing
about these changes, Bernard Siegel notes, "For a century and a half whatever
demands [poor backlanders] could make and rights they might expect to be
fulfilled occurred within a complex patronage network to which they suddenly
no longer had access" (1977, 329). Indeed, as Todd Diacon (1991) points out,
this led to a profound sense of deception and moral outrage. Rural folk came to
realize that the very figure of the patron—long associated (at least normatively)
with facilitating their subsistence and protection—had ominously become not
only an instrument of the new capitalist class but also the most immediate
threat to their clients' ways of life and even to their clients' very survival.

At the height of railroad construction in the Contestado region almost 8,000
workers labored on the line; many of these were European immigrants or migrants recruited from other regions. The railroads produced an explosion of
violence, with accounts of murder, robbery, and towns terrorized by gangs of

track workers filling local newspapers. Violence also escalated as certain members of the local elite who had earlier cooperated with railroad and lumber industrialists turned against these newcomers, who came to be viewed as usurpers who threatened the local elites' power base (ibid.).

Furthermore, for Northeastern backlanders a series of droughts between 1877 and 1919 became a major scourge. Before midcentury the human consequences of drought had been limited, since the cattle economy absorbed very little labor. The situation changed radically from 1850 onward, when a drought-resistant type of arboreal cotton was introduced and marketed internationally. Cotton required a far larger labor force than cattle, and as the crop prospered it attracted large numbers of rural workers from the neighboring *agreste* zone. Residents of cotton-producing areas cultivated food crops (corn, beans, and manioc) in conjunction with and frequently on a similar sharecropping basis as cotton production. Unfortunately, the cotton boom proved short-lived, and after 1871 cotton prices dropped, as did local wages and profits. Conditions spiraled perilously downward when drought deprived country folk of their subsistence crops as well (Anthony Hall 1978; Villa 2000). Unable to feed themselves through their own efforts and abandoned by local patrons, massive numbers of desperate backlanders fled to cities. The Northeastern city of Fortaleza grew from its predrought population of 20,000 to between 130,000 and 140,000 in 1878 (Villa 2000, 70). Little relief was to be found there, however. Newspaper journalists reported on desperate parents forced to peddle their virgin daughters into prostitution and even cases of starving parents cannibalizing their own children.[18] A series of epidemics was the final blow, leaving in its wake some 30,000 dead in Fortaleza in 1878 and 1879 alone (ibid., 67–72).

If the increasing commodification of land and labor in the late 1800s and early 1900s unleashed what Eul-Soo Pang (1981–1982) calls an "agrarian crisis," the crisis in the countryside only intensified with the founding of the republic. The institution of *coronelismo* proved central to the disorder plaguing the countryside during this period. Coronelismo refers to that system of monopolistic control exercised at the local level by the figure of the *coronel* (colonel; plural *coronéis*), commonly a large landowning planter or rancher.[19] As one of the very few, if not the only, dominant patrons in a given locality, the coronel built his power base by creating broad horizontal and vertical ties of patronage, enjoying a privileged social and economic status, and controlling access to force and the law within his municipality. The municipality was the political-administrative bastion of the coronel and under the First Republic the benefits associated with gaining and maintaining control over it intensified, as did the competition among rival local coronéis and their retinues.

The state governors solicited the coronel's support for designated federal and state candidates in exchange for complete liberty in running the affairs of the municipality, including control over the granting of bureaucratic sinecures at the local level (tax collectors, clerks, public prosecutors, judges, teachers). With political rewards so attractive, members of the rural elite turned against each other, frequently contracting the services of ruthless bandit bands.[20] Referring to these times Pereira de Queiroz observes, "In many zones of the sertão, the old great families became almost pulverized, subdivided into countless alliances which disaggregated once again in an atmosphere of uncertainty and instability" (Queiroz 1965b, 293).

Finally, when the rural poor needed help most, they found yet another institution undercut. By the start of the twentieth century the church could no longer depend on the largesse of its traditional allies, the state and the latifundiary class, to help subsidize its social welfare activities. Indeed, in the Collective Pastoral Letter of 1915 church authorities turned to their own parishioners and exhorted them to provide charity for the poor, adding that charity was a virtue worthy of salvation. To exacerbate matters, high-ranking church authorities only fueled parishioners' concerns when they depicted their republican foes in patently eschatological terms. For example in his 8 December 1889 Pastoral Letter, Dom Luíz Antoônio dos Santos, archbishop of Bahia, warned of an international plot authored by political radicals associated with masonry. He claimed that they had "assaulted . . . the faith, dogma, and all the supernatural with the aim of excluding God from all social relations, robbing the Pope of all the power that earthly power had long guaranteed; closing the convents, banning the Religious Orders . . . confiscating [the church's] wealth, [and] erasing God's name from all the acts of human life, from the very buildings and public monuments" (cited in Bastos 1995, 110). The archbishop went on to label these developments as part of "the new Religion of Satan" (ibid., 111).

The Sundering of the Pact and the Emergence of Millenarian Movements

For many centuries a hegemonic pact of sorts had been struck between poor backlanders and members of the dominant classes, a pact predicated on a basic conception that time on earth was brief and inconsequential. Secular and church leaders were thought to be facilitating their dependents' attainment of the true reward of salvation after death in return for their obedience (Otten 1994). Nonetheless, as humble backlanders fought against sin and sought salvation, they faced the tension between the demands of the spiritual order and the realities of mundane life. Remarking on this tension de Groot writes, "Many world religions profess the need to make social life congruent with the models presented by the heavenly order in as many respects as possible. . . . The question is: do people think that their religious culture accomplishes this task? Do they think the tension is resolved and that society offers the individual a proper stage for salvation? Or do they feel that the tension is acute and requires more specific action?" (1996, 3).

For most people during much of the colonial period, this tension was sustained at a manageable level. Elite and popular discourses that asserted the providential power of the monarch and his representatives, as well as ecclesiastical and folk Catholic rituals that communicated the sanctity of hierarchy and relations of loyalty and protection, helped in this regard. Yet this was a system of meanings and social practices best suited to a seignorial regime. Over the course of the 1800s and early 1900s this regime was challenged and ultimately overshadowed by new systems of production and governance controlled by members of the agrarian and industrial bourgeoisie. In the midst of these profound changes, a hegemonic crisis ensued.[21] The crisis deeply shook backlanders' trust and confidence in their superiors' willingness and capacity to assist them in attaining spiritual rewards and material security. Indeed, decades passed before new hegemonic discourses and sets of habitual practices were fully elaborated and broadly disseminated among the elite and subaltern classes alike. These discourses, when they emerged, were designed to make the capitalist order and the republic appear equally preordained, efficacious, and moral as previous regimes, if not more so.[22] Or, to paraphrase Pierre Bourdieu, that "ideological alchemy" whereby necessity becomes virtue was constructed (1971, 300). In the meantime, many turn-of-the-century backlanders found meaning and solace in that corpus of beliefs and practices that had for so long sustained their faith and promoted their material well-being.

Backlanders initially turned to such routine religious practices as performing acts of penitence and making promessas to powerful saints in the hopes of gaining divine assistance (Pessar 1982). Tragically, the misery and exploitation continued. For many it must have appeared that the saints had chosen to abandon them just as had their once-trusted patrons. Under these dire circumstances, traditional Catholicism's narrative of the imminent apocalypse appealed to many thousands who lacked a new language or set of routine practices (for example, citizens' rights, strikes, and the creation of labor unions) to interpret and negotiate their changing times.

A Millennial View of Destiny

Prior to the ultramontane reforms most priests emphatically warned that God and the saints were becoming increasingly alienated from humanity due to its sins. This was also the message disseminated by those lay practitioners who filled the breach in the absence of an official church presence in the countryside. Clergy and laity, alike, came to rely on Padre José Gonçalves Couto's almost thousand-page *Missão abreviada para despertar os descuidados, converter os pecadores e sustentar o fructo das missões* (*Short Missal to Awaken the Careless, Convert the Sinners, and Sustain the Work of the Missions*). By the time Antônio Conselheiro purchased his copy in 1878, it was in its eleventh edition. It was also the text that is said to have inspired Pedro Batista some sixty years later to embark on his career as a thaumaturge. One of the *Missão abreviada*'s many apocalyptic passages reads, "This is the truth, that after the time that is rapidly drawing to an end, an eternity will arise that will never end. The eternity must be happy or sad; there will be nothing between" (199).

Beyond such biblical texts, apocalyptic thought was incorporated into popular hymns (*benditos*), chap books, and everyday discourse.[23] Consider the following traditional bendito sung at times of drought.

My Father, my lord,
We have so much suffering.
The drought is great.
All is dust.
It is all dust
Because of our sins.
Because they are so great
We are all castigated. . . .
Without your grace
We are all starving to death.
In the homes of the poor
No one eats. . . .
Do not abandon us.
Look down at the earth.
She is scourged
With hunger and war . . .
And pestilence too.
Have mercy, Our Lady
Forever, Amen.

Given the advanced age (in 1974) of the people who furnished this and other benditos about drought and given their claims to have learned these hymns as young children, it is likely that such prayers existed in the late 1800s. All contain references to drought as the precursor of hunger, pestilence, war, and death—those same scourges referred to repeatedly in the apocalyptic biblical text Revelation. These hymns, therefore, likely served to alert people to the dire connection between droughts and the unfolding of the apocalypse.

Such scourges were also prominent in prophecies delivered by itinerant prophets, some of which were transcribed in popular chapbooks. One such text, about a prophet who announced the end of the world, states,

> Then he began to advise
> All that was about to unfold.
> That the pestilence, hunger, and war
> Were about to appear. (Fernandes 1938, 161)

These words are reminiscent of those attributed to the early-nineteenth-century friar Vitale da Frascarolo. As the highly popular cleric traveled throughout the Northeast, he warned of "a drought accompanied by a dark sun" and "a multitude of pests that left few tracks." These marked the start of the great agonies that would be unleashed, according to Vitale, because humanity dared to scorn God's law (Otten 1994, 68).[24]

These observations suggest that the devastating and recurring droughts of the late 1800s and early 1900s, coupled with profoundly aberrant behavior (such as cannibalism and child prostitution), a high incidence of crime, and epidemic diseases, were interpreted by many as signs of the long-awaited apocalypse. Much of the attraction for messianic figures like Antônio Conselheiro and José Maria must have been their willingness both to confirm and authenticate these fears and to provide counsel on how to attain salvation. For example, a letter removed from the pocket of one of Conselheiro's followers in 1897 before he was executed by the military read, "Our Conselheiro said that whoever doesn't leave for here will come to ill, as it is now the time of Salvation" (Levine 1992, 169). And a prayer found on the body of a dead Contestado rebel clearly stated that God threatens hunger, pain, and suffering to all who sin and do not follow his orders. It continued, "I will send kings to battle each other, armies to fight one another, and sons to fight fathers and mothers. [It is only] thanks to my Paternal love that you have been saved thus far, [for otherwise] you would have already been condemned for your injustices" (Diacon 1991, 118).

Certainly in the millenarian communities members were encouraged to compose and share apocalyptic narratives. A striking example is found among the writings left behind by followers of Antônio Conselheiro, which explain that Jesus is tiring of the sins of the world and is sending warning signs and a prophet, Antônio Conselheiro, who encounters much opposition among men. The eschatological signs cited include the construction of the railroad, the deposing of the emperor, the advent of the republic, and the population census (Otten 1994).

Fears that the church hierarchy had also been undermined by satanic forces only added to the dread. Indeed, as early as 1874 poor parishioners, alarmed by such rumors, assaulted churches and destroyed books and furnishings in Pernambuco and Ceará (Levine 1992, 211). Distrust in the official church and its capacity to lead its flock along the road to salvation also led one of Conselheiro's chief lieutenants to advise visiting priests, in no uncertain terms, that "when it came to matters of eternal salvation, the population of Canudos had no need of their ministrations" (1895 report by Friar João Evangelista, cited in Levine 1992, 150).[25]

Finally, to fully appreciate why millenarian movements developed at the turn of the twentieth century, one must also consider the principle of "resentment." As Max Weber (1963) noted, the religions of the dispossessed classes often encompass the promise of divine vengeance against members of the elite. In Catholicism, for example, the pious poor are to be rewarded after death and again on the Day of Judgment for their faith and resignation. On the other hand, eternal torment awaits those who have abused their power and wealth. As a traditional bendito proclaims,

> The mighty of this world
> In the next they will find
> Our Lady crying
> And the devil well contented.

In his writings, too, Antônio Conselheiro cited the biblical example of Lazarus to underscore the need for charity on the part of the rich if they were to have any chance at attaining salvation (Nogueira 1978). More darkly, Padre Cícero purportedly prophesized that "nation will fight against nation . . . the people will revolt against their governments . . . and the poor will turn against the rich, and they will kill and overthrow the nobility and the powerful. [Ultimately, all will be subject to God's will on the Day of Judgment, as] neither rich nor poor will escape" (Otten 1994, 68).

For most poor backlanders resentment was held in check as long as elite Brazilians held up their end of the patriarchal pact. Indeed, under these circumstances, they were, as Antônio Conselheiro himself wrote, "Ministers of God for the [general] good."[26] Accordingly, they should be respected and obeyed as if they were God himself (Nogueira 1978, 566). Yet, when many earthly protectors chose to abandon their sacred and social trust, and when their actions proceeded to undermine spiritual and social harmony, then it was only just and prudent to denounce them and to replace them with a more ethical brand of leader.

This interpretation helps to clarify the promonarchical ideology evident in the Canudos, Contestado, and Juazeiro movements.[27] Who after all best epitomized those hegemonic meanings and values that morally united the vulnerable poor with the elite than the monarch? As Levine (1992, 210) notes, for rural backlanders Emperor Pedro II was a father figure and a kind of earthly saint; discreetly, messianic leaders never commented on his masonic connections nor on his passivity over the Religious Question. Instead, José Maria read aloud to his followers passages from *The History of Charlemagne*, in order, one imagines, to encourage monarchist feelings and rekindle beliefs in divine right and destiny. One survivor accordingly explained to his interrogators, "Our families require the protection of religion to be content; the monarchy is the only law that can help the lives of sinners, and that is what José Maria wanted for the happiness of his people" (Diacon 1991, 117).

Millenarianism as Popular Culture

So, again, how is it that millenarianism moved over the course of several centuries from an elite discourse of empire building, messianic warriors, and providential destiny to an ideology that emboldened scores of poor backlanders to denounce government and church authorities and to create alternative communities largely beyond the reach of estate owners and the emerging agrarian bourgeoisie? Part of the answer lies in the very success enjoyed by members of both the dominant and the subordinate classes. Together they drew on religious meanings and rituals to produce a hegemonic notion of harmony and symmetry between the supernatural and social realms. This construction contributed to a begrudging, if not more ardent, acceptance of the morality and immutability of the long-lived seignorial order. It also promoted ongoing negotiations between the dominant and dominated over their mutual responsibilities and obligations within this larger scheme.

It is little wonder, then, that when confronted with those hardships and uncertainties attendant to major political and economic transitions and with a subsequent hegemonic crisis, many backlanders turned to traditional Catholicism. There they found meaning and succor in the very same religious mean-

ings and practices that had long promoted order, spiritual rewards, and material security. Even if some backlanders might have entertained the idea of
struggling to reform key social institutions through collective, overtly political
means, to many the task of reforming society must have seemed at this juncture
"more overwhelming and less rewarding than the task of reforming their own
souls, particularly since they believed that in this effort they would have God
on their side" (Costa 1994, 9). Indeed, in a context in which even their saints
seemed to have forsaken them, thousands of backlanders turned for protection and guidance to an even higher spiritual order: popular spiritual leaders
whom they believed were either God himself or his special emissaries on earth.

On the face of it, there was nothing necessarily radical about these backlanders' reembrace of a sacralized and highly personalistic order. Nonetheless, large landowners in the communities surrounding Juazeiro, Canudos, and
Contestado vilified the messianic leaders who had reconstituted highly personalistic and precapitalist values and relations. For example, Antônio Conselheiro's nemesis, the Baron of Jeremoabo, criticized Conselheiro's followers
for having sold their lands, homes, and livestock at significantly below market
prices. He further chided them for spending so much time in prayer rather than
providing much needed labor to him and other estate owners (Bastos 1995,
178–79). In all the holy cities monetary charity, as well as shelter and land,
were provided to the destitute by the religious leaders and certain of their followers (Della Cava 1970; Levine 1992; Monteiro 1974). These measures miti-
gated those steps toward greater proletarianization favored by many members
of the bourgeoisie.

At that moment in time there could be little tolerance for the millennial beliefs, mystical/"irrational" subjectivities, and communal practices that flour-
ished in the holy cities. They gestured far too appealingly and defiantly to an
all-too-familiar "past," while challenging the new elites' uncertain future and
their authority to set the nation's course. Initially, turn-of-the-century modernizers attempted to co-opt popular millenarian leaders. This strategy proved
generally successful in Juazeiro.[28] In Canudos and Contestado where it failed, a
war of words that effectively stripped the backlanders of reason and humanity
ensued. With the stroke of a pen, they became "fanatics," "insane," or as a
cousin of the Baron of Jeremoabo wrote, "all miserable ex-slaves and crimi-
nals from every province, without a single one who is a human being" (Levine
1992, 140). This discursive assault drew a line between a subhuman and dangerous race of rural folk and their enlightened superiors who championed scientifically informed and restructured national markets, state power, and modes
of producing "truths." This fashioning of poor backland subjects into fanat-

ics and nonhumans calls to mind Michel de Certeau's observation (2000) that deviltries are both social symptoms and transitional solutions.

Such demonization at periods of major transition is often a preamble to physical and social erasure. Thus, in the name of and in service to Brazil's national bourgeoisie, da Cunha writes, "Canudos . . . was a parenthesis, a hiatus . . . a vacuum. It did not exist" (da Cunha 1944, 444).[29] Indeed, obliteration was ensured when 8,000 men were placed under the command of the war minister and ordered to finish off the starving rebels at Canudos (Levine 1992) and when a batallion of nearly one-half of the Brazilian army was deployed in Contestado and charged with carrying out a "scorched-earth" policy (Diacon 1991). It was in this very same spirit of excision, containment, and scientific reason that Antônio Conselheiro's severed head was paraded on a spike through the streets of Salvador, examined for congenital abnormalities by a leading medical proponent of eugenics, and finally preserved and displayed at the Medical Faculty (Levine 1992, 184).

From Elite to Popular Discourse and Practice

Over the sweep of several centuries Brazilian millenarianism moved from an elite to a popular set of discourses and practices. In the mid-1800s republican leaders and officials of the Catholic Church embarked on projects of modernity, which among other things entailed a repudiation of all vestiges of that mystical enchantment associated with folk Catholicism—including millenarianism. The most stalwart republicans even spurned the Catholic Church and joined new religions based on Positivist teachings. Key republican leaders also spearheaded the creation of national and state constitutions devoid of references to God (Azevedo 1981). Some clearly found such innovations appealing. Yet others, including the many thousands of backlanders who joined millenarian movements, perceived these ideological changes and their accompanying social, political, and economic initiatives to be illegitimate and dangerous to their spiritual and material well-being.

If Peter Berger's (1967) felicitous term, the "sacred canopy," characterizes those earlier times when many Brazilians were inclined to convert unequal power relations into something that was at best sanctified and at worst routinized through practice, then by the end of the 1800s this canopy had become largely threadbare. With little if any assurances that their patrons and national leaders would deliver on past understandings and promises, thousands of poor backlanders found meaning and guides for action in time-honored folk Catholicism. Moreover, the resentment this belief system harbored, yet managed for the most part to keep in check, was unleashed when members of the elite systematically reneged on past, mutually held understandings about the ethics and practices of patrimonial authority. For their part, members of the fledgling bourgeoisie tried to co-opt rebellious millenarianists, but when this failed the might of the pen and the sword followed.

THE POVO MAKE A SAINT

Such self-styled modernizers as the physicians who turned Conselheiro's severed head first into a laboratory specimen and then into a museum curiosity sought to contain and ultimately to extirpate "fanatical" behavior from what they perceived to be their less enlightened countrymen/women (o povo). Yet well into the mid-1900s backlanders like those who flocked to Pedro Batista continued to contest the elite's denigration of them and to resist efforts directed at forcing them to abandon their religious convictions and practices. They also pursued, whenever possible, opportunities to contest and to negotiate the terms of both hegemonic rule and modernity. The followers of Pedro Batista managed to do so by hitching their stars to an elderly penitent whom many believed to be the incarnation of both the deceased Padre Cícero and Jesus Christ.

Previous studies of Pedro Batista and other millenarian leaders begin with the charismatic figure firmly in place. This overlooks one of the crucial steps in the social production of popular millenarian movements: the "sacralizing process," as I call it. Had the events of my 1970s fieldwork not foisted its significance on me, I too might have failed to address this process. At that time a would-be replacement for the then deceased Pedro Batista faced his own crucible of sacralization. My ability to observe firsthand this patterned, yet highly contentious process convinced me of the need to reconstruct, with the help of romeiros and nonromeiros alike, the initial process by which Pedro Batista was accepted or rejected as a figure with extraordinary spiritual power (mistério). In combining my findings about this initial phase of the Pedro Batista movement with analogous (but heretofore unanalyzed) materials from the Jua-zeiro, Canudos, and Contestado movements, I reveal the intertextuality among movements within the backland millenarian genre and offer a more general model of the social construction of Brazilian millenarian leaders.

Pedro Batista and His Mission

Pedro Batista's past—that is, his life before he embarked on his penitential mission in the late 1930s and came to the attention of a broader public—is a subject relevant both to a more general account of the movement and to the particular subject at hand. Unfortunately, I (and others) have been unsuccessful in uncovering "official" documentation (such as a birth certificate and military records) relating to his youth and adult life prior to his emergence as a beato. Moreover, written accounts and oral histories that treat Batista's early years dif-fer in important details. While such discrepancies are frustrating empirically, from the vantage point of those who recognize Pedro Batista as a divine emis-sary such discrepancies are to be expected. Indeed they are perfectly consistent with popular understandings of a person with divine gifts (*dom*) and mistério, since part of what separates them from everyday people is their lack of relatively transparent pasts.

In her writings Pereira de Queiroz reports that Pedro Batista was born in Alagoas, but his family soon had to flee to neighboring Pernambuco owing to his father's political problems (Queiroz 1965b). A competing account told to me by a romeiro confidant of Batista alleges that the beato was born sometime in the 1880s in Porto do Calvo, Alagoas, and remained there during his youth.[1] He never knew his father who was a large landowner and a *branco* (light-skinned individual). According to this second version, Batista's mother, "a full-blooded Indian," died when he was a baby, leaving him to be raised by her brothers. Many years later Batista attempted to reclaim some of his then deceased uncles' lands. Unfortunately, by then the property had fallen into the hands of powerful and unscrupulous mill owners. Batista purportedly did manage to find a judge willing to acknowledge his familial ties to the land. Nonetheless, neither the judge nor anyone else was willing to help Batista press ahead with his claim. A disappointed Batista had no choice but to move on (Fernando Reis 1999).[2]

Although these two accounts differ on the location of Batista's upbringing and the prominence of his parents, they do agree on the very basic fact that he was a son of the Northeast. Yet even this detail has been challenged of late, to the considerable chagrin of many romeiros. The latest, highly controversial version holds that Pedro Batista was born and raised in the Southern state of

Paraná, where an alleged elderly niece and other family members continue to reside. What is certainly true is that an important component of Pedro Batista's mistério was that he appeared to have no known kin.

There is greater agreement on the details of Batista's early and mid-adult years. As a young man Batista apparently served in the army, having been posted in the Northeast and in the South. While stationed in Maceió, the youthful soldier was ordered to destroy ritual objects owned by practitioners of Afro-Brazilian religions. In doing so, he served at the bequest of a federal government that classified Afro-Brazilian and spiritist (e.g., Kardecist) religions as marginal, deviant, and potentially subversive; once settled in Santa Brígida, Batista and many of his romeiros continued to hold distrust and disdain for Afro-Brazilian practices and practitioners. Soon after his mission in Maceió, young Batista was sent on another mission, again to protect the fledgling republic from religious "fanatics" and "subversion." This time his unit was called into action to fight the millenarianists of Contestado. Some claim the battle ended before his contingent arrived; others contend that he deserted rather than participate in the fighting. A few romeiros have speculated that Batista's memories of the carnage there so profoundly affected him that he later committed himself to a life of penitence. Others suggest that Batista's years in the military contributed to his insistence on discipline and order within the romaria as well as to his eagerness to cooperate with military and police officials. After his stint in the army, Batista remained in the South, working in Rio de Janeiro and Santos as a seaman, a stevedore, and a fisherman (Zezé Ramos 1999; Fernando Reis 1999).

Pedro Batista told his followers that after his many years at sea he decided to settle down in Paraná and turn his hand to farming. It was during this latter period that he contracted a mysterious illness that no doctor seemed capable of curing. As he recounted, one day long into this debilitating illness, he felt the sudden urge to arise from his sickbed and leaf through the pages of the *Missão Abreviada*, a book the illiterate Batista always kept close by. It immediately opened to an illustration of Jesus kneeling before an angel, and the image riveted his gaze for a good long time, seeming to speak directly to him. Perplexed and fatigued, Batista returned to his sickbed, where he fell immediately into a deep sleep. He soon had a dream in which the same angel pictured in the illustration stated, "Yes, my son, it is not by chance that you opened to that page in the holy book. Your mission and Jesus' are one and the same" (Alzira Bezerra 1974).

When he awakened from the dream, Pedro Batista realized that he was totally cured. He was later to explain to his followers that during his long illness the spirit he had been born with had been totally burned away. He had received another spirit whose identity he was not at liberty to divulge. It commanded him to preach God's warnings about the imminent apocalypse throughout his native Northeast Brazil (ibid.). A revitalized Pedro Batista exchanged his invalid's bedclothes for the beatos' long dark tunic, and in 1938 he headed north on foot to fulfill his mission. During the seven years of his penitential journey (*caminhada*), he attracted thousands of followers whom he began to resettle in the small town of Santa Brígida, Bahia, in June 1945.

The Thaumaturge Years, 1938–1945

Just as a shortage of documentation makes it impossible to reconstruct a "definitive" history of the first five decades of Pedro Batista's life, so too is there a dearth of material with which to lay out a precise itinerary or exact chronology of the beato's seven-year caminhada.[3] What we do have, however, is a written account, in verse, about the beato from the perspective of one of Pedro Batista's most-trusted associates within the romaria. João Oliveira's "Vida e Morte do Meu Padrinho" (Life and Death of My Godfather) offers a glimpse not only into these extremely important early years in the beato's career but also into one of the sacralizing venues through which Batista's status as a spiritual leader was asserted and set out for wider public consumption.

While more secular histories may begin by begging the reader's indulgence for certain shortcomings, such as unavoidable gaps in archival material, Oliveira elects to begin his account by admonishing,

> I request of my God
> With hope and living faith
> That God helps me
> And the devil stays away
> So that I can write correctly
> The history of my Padrinho
> Pedro Batista da Silva. (n.d., 1)

Clearly Oliveira sees his task as something far more momentous and daunting than the mere presentation and analysis of empirical facts. In assuming responsibility for recounting the life of Pedro Batista, he understands that he has entered into a moral contract with his protagonist and with his readers/audience. He recognizes, too, the weighty obligation of bearing witness to the life of a man who is for him a divine emissary. He also acknowledges what is for him and his readers the ever-present danger of falling prey to satanic deception. Before presenting details about Pedro Batista's penitential journey, Oliveira also takes care to address the unknowable nature of Batista's past, stating,

> Where he came from no one knows.
> No one can comprehend.
> The common folk would ask him,
> He would not say.
> These were his obligations
> For God's secrets
> Are for no one to know. (ibid., 4)

With this verse Oliveira seems to be alerting his audience to the fact that while the rest of the narrative will contain memorable episodes drawn from the beato's more recent past, the bulk of Batista's life and very being remain shrouded in mystery, as befits a divine being.

The romeiro author also comments at the outset of his narrative on the epochal nature of Batista's mission, on his extraordinary powers—indeed suggesting that he is God ("the great pardoner")—and on the gravity of his apocalyptic message.

> He departed the state of Paraná
> In order to fulfill the mission
> Of the Eternal Father,
> Counseling the Christians
> That the world was coming to an end.
> All should take care to pray
> To avoid the great engulfing.
>
> He who drinks, drink no more.
> All turn to prayer
> And take heed to perform acts of penitence.
> All stop smoking
> And stop sinning
> Because the time has arrived
> For the total consummation.
>
> Providing this counsel
> Blessing water too,
> Curing the sick and the possessed

Of all the bad that they have today.
In less than a second expelling the spirit . . .

The spirits shouted,
This is the judge
Who has come to exorcise the spirits
From the bodies of the sinner.
He has come to give universal forgiveness.
All should believe
That this is the great pardoner.

It is the order of his mission
To not use any form of transport,
But to travel on foot
From the South to the North
Mortifying himself
To fulfill this mission,
Even if it were to cost him his life. (ibid., 4–5)

It is at this point, after having introduced his audience to the remarkable powers and importance of the narrative's protagonist, that Oliveira changes gears a bit to map out a rough itinerary of the beato's seven-year journey. He states that Batista headed north passing through São Paulo, Rio de Janeiro, and Minas Gerais, on his way to Ceará. Along the way he "cured from morning until night . . . curing the crippled and the blind" (ibid., 6). Once in Ceará, Batista made his way to Juazeiro.

[When] he was within the city
He looked around
Noticing the great loss
Without Padre Cícero.
The city grew
But it was lacking its pastor.
Only God can send another. (ibid.)

While all devotees of Padre Cícero would likely concur with the last line of the verse, Oliveira strives to awaken in his audience the conviction that Pedro Batista is none other than this anxiously awaited replacement. In his assertion that Juazeiro is "lacking its pastor," Oliveira is also offering a popular and transgressive reading on the state of ecclesiastical affairs in Juazeiro. Following Padre Cícero's death, local church leaders redoubled their efforts to stifle folk

Catholic beliefs and practices, especially those related to the miracle and the priest's supernatural powers. Many romeiros resisted. A particularly dramatic confrontation in 1935 found twelve self-styled romeiro guards refusing to permit the then resident priest from entering Our Lady of Sorrows (Juazeiro's main church) on the grounds that he was a communist. Ten soldiers arrived on the scene and fired on the guards, killing six (Slater 1986).

Not surprisingly, Batista met a chilly reception with authorities in Juazeiro, and accordingly headed east to Recife, the capital of Pernambuco. From there he fanned out to many towns and hamlets in the state, finding himself imprisoned in many of the towns he passed through. According to Oliveira,

> The jailers would leave the jail unlocked at night.
> He would always awaken there the next morning
> Never thinking of evading the sentence he was given.
>
> In the city of Águas Belas
> His suffering was great.
> Eleven months in prison
> Because of the people.
> Many people followed him;
> The government did not want this;
> They imprisoned him in many places.
>
> He was locked up
> Without bread or water
> As they tried to get him to give up
> His great mission.
> But he did not succumb.
> The more they tried to punish him
> The greater his satisfaction grew. (n.d., 7)

These verses capture a move by authorities to define and treat Batista as a criminal, a symbolic framing and treatment contested by Oliveira and other devotees who read these actions as examples of martyrdom and as proof of Batista's obedience to a higher authority.

Oliveira states that as word spread of miraculous cures ever-growing numbers were attracted to Batista, which only fueled greater persecution by Pernambuco state authorities and even assassination attempts. The beato then journeyed through the states of Sergipe and Alagoas where he continued to attract many supporters, some of whom elected to accompany him on his continuing travels.

High ranking authorities
Ordered him to cease curing
And giving counsel
So that the people would leave him.
He responded thusly:
It is for this that I have come;
No one can hinder me.

It is an order from the Eternal Father
I am destined to complete.
Where ever they do not accept me
I will prepare to take leave;
The world is vast for me.
With Jesus they did the same;
I, too, will persevere. (ibid., 9)

Oliveira tells of one last jailing in the town of Água Branca, Alagoas. Having been expelled from that state, Pedro Batista made his way into Bahia where he finally settled.

These select verses describe the places Batista frequented over the course of his caminhada and the type of people he encountered. They also offer an appreciation from a romeiro point of view of Batista's successes and tribulations. Yet readers are privy to much more. All histories are to some extent ideological narratives, no matter how objective — or in this case, inspired by spiritual powers — they aspire to be. As critical scholarship in social and cultural history points out, historical texts suffer from intentional silences (Trouillot 1995) as well as unfortunate erasures due to a lack of documentary material for certain people and events. The chapbook genre in which "Vida e Morte do Meu Padrinho" is written recalls those poor, often illiterate, rural Brazilians whose pasts and current experiences are rarely inscribed in archival documents or entered into official histories. At one level, then, what Oliveira provides is a popular history of Pedro Batista and his social movement, complete with local colloquial turns of phrase and (in the original Portuguese) the rhyming verse format so easy on the ear for the many who would hear rather than read the text.

At another level, though, the narrative accomplishes far more than merely informing and entertaining its audience. The text also advances moral claims about who Pedro Batista is and how he fits into the Northeasterners' cosmological, ethical, and social systems. As Candace Slater observes, cordel stories "do not simply record events but play an active role in shaping these. . . . At heart, a cordel story is a moral question whose answer becomes evident through a largely ritual narrative process" (1982, 212–16). This narrative process occasionally features a battle between good and evil and contends that while poverty and injustice plague the poor, intermediaries in the form of saints, ethical priests, holy persons, and good patrons do intervene between God and those in need; consequently, miracles can and do occur.[4] In Oliveira's decision to feature certain key episodes in Batista's journey—his martyrdom at the hands of members of the elite, his obedience before unjust authority, his embrace of poverty, his penitential practices, his many miracles—he contributed to that popular project wherein a "stranger" is refashioned into a beato/conselheiro and, still more significant, into a santo.

The Santo

Among backlanders the distinction between a beato and a santo is an important one. The beato, much like a priest, furnishes religious teachings and ethical counsel. Moreover, owing to the beato's extraordinary goodness and faith, he or she proves to be particularly efficacious when solicited to intercede with God on a petitioner's behalf. A person who is considered a santo, by contrast, is not viewed as an intermediary at all. Rather, these charismatic figures are believed to be so close to God and so powerful that they perform miracles themselves without requiring God's intercession (see also Zaluar 1983, 104–5). In rare instances, the belief in the santo's closer proximity to God encourages people to take the far more dramatic step of concluding that the santo is in fact God. Yet, as Luitgarde Oliveira Cavalcanti Barros points out, the santos' many virtues, including humility, goodness, poverty, and penitence, "distinguish them from common men but it does not separate [the santos] from them" (1997, 52). Instead, santos hold great attraction for backlanders who come to see themselves reflected in these victimized yet beatific penitents. What they find, according to Zaluar, is "a positive social identity for those who are poor, dispossessed, subordinated, and socially inferior" (1983, 105).

Studies of millenarianism in Brazil and elsewhere commonly introduce a figure called the "prophet" or "messiah," reflecting an eagerness to categorize and label that, in effect, obscures the local terms and meanings attached to such figures. While in my earlier work I was also guilty of this practice, I now join Zaluar in carefully scrutinizing the use of the term *messiah* for individuals who were often referred to explicitly by their followers as santos: São João Maria, São José Maria, and Bom Jesus Conselheiro (Zaluar 1983, 106).[5]

There are two separate and frequently opposed projects involved in the act of bestowing sainthood. Official canonization falls to high-ranking church au-

A statue of Padre
Cícero in front of the
altar of a romeiro
home. Photo by the
author.

thorities who follow strict and highly codified tenets. The other project, as Barros states, "represents a social construction of common people (povo) who
themselves make saints" (1997, 52). On the one hand, the church's actions have
occasionally so disturbed backland parishioners that they have steadfastly refused to adopt a newcomer into their pantheon of saints, as was the case in
rural Brazil for Christ the King (Cristo Rei), Our Lady of Lourdes, and Our Lady
of Fátima. On the other hand, backlanders' attempts to sanctify penitential
figures like Antônio Conselheiro, Padre Cícero, and Pedro Batista gravely of-
fended and violated the teachings of the Roman Catholic church. Clerics have
commonly stepped forward to denounce such "heresy."[6]

Although Barros astutely draws attention to the rural peoples' agency in
socially constructing their own saints, she fails to describe exactly how this
social construction develops. Closer analysis isolates four activities central to
the sacralizing process: the separation of the religious figure from the political
sphere by the obscuring of his family ties;[7] the leader's presentation of himself to potential followers as an ideal patron; his capacity to create a performance that showcases his divine power and teachings; and the development of
miracle stories by his devotees. While my analysis focuses on Pedro Batista's

early career, I make reference to other successful charismatic figures to illustrate the broader utility and applicability of this framework for the study of the popular construction of Brazilian millenarian leaders.[8] I also contrast the povo's acts of social construction with those of elite actors, such as journalists, who denounce and disenchant the subaltern project. This dialectic of cultural struggle is yet another feature in the social construction of a santo. It pits members of the dominant and popular classes against each other. At stake are the appropriate meanings to affix to the actions and motives of popular santos, their devotees, and their detractors and to contesting claims concerning likely outcomes of such subaltern activity.

THE SEPARATION OF THE SANTO
FROM THE POLITICAL REALM

The figure of the santo gains its distinctiveness and much of its power among backlanders by what it is not. The santo belongs fully and unambiguously to the world of *religião* (religion). As such, he or she is elevated far above the more mundane and divisive political sphere. In this classificatory system religião is understood to encompass such ethical elements as piety, devotion, sacrifice, altruism, and redistribution (many of the characteristics Victor Turner [1969] associates with antistructure and "communitas"). Politics (*a política*), by contrast, are those behaviors that contribute to contestation and sustain differences in power and wealth.[9]

A santo must demonstrate through words and actions as well as through claims advanced by others that he or she belongs solely to the world of religião. As the following statement by Dona Dodô attests, dire consequences follow if the line between religião and política is breached: "I was with my Padrinho Pedro Batista in 1940 when we met a very extraordinary man. This was the only person I've ever seen my Padrinho take a blessing from! This man who was filled with mistério, advised my Padrinho that his mission was not to enter into the world of men. His mission was another. This man said that many would try to murder my Padrinho, but none would succeed. He warned that my Padrinho could only be undone if he entered into politics."[10]

As the povo proceeded to construct their own saints they attempted to remove those whom they suspected were divine from the sullied domain of política. In doing so, they had to successfully navigate matters of kinship, because in rural Brazil at the time of Pedro Batista and the other santos considered herein politics and kinship were very much intertwined. As Pereira de Queiroz writes, "To explain who a man was, it was essential to say whose son and kinsman he was. Only then was it clear what relations held between any two

people; whether of cooperation or conflict. . . . In the Northeast as in the Contestado, kinship determined the socio-political affiliations. . . . The idiom of
the region itself still tends to express this intra-kinship solidarity and the importance of kin for the socio-political localization of the individual. To ask a
jagunço [bandit] of the South who he is, is to invite the answer 'I belong to
"colonel" so-and-so's folk,' and in turn the 'colonels' tend to use the expression
'my people' " (Queiroz 1965a, 68–69). If the cultural logic behind backlanders' concepts of charisma held that mundane politics were anathema and if an
individual's kin ties situated him or her within a sociopolitical landscape, then
those who claimed otherworldly powers did best to obscure and mystify their
kinship roots.

A surname and parentela (extended bilateral kindred) locate a rural Brazilian
within a sociopolitical space. Having no such name and kinship bonds removes
an individual from this sphere. An erasure of familial ties and, by extension, of
a fixed location within the political landscape appears to have been one of the
ways in which a religious figure might stake his or her claim to popular sainthood or have others advance such claims. For example, a verse from a literatura
de cordel about Padre Cícero claims,

> Mãe Quino gazed at her new born babe
> and the nurse went out to change her robes.
> An angel came down to close the sainted mother's eyes.
> She exchanged the babe for baby Cícero.
> Baby Cícero born not from woman, knowing no sin.
> Mãe Quino, his sainted mother could never see again.[11]

The denial of kinship ties can also occur through the dropping of the beato's
surname. Antônio Conselheiro, for example, shed the name, Antônio Maciel,
which allied him with the politically active Mendes Maciel clan of Ceará. In its
place he adopted several names, such as Brother Antônio, Antônio dos Mares,
and Antônio Conselheiro. Most elite commentators mocked these nomencla-
tures and the gullible people who accepted them (Diaz 1997). A notable exception is the renowned literary figure Machado de Assis, who at the very least
grasped the povo's intentions when they commenced to call their leader Conselheiro. He writes in an article dated 22 July 1894, "The telegram from Bahia
makes known that the Counselor is in Canudos with 2,000 men . . . fully armed.
What Counselor? They do not give him any name but one that sallies forth from
poetry and mystery" (cited in Diaz 1997, 92). Levine notes that when local politicians and clerics sought to discredit Conselheiro while he was still wandering

through the backlands and attracting large numbers of followers, they came up with what the historian calls "the preposterous charge that he had murdered his mother and wife in Ceará some years before" (Levine 1992, 137). But perhaps the apparently groundless charge was not so preposterous after all. Could it have been a strategically aimed broadside delivered by an elite who recognized the taint that kinship held for an aspiring charismatic leader and who therefore sought to remind the counselor's "gullible" followers that he like them had very real family connections?

Oliveira's narrative, too, obscured and rendered mysterious matters of Pedro Batista's true identity and past with such lines as "he would not say" when people asked him about himself, because "this was his obligation / For God's secrets / are for no one to know" (n.d., 4). To perpetuate the aura of the elusive nature of Pedro Batista's kinship, his followers emphasized that in all the years that they knew him not one person appeared claiming to be his relative. According to romeiro Fernando Reis (1974), "My Padrinho Pedro Batista's adopted family was unknown and his real family was not of this world."

Within the dialectic of cultural struggle, elite Northeasterners assigned very different meanings and motives to Batista's lack of roots. For them the absence of social ties rendered him antisocial, shiftless, and suspect. For example, in a very critical newspaper article written during the period of Batista's caminhada, the journalist followed a section that describes the beato as little more than a quack and pilferer with this observation: "Since Batista stated that he had relatives in Porto de Pedras, the sheriff Valdemar Silva sent a soldier to that town, where he found nothing that confirmed this statement" ("Encontra-se, atualmente na Baia, o beato Pedro Batista," *Jornal de Alagoas*, 25 February 1942, p. 6). An earlier article in the same journal condemned Batista for his apparent vagrancy, and it spoke of the "family of the sertão," who it claimed were jeopardized by the beato's fanaticism and who needed to be rescued by their paternalistic guardians (i.e., the newspaper's literate readers). "The sertão is once again agitated by the religious activities of a beato, one of these who have mobilized our population in the interior many times, fanaticizing them and creating a problem to be resolved in order to restore the tranquility of the *family of the sertão*. This time it is the beato Batista, *of unknown origin*. . . . Pilgrims follow him on foot, for leagues and leagues. . . . The pilgrimage . . . *does not have a definite destination*" ("As milagrosas curas do profeta Batista," *Jornal de Alagoas*, 14 February 1942, p. 6; emphasis added).

Although Batista's romeiros were certainly eager to separate him from the conventional domain of kinship, they even more readily placed him within that divine pantheon that included Padre Cícero, whose spirit Batista was believed to have received. It was this belief that encouraged many to apply the same honorific, Meu Padrinho (My Godfather), to both men.[12] As evidence of Batista's true identity, his supporters pointed to a pledge purportedly made by the priest shortly before his death in which he promised to return, as commemorated in the following bendito.

> In the year of '34
> He told us
> My children, I am going on a journey;
> My Father in the sky has told me.
>
> I am going, but I will return.
> Follow my commandments
> With faith recite your rosaries
> So you will be able to recognize me.

Romeiros were eager to tell me that when a zealous devotee or (exorcised) spirit presumed to call the beato either Padre Cícero or Our Father, he would thunder back, "My name is Pedro Batista da Silva, *curador*." Although this might seem to be a move on Batista's part to explicitly deny his divinity, the following statement about Padre Cícero is illuminating: "Because Northeasterners fully expect a saint to deny his or her sanctity, they would have seized upon any disavowal of his own powers . . . as added proof of his privileged spiritual status" (Slater 1986, 39).[13]

Moreover, Pedro Batista's denials were occasionally contradicted by tantalizing episodes, such as the time Dona Dodô was inspired to compose the following bendito (which, like João Oliveira's narrative, also mentions Batista's disheartening visit to Juazeiro early in his caminhada).

> God, hail Juazeiro,
> Send it a blessing.
> We come on a visit
> To my Padre Cícero Romão.
>
> God, hail Juazeiro,
> Land of the Blessed Saint.
> We remember my Godfather;
> Here he made his home.
>
> My Godfather appeared
> In an unknown place;

He could not remain here
Because he was not well received.

The romeiros do not remember
That my Godfather always said
When he reappeared
No one would recognize him. . . .

Dona Dodô told me that she immediately shared this bendito with the beato and that her recitation caused him to weep uncharacteristically and turn red in the face. After hearing the hymn in its entirety, Batista got up and secluded himself briefly. When he returned he asked, "Dodô, do you have the courage to sing that hymn? If you do, do so; because you have completely captured the truth." Not surprisingly, Dona Dodô's hymn immediately became popular among the romeiros, who reminded their listeners of the popular belief that only the most deserving and faithful possess the power to recognize Padre Cícero's replacement.

THE SANTO AS PATRON

Whether envisioned as an exchange entailing either devotion and obligation or loyalty and protection, poor backlanders forge ties with superiors in both the sacred and secular realms. While both types of exchange may lead to the forging of asymmetrical bonds of patronage and dependence, only the secular variety is understood by all to create a surplus of power and wealth for the dominant partner (Forman 1975). Consequently, segments of the rural masses and the elite evaluate the authenticity of would-be santos by observing how they manage their patronage relations. Santos are expected to follow the example set by celestial saints and therefore to reject riches and worldly power.

Often the bond of patronage between a devotee and a religious figure, like a penitent or curer, is forged through an initial act of charity—most commonly in the form of money, agricultural products, or livestock. The bestowing of charity is viewed by many as a form of recompense for those people who dedicate long hours to helping others yet might lose their powers were they to actively solicit payment. Many also believe that in giving charity to a poor penitent the donor will later receive grace and be pardoned for past sins.[14] Antônio Conselheiro purportedly preached that "those who aided his efforts by personal service or gifts of money would be forgiven their sins by God" (Queiroz 1965a, 82). On the other hand, some claim to be fearful about refusing aid to a legitimate penitent since these people possess great power and may punish those who anger them. João Maria is alleged to have received a small, putrid block of cheese as an offering from a rich farmer who intended to mock him. When the beato saw he could not eat the cheese, he placed it under a rock on the farmer's land. It is said that from that day on, the farmer and his sons lost money on their land, and the farmer ultimately died a poor man (Queiroz 1966, 58).[15] In the shift from beato to santo two operations associated with charity must be successfully accomplished. First, the beato must be so charismatic that he or she accumulates more money and goods than are needed for mere subsistence. Second, rather than accumulate the wealth, the religious figure must be willing to redistribute gifts of charity (*esmolas*) among the poor. This is what distinguishes those divinely ordained leaders from everyday patrons or, worse, charlatans who prey on the weak.

Making reference to the first operation wherein a beato successfully leaves the ranks of simple mendicancy, Mariano Alves drew a clear distinction between Pedro Batista who had managed this transition and another would-be santo who had not: "[Unlike my Padrinho Pedro Batista], the old man did not support the people. The people supported him. . . . He was a beggar. . . . He was also a good conselheiro. [But] he wasn't like my Padrinho, because my Padrinho was an exceptional case" (2000). And, alluding to the second operation, elderly romeira Alzira Bezerra (1974) took me aside right before I journeyed with Dona Dodô and several other romeiros to visit a contemporary curer in another state who was beginning to receive many devotees and a large cache of donations. Bezerra advised,

> This is the time we poor watch these curers and penitents most carefully. There are always the ignorant fanatics who will be deluded no matter what. But most watch to see what the person does with the charity from the poor and rich alike. Satan has his way with so many. I can't tell you the number of charlatans I have seen who thrive on people's ignorance and misery, taking their money and fleeing without having helped anyone. We have a saying, "Give charity and it will multiply one-hundred fold." With people like Dona Dodô, Dona Maria [the popular curer we were about to visit], and my Padrinho Pedro Batista, you can actually see this. The small amounts they receive are joined with the charity from others, and then given in small amounts to all the many poor creatures. . . . I have never seen a politician do this, except maybe Getúlio Vargas, and some say he too was God's messenger.

Consistent with this model of charismatic leadership, Antônio Conselheiro also divested himself of surplus wealth early in his career by giving charity to the poor (Montenegro 1954, 22) and by paying laborers who worked on construction projects he sponsored. While his followers viewed such generosity as in keeping with his mistério, a very different reading of these practices is found in a letter to the chief of police in Bahia. Written in 1886 by the deputy of a town that Antônio Conselheiro often frequented, it labels the beato's followers as ignorant, indolent, and criminal while it charges Conselheiro with inflating local wages. "On the days of sermons, beads, and litanies, his congregation mounts to a thousand persons. In the building of this chapel, the cost of which in labor is nearly a hundred milreis, or ten times what it ought to be, this Antônio Conselheiro employs individuals from Ceará. . . . All this money comes from the credulous and the ignorant, who not only do no labor for themselves, but who sell the few goods that they possess and even steal in order that not the slightest thing may be lacking which the Counselor requires. This is not to speak of the sums paid in for other works" (da Cunha 1944, 138).[16]

José Maria, too, redistributed the charity he received among those poor people who sought a cure or counsel. According to Maurício Vinhas de Queiroz, the most important cure in the beato's career was performed on an old landowner and his wife who had been deceived by doctors. "It is said that Francisco de Almeida remained so appreciative that he offered José Maria land and many ounces of gold. José Maria refused and thus it was through this indifference that his fame as a curer was further heightened" (Queiroz 1966, 84).

Padre Cícero clearly distinguished himself as a gifted patron, finding jobs in the manufacture of handicrafts and in farming for the scores of newcomers attracted to Juazeiro. Moreover, he managed to make a number of sound investments with the money donated to him. And even his detractors had to concede that the profits from these "did not go into his own pocket but were placed at the service of the needy" (Slater 1986, 36).

Finally, in Pedro Batista's early wandering days he would only accept charity from a person whom he was sure could afford the sacrifice. According to informants, he gave the needy money and goods that he had received from the more fortunate. An early follower of Pedro Batista estimated that on a day in which he would collectively cure hundreds of people he might receive one hundred dollars. But Eugenio Santos (1977) assured me that, "It passed from the right hand to the left" as Pedro Batista distributed the money among the poor. A representative comment about Pedro Batista's early redistributive activities came from Maria de Jesus (1973), who recalled,

> I was a poor, sickly widow. I saved my last pennies to buy food to eat on my pilgrimage to see my Padrinho. I kept one coin, however, to give to my

Padrinho in gratitude for bringing his divine gifts to us poor sinners and for opening the way for our salvation. . . . After I had heard such pure and beautiful words from my Padrinho I put my small coin in his hand. [He stated,] "You are a poor, devout follower of Our Lady. It is I who should be honoring you for your courage and faith." And then despite my protests he placed ten cruzeiros in my hand and gave me a large turkey that someone had just presented him. He said one day he would be given permission from Our Father to settle and then he would be able to care for me and my children. And thank God, that is exactly what happened.

At this late date it is impossible to know whether popular santos like Antônio Conselheiro and Pedro Batista consciously imitated God and the saints when they engaged in such selfless, redistributive acts. What is clear is that many of their followers drew this parallel. Gazing at a portrait of Pedro Batista set above the small altar in his home, Antônio Villa (1977) remarked nostalgically, "Just as God receives my devotion and faith and distributes it in graces to me and all of the needy, so my Padrinho [Pedro Batista] received charity from his devotees and divided it among all the poor, keeping none for himself."

While Batista's followers describe a saintly figure who received with one hand and gave with the other, his detractors painted a very different picture. *Gente fina* (upper-class people) were inclined to view poor sertanejos as little more than a pitiful "legion of automatons" ("Encontra-se, atualmente na Baia, o beato Pedro Batista," *Jornal de Alagoas*, 25 February 1942, p. 6), blinded by their ignorance and childlike gullibility into selling their property and goods and handing them over to the beato. Basing his claim on the statements of a local sheriff, a journalist states that Batista's pilgrimages "have no other purpose than to exploit the people. The claim that all the money he receives is distributed to the poor is a tall tale. On the same subject, lieutenant Valdemar informed us that in a certain locality in the interior, Batista was able to collect the quantity of one million reis. He only distributed two hundred thousand reis among his followers" (ibid.).

On one hand, in the struggle over assigning agency and meaning to Pedro Batista, the povo bore witness to saintliness and to actions that were reminiscent of the best of the fast-disappearing rural *bons patrões* (good patrons). On the other, at a time when the center of national life had moved materially and symbolically from the Northeast to the central South and the figure to be emulated was the wealthy urban entrepreneur (Ianni 1992), journalists did their part to dismiss contending images of worth. Not only did they reject the more popular image of Pedro Batista as a saintly, patronal figure, but they insisted on a more contemporary trope. That is, they turned Batista into the entrepreneur's reviled opposite: the unsavory flimflam man who preyed on rural bumpkins.

The third activity a santo must undertake is a performance that successfully communicates his mistério and allows him to articulate his spiritual message. Although all four sacralizing actions proved significant in the construction, evaluation, and authentication of Pedro Batista as a santo, his romeiros consistently cited his curing ritual as the act that most impressively showcased his mistério. In fact, for many the decision to dedicate themselves to Pedro Batista and his mission followed a successful cure.

While there were no established rules about the setting for the ritual as long as the surroundings were appropriate for calling on God and the saints, the prophet preferred to cure during the day. Evil spirits were believed to roam at night, and they might attempt to undermine a cure. People could be cured individually or collectively, and bystanders were permitted to attend in silence, except when their redemptive prayers were solicited by a spirit. To render the body open to receive the Word of God and to expel intrusive spirits, hairpins were to be removed, so that women's hair might hang freely; men's hats were removed. The person was seated with feet bare and palms cupped upward on his or her knees. Many dangerous boundary crossings ensued—the Word of God and the "currents" of the saints came into contact with the petitioner, and they pushed out evil spirits and spirits of the dead. The spirits, in turn, would pass through the beatos's body on their way to the Red Sea or to a better place in purgatory like the "Foot of the Cross."

After the individual petitioned "A cure for the love of God," Batista would formally initiate the curing ritual. He instructed the individual to join him in making the Sign of the Cross, followed by Batista's recitation of the Lord's Prayer, Hail Mary, and the Apostles' Creed. The beato then proceeded to intone prayers that were barely audible. These were interpreted as a call to God and the saints for assistance to rid the sufferer of the spirits that had invaded his or her body, as Josefa Gomes (1974) explained: "Just as Jesus called to his Father to give him strength and guidance, so my Padrinho appealed to God and the saints while he prayed. His soul would rise up and gain power from heaven; and he would bring the power of the Lord and forceful saints like São Jorge [Saint George] down with him, so that his words might exorcise the demons residing within the bodies of the faithful: 'Get away, Satan' [he would yell]; or he would pardon the poor suffering spirits yearning for a better place in purgatory—'Stay chained beneath the Red Sea until the Day of Judgment.'"

As he said these prayers, the beato would make crosses all over the individual's body, along with occasional shushing noises that served to surface the offending spirits. Raimundo Alves (1977), a nonromeiro who attended Batista's cure for a man who arrived so demented that he had to be restrained with heavy ropes, reported that Batista began by commanding the man be untied. As soon as the beato commenced his prayers, the man settled down. Alves observed that Batista applied pressure points on the man's ears in a fashion consistent with Afro-Brazilian curing rites, which led Alves to speculate that Batista may have picked up this technique while attending Macumba curing rituals in Southern Brazil.[17]

Many informants likened Batista's curing rituals to epic battles. Spirits who spoke through their victims would begin to ramble, and Batista would bellow, "What is your name?" After circuitously attempting to avoid identification each spirit would climactically declare its name, tell its life history, and beg for mercy and pardon. My observations of more contemporary curing rituals reveal that sometimes such public declarations of the spirit's identity prove cathartic for the sufferer and his or her kin, while at other times the denunciations greatly exacerbate already-brewing social conflict. For his part, Batista asserted his paramount authority by alone judging the authenticity of the spirit and its claims. For example, a spirit might have entered the body of an individual with whom he or she had quarreled years ago in order to receive the latter's pardon; or, more insidiously, the spirit might claim to have been sent by an enemy through black magic (or *macumba* in local parlance). According to romeiro curer Raimundo da Silva (1977), evil spirits routinely lied about their identities in order to trick the beato into giving them his pardon. Under these circumstances the interplay between Pedro Batista and the spirits became highly charged, as well as often entertaining for those who were drawn to the ensuing drama.[18]

> If the spirit was a good one, just desiring to partake in the substance of one of the faithful, my Padrinho would compassionately pardon the spirit and send it off to the Foot of the Cross or chain it beneath the Red Sea until the Day of Judgment. But, mind you, many spirits were deceitful, and they would lie. They would begin flattering my Padrinho, saying he was Padre Cícero and Our Father. My Padrinho would thunder, "I am Pedro Batista da Silva, curador, and you are Satan! Tell us your real name, you demon!" The stronger spirits would keep on lying, and my Padrinho would begin praying the Words of God, drowning out the evil words of Satan. The demon's voice would gradually grow weaker. Finally the spirit would declare that the power of my Padrinho was greater than that of his master! "Please

Padrinho Pedro, give me your blessing and pardon me for my sins." But my Padrinho would not be swayed, he would chain the demon to the bottom of the Red Sea until the Day of Judgment, when he might be judged again.

When all the benign and evil spirits had been dramatically exorcised, an orderly and understated denouement consisting of blessings concluded the ritual. Batista "closed the body" that was now ritually purified. He attempted to render it spiritually impervious to evil and suffering by calling down various saints to apply a "blessing of protection, health, and prosperity." The beato and petitioner then terminated the ritual as they had opened it, with the Sign of the Cross. The petitioner would complement his opening supplication with "May God repay you."

If as Anthony Wallace (1956) claims, one of the ways a charismatic figure displays his special power is by enunciating peoples' concerns and suggesting redressive measures, Batista's curing ritual certainly assumed this important function. Moreover, the beato astutely made growing numbers of people complicit in his mission by involving sufferers in helping him to identify the agents responsible for their distress and then by convincing them to accept those commandments (*mandamentos*) needed to remain well and spiritually sound.

Similar to his predecessors, Batista advised that the larger society was inflicted with grave social ills that he associated with such aspects of modernity as individualism, vanity, vice, and usury. These behaviors had so incited God's wrath, the beato counseled, that the Day of Judgment was near, and as a consequence spirits eager to be saved had sought out the bodies of devout Catholics. The diseases these spirits caused were immune to modern medicine; they were only responsive to the Word of God.

In Batista's commentaries about the curing ritual are clear traces of resentment. Alzira Bezerra (1974) recalled,

> My Padrinho said, "The large circle has entered into the small one."
> "What does that mean, my Padrinho?"
> "The judgment of the dead will take place within the bodies of the living. A captain, a millionaire, those who never had need of the poor will entrench themselves in the body of one who has nothing to wear, nothing to eat, so as to gain pardon from that poor creature." [19]

This inversionary image helped to steel Batista's followers against the derision and abuse leveled against them by political bosses, priests, large landholders, merchants, and so on.

After exorcising the offending spirits, Batista introduced the petitioner to the *antiga lei* (the old laws), a variant of traditional Catholicism. Its teachings had to be obeyed lest the individual be attacked even more virulently by intruding spirits of the dead. The cured subject was accordingly obligated to desist immediately from such evil habits as smoking, drinking, gambling, and adultery, and to replace "immodest" dress with long-sleeved clothing and to wear a rosary as a necklace; women were also to wear long skirts and to forsake hairpins and makeup.

It is surely not happenstance that a curing ritual is that vehicle most often remembered by Batista's followers as the most significant demonstration of his spiritual powers and the act that convinced many to accept him as their leader. Illness is one of the most imposing and alienating of life experiences. Private anguish may evolve into social and existential detachment unless the intrusive pains are controlled and made meaningful. Illness thus presents powerful experiences that call for some form of "domestication," the immediacy and profundity of this personal need rendering the afflicted especially receptive to the meanings and proscriptions offered by a curing ritual. In Claude Levi-Strauss's analysis of the Cuna shaman's song of childbirth, he writes,

> The cure would consist then in making an emotional situation thinkable; and in making the mind accept pains which the body refuses to bear. It is of no importance that the mythology of the Shaman does not correspond to objective reality, the patient believes in it. The protective powers and the malevolent ones, the supernatural monsters and magic animals form part of a coherent system which underlies the native conception of the universe. The patient accepts them or rather she has never doubted them. What she does not accept is this incoherent and arbitrary pain which is an intrusive element in her system. By appealing to the myth, the Shaman places it in a unified schema, where everything belongs. But the patient, having understood, does not resign herself: she gets better (1967, 192).

Emília Santana (2000), who is not herself a romeira but whose mother was until her death several years ago, described the effect of Batista's cure and its aftermath.

> She got sick, went to Recife, saw all the doctors in the region, and every medicine she took made her sicker. We said it was nervousness. . . . At that time many people would advise you to have someone pray over [you]: "So and so does that type of work and prays." One day, a man arrived at our farm and said, "There is a man in Bahia who cures people. Why don't

you try taking her there?" We were already desperate by then. So my father decided to take her.

Pedro Batista prayed over her and said that doctors could not cure her disease. There would be no doctor who could make her better, and she would end up being put into a psychiatric ward. . . . [After she visited Pedro Batista several times,] she was able to improve so she could stay by herself without being cared for by anyone else. He helped her a lot. These are things we do not understand. They are supernatural and we can't understand them. She was able to live without her doctors again; he was the person who improved her health.

[After that] she considered herself a romeira, and we moved to Santa Brígida. We also accompanied the romaria not because we believed in it, but rather because she forced us to do it to express her thankfulness for the grace she had received; she wanted us to accompany her. We didn't really enjoy it—all that praying, and those proper clothes, long sleeves, and long skirts. We did it because she was our mother.[20]

While many poor backlanders marveled at Batista's miraculous cures and his willingness to heal without charging for his services, most gente fina adopted a far more jaundiced and denigrating view. For example, one newspaper article reads, "They tell marvelous things about this man. His supernatural powers are exalted by hundreds of devout followers who come in pilgrimages. The believers report that blind people have their vision restored, the crippled walk again, and the injured are cured simply by the saint having laid on his hands" ("As milagrosas curas do profeta Batista," *Jornal de Alagoas*, 14 February 1942, p. 6). These statements were followed up some days later by another article, which advised, "As to his miraculous cures, they consist of blessing water and giving it to sick people to drink. In fact, Lieutenant Valdemar has never had the opportunity to verify the authenticity of a cure made by Batista. In Água Branca several blind and paralyzed persons used the holy water without obtaining any results whatsoever. Through the statements made by the sheriff [Valdemar], we can conclude that the pilgrimages of my godfather, as his admirers call him, have no other purpose than to exploit the people" ("Encontrase, atualmente na Baia, o beato Pedro Batista," *Jornal de Alagoas*, 25 February 1942, p. 6).

As these articles illustrate, in addition to lamenting the ignorance of the povo, journalists denounced Batista as a charlatan who took advantage of the childlike masses. An excerpt reproduced below from a church-supported newspaper is representative of the solutions elite Brazilians favored. Charlatans had to be policed and separated from the masses while the folk were formally educated. As the journalist cited below advised, this social engineering had to be done lest "backward beliefs" contaminate the entire citizenry and reinforce beliefs among foreigners that Brazil was an underdeveloped and superstitious nation.

> There is a necessity for strong police repression, which is already taking place. The police should act with no tolerance and go . . . directly to the heart of the practices of the beatos in order to eliminate these practices completely. . . . The truth is, as was stated by the young Alagoan scientist Lages Filho, this is one of those phenomena that the police and the penal code cannot repress fully. It can only be done through the mind, when schools are given to the beatos so that they can be educated and improve their living, economic, and environmental conditions. However, under these circumstances, the use of strong police intervention as a preliminary measure is absolutely necessary until other cultural and educational measures can be enacted. At the moment we are far from being able to establish these rationally and immediately. . . . The epidemic of unhealthy mysticism will spread among the ignorant masses, further weighing down their fragile psyche. This epidemic would make the aberrations of a sect of crazy people become accepted by the collective psyche. Let us then do away with the belief system surrounding beatos with all the coercive instruments we have at our disposal in order to destroy this evil that is afflicting the social order. If we do this, we will be defending ourselves. . . . We will be restoring to normal the rural area where the dangerous and abominable folk healing prevails. As a consequence . . . we will rid ourselves of our reputation for having backward beliefs, removing the perception that some have that we serve as a breeding ground for beatos. ("Vamos decompor o beateiro," *Gazeta de Alagoas*, April 1942, p. 8)

While politicians, clergy, social planners, and journalists, among others, plotted a course for the nation and set down terms for inclusion, the followers of Pedro Batista were engaged in a far different project: to determine whether they were in the presence of a santo and, if so, who would be among the elect of the heavenly kingdom.

SACRALIZATION THROUGH MIRACLE STORIES

Those who believed that they had indeed encountered a santo and who sought to convince others of this momentous fact engaged in an additional step in the sacralizing process: they fashioned Batista's deeds into miracle stories. When managed effectively the creation and retelling of miracle stories helped to turn a common man or woman into a santo.[21] Two of the most frequently told stories about Batista follow.

Pedro Batista and His Assassins

The first story was related by Dona Dodô and describes a miraculously foiled assassination attempt directed against Batista and instigated by politicians in Juazeiro. Other similar accounts of unsuccessful assassinations are set in Santa Brígida and involve such mysterious happenstance as guns falling to the ground or failing to fire and knives that are somehow immobilized (see Oliveira n.d., 12–13).

> My uncle was an important political figure in Juazeiro. "Dodô, you like such things. Come with me to that old woman's farm to see a penitent who is curing and preaching." My uncle was amused by this. He insisted that being as I was a young penitent, I should accompany him. We were joined by the political chief.
>
> The first time I saw my Padrinho my whole body went cold; tears brimmed in my eyes. I knew from the first moment that my mission and his would be one. But I remained quiet. I just stood and watched him cure the poor.
>
> Suddenly two hired killers appeared. The woman who owned the house ordered the men away: "Get away from here, you sons of the devil; this is my home." I'd never seen a woman talk so forcefully to men! When they paid her no heed, she turned to the political chief and asked for his help. [He responded,] "These are armed killers, what can I do?" It was clear that they had been sent by him! The woman began to berate the men again, saying very forceful words. "Remain silent," my Padrinho told her. "Place your faith in God."
>
> The assassins approached him: "Are you Pedro Batista da Silva, curador?" "I am called———." He said a name, but to this day, neither I nor anyone else who was there can replicate it! Such is the mystery of my Padrinho. Then they said, "Are you prepared to die?" "If God wills it," he replied. Then standing right before him, they began to shake violently, and in a moment, their guns and holsters had fallen to the ground! Shocked, they fell to their knees and begged for his pardon. My Padrinho responded, "You receive the pardon from Pedro Batista da Silva here. But the next time you ask for my pardon, you will call me by another name!"[22]
> (Maria das Dores 1974)

Pedro Batista's Imprisonment in Água Branca and the Miraculous Donkey
The second tale is among the most popular told about Pedro Batista. Like the
preceding story, it also belongs to a particular genre: those stories that describe Batista's mistreatment and humiliation at the hands of politicians and
government officials and that feature his ability to overcome and trump his oppressors. This story depicts a miraculous event involving Batista and a donkey;
although Batista navigated most of his penitential journey on foot, he is said
to have finally petitioned God for permission to travel by donkey toward the
end of his mission. As the following miracle story attests, the donkey proved
to be no ordinary animal.

My Padrinho had been in Água Branca for a few weeks curing the sick
and counseling the sinners.[23] Without any apparent reason, the colonel
ordered him arrested. Now my Padrinho had tremendous support in Água
Branca. I would say at least one-third of the people were with him. So I
guess the colonel wanted to demonstrate that he had more power than my
Padrinho. But this was the devil's doing, because the colonel was smart.
He knew that no mortal has more power than God. As the hymn says,
"Satan has force, but he doesn't have power."

My Padrinho was placed in solitary confinement and deprived of food
and water. But he didn't complain. Those people who did not like my
Padrinho smiled like the Jews during Jesus' suffering at the hands of Pontius Pilate. "Just wait a few days to see how the bones of your Savior begin
to rot."

The jailer had also been ordered to kill my Padrinho's donkey. So on
the fifth day of my Padrinho's imprisonment, the jailer took the beast into
the woods to slaughter it. Suddenly the jailer's son came running up to
his father.

"Why did you set that old man free?"

"Stop, your foolishness, boy. Why would I ever do that!"

"But I just saw him in the field over there grazing his donkey."

The jailer quickly mounted my Padrinho's donkey and accompanied
his son to that field. And sure enough, my Padrinho was there grazing his
donkey! The jailer became frightened and while keeping his eye on my
Padrinho, he ordered his son to run back to the jail to see if my Padrinho
had escaped.

"Father, he is still there in the jail."

Imagine, the jailer sped back to the jail. "Forgive me, Padrinho, I now
recognize who you are."

When the colonel heard the story, he arranged a two-man guard to escort my Padrinho out of Alagoas. They were ordered to take him across the Rio São Francisco into the state of Bahia. My Padrinho was never to return to Alagoas under the threat of death were he to disobey. When they reached the river it was cresting, and the soldiers decided that they would have to cross at a spot further down the river. But my Padrinho didn't care, he crossed right there.

"Silly old fanatic, you'll get drowned just as you deserve."

But their mocking ended when he reached the far side without even dampening the bottom ridge of the animal's saddle! The soldiers immediately threw down their weapons and fell to their knees.

"Pardon me, my Padrinho" (Antônio Villa 1977).

The first thing that is striking about these two stories and similar miracle stories told about Batista is their particular narrative structure, which communicates and embodies the protagonist's authority. They adopt what Slater calls, a "four-step challenge sequence, [that] ensures the miracle narrative['s] underlying unity, disposing individuals to see the most varied episodes as displays of that supernatural power known as mistério" (Slater 1986, 112). In the first step, both stories begin with a statement or statements that are implicit affirmations of Batista's authority, as with mention of how the beato ministers to the poor who seek him out. In the second step, members of the elite and their retainers, who seek to reassert their power through acts of aggression and subordination (e.g., assassination or imprisonment), issue a direct challenge to Batista's authority. In the third step, Batista manages a miraculous response: miraculous from the vantage point of sertanejo phenomenology because it confounds understandings about the expected outcomes of brute power exercised by the elite against those they view as weaker. This unexpected outcome leaves room for no other explanation than divine intervention (see also Zaluar 1983, 99–100). Whether Batista comes to exact divine retribution against his tormenters (as he does in tales in which his rivals are incapacitated) or whether he humiliates an offending political chief and reveals his weakness (as in his purported escape from jail), the underlying message is that Batista's power is far superior to his rivals'. Or as the second story so colorfully states, "Satan has force, but he doesn't have power."

Unlike many conventional saints' tales, which feature martyrdom and resignation, none of the stories about santos I am familiar with adopt this narrative line. Rather, they are foremost about *authority* and the santo's absolute refusal to brook challenges or affronts from those who misguidedly believe they possess greater power and authority than he. Accordingly, in the fourth and final step, the aggressor repents or is neutralized through humiliation or misfortune, and Batista's authority is reaffirmed.

Referring only to stories about Padre Cícero, Slater also notes the difference between these and conventional saints' legends. She writes, "In contrast to the martyr and later confessor saints [whose miracle stories find them] regularly call[ing] out to heaven for help and guidance, the priest exhibits a remarkable self-sufficiency. Whereas the martyr's tale sees divine intervention as a reward for human beings' continuing faith in the face of persecution, the Padre Cícero stories reiterate the priest's ability to help his followers and strike down detractors" (ibid.) What Slater fails to note is that Padre Cícero's "remarkable self-sufficiency" is totally in keeping with sertanejo beliefs about santos: these figures are so special precisely because their power does not depend on divine intervention, on "calling out to heaven" for assistance.

Just as the structure of the miracle stories contributes to Pedro Batista's mistério and stature as a santo, so too does the content of the tales. Elements such as Pedro Batista's bilocality (being in jail and grazing his donkey in the field at the same time) and his levitation over water are common to European holy figures such as Mary Magdalene of Pazzi and Jesus Christ. Yet the pattern of drawing on earlier religious themes and episodes is especially pronounced in Batista's case, since a good many stories told about him replicate entire episodes in popular stories about Padre Cícero. For example, both santos are featured in a tale in which the weapons fall to the ground due to the uncontrollable shaking of repentant assassins; in another account, the entombed bodies of both men miraculously disappear with only a slipper or sock left behind (ibid.).

It might be argued that the striking similarity between these miracle stories is due simply to the fact that their producers have drawn from a shared corpus of meanings and themes available to those sertanejos bent on establishing charisma. But the more pointed borrowing from Padre Cícero tales bespeaks a second and far more specific goal: the producer and retellers of the miracle story seek to establish the fact that Pedro Batista *is* Padre Cícero. Thus, it is perfectly appropriate that events that happened to one should reoccur for the other and that both should respond in the same miraculous fashion.

Finally, there is another reason why the legends about both men — and probably other santos as well — are so similar. As the following vignette from my fieldwork illustrates, many backlanders conceive of an ultimate unity among all things that are holy and mysterious. The "sameness" of miracle stories captures and reproduces this fundamental unity. While participating with some forty romeiros on a three-week pilgrimage on foot from Santa Brígida to Juazeiro,

I was fortunate enough to hear many spontaneously told stories about both santos. Once, over the course of a day, I heard almost identical stories about foiled assassination attempts and about petitions for help made to one or the other man that were fulfilled in miraculous fashion. I commented casually to my companions on the striking similarities between the stories. They seemed pleased with my observation, and several smiled that particular smile that I have come to associate with their pleasure at my having grasped something important and essential about Batista's powers and mission. As if to reinforce my growing awareness of this profound truth, Agripino da Silva volunteered, "Well, of course, isn't it so that they share in the same mistério, that they are one." For many romeiros, then, holy beings like Padre Cícero and Pedro Batista and their demonstrations of divine power are *interchangeable*, since they partake of the same spiritual essence. For these narrators of miracle tales, there is nothing of what an outside observer and nonbeliever would call artifice or rhetoric; rather, they are speaking about the divine as one should and must.

Against Batista's followers, who drew on a conventional structure and themes for relating what they believed to be miracles, critics turned to the pages of elite press to tell their version of the story. Consider, for example, how *Jornal de Alagoas* related the affair of Batista's jailing in Água Branca. According to a 1942 newspaper article, the beato was ordered to depart the municipality immediately "when the authorities found that they could no longer tolerate . . . the Moses with an almost supernatural voice . . . who [told his followers] they should fear nothing because the heavens would protect them" ("O beato 'autorizado' a fazer propoganda contra Cristo-Rei," *Jornal de Alagoas*, 22 February 1942, p. 8). Apparently, Batista crossed over to a neighboring town for a few days before heading back to Água Branca. This is an interesting episode since it contradicts his followers' repeated assertions that he never stayed in a place where the authorities had ordered him to leave. The return occasioned Batista's immediate arrest. Using the subheadline "The Multitude Invades," a journalist had this to say about the arrest: "Having heard that the 'saint' was imprisoned, the fanatics protested. They said that what was being done to their 'redeemer,' who was a messenger from God and the reincarnation of Padre Cícero, was unjust. At a certain moment, they all invaded the police station. Lieutenant Valdemar, after coming to an agreement with the other authorities, was forced to order that the people be dispersed. He returned the beato to the cell after his immense beard was shaved off during the protests of the multitude" (ibid.).

Both the removal of Batista's beard and its coverage in the press were hardly incidental. Earlier articles had alerted readers to the fact that the beato's "fanatical" followers collected hair from his long beard and used it for medicinal teas. The act of publicly and forcefully shaving Batista's beard carried multiple meanings, and it asserted elite dominance. It erased a powerful, biblical allusion to Batista's status as a holy man, and it deprived him of an instrument for miracle making. It also staked a claim for modernity. One of the popular icons of the past had been Emperor Pedro II's flowing beard, which represented monarchy and patriarchal oligarchy. By contrast, modernity called for trimmed or no facial hair. In removing his long beard, Batista's captors inscribed modernity onto his body. The humiliation and violation of the act were hardly lost on his devotees, who to this day describe the incident in voices tinged with sorrow and anger.

In 1945 Pedro Batista was forced by Alagoan state police to cross the Rio São Francisco into Bahia state. This time Batista managed to find, in the isolated hamlet of Santa Brígida, a place to settle permanently, and in short order he was joined by several thousand backlanders. Over the preceding seven years of his penitential journey Batista, his devotees, and his detractors had engaged each other in the social production of a popular saint. For the romeiros who joined him in Santa Brígida, he was a miracle worker, a sage counselor, a man who was above politics and without kin ties. He had, heroically, emerged unscathed from the physical and rhetorical assaults of elite actors. Indeed, it can be argued that the two opposing sides in the cultural struggle surrounding Batista's popular sanctification needed each other. On the one hand, the authors of the modernizing project depended on constructions of backward and fanatical "others" to delineate their "progressive" mission and emphasize its urgency. On the other hand, those passionate adherents of folk Catholicism who accompanied Batista needed their localized embodiments of Herod and the Antichrist to fortify their own beliefs and resolve. These devotees followed Pedro Batista to Santa Brígida—"the Second Juazeiro"—where their hopes for attaining heaven on earth and eternal salvation were now focused.

THE CORONEL AND THE BEATO

The original inhabitants of Santa Brígida (the baianos) and the newcomers (the romeiros) are in agreement that at first blush Santa Brígida was an unlikely spot for the peaceful beato to settle. It was known to be the home of feuding families and, until recently, one of the sanctuaries of the infamous bandit, Lampião.[1] In fact, Santa Brígida was not a site that Batista's hosts initially deemed appropriate for him. Rather, as old-timers tell the story, after Batista had cured his wife, the grateful overseer of a farm in the municipality of Glória invited the beato to settle nearby.[2] Batista demurred, inquiring instead whether the overseer might speak to his employer, Manuel Pereira de Souza, a powerful political figure in the town of Paulo Afonso, to see if he might arrange for Batista to settle in the neighboring community of Santa Brígida. Romeiros delight in emphasizing that due to that town's notoriety the overseer tried hard to dissuade Batista from settling there. The beato remained firm, however.[3] Shortly thereafter the necessary connections between Batista and the leading families of Santa Brígida and Jeremoabo (the municipal seat) were successfully brokered.

This is how one nonagenarian remembers the beato's arrival one June afternoon in 1945:[4] "I remember [when] he arrived here, he was very poor. He was on a brown donkey. He had a leather hat on his head and a full beard. He was followed by a youth on foot. He said he was a table maker. He stayed here and later Major Felipe and Major Annibal decided they didn't want him to stay. . . . This was a quiet place. They wanted to get him out of here. My uncle Jacob Marques da Silva and Coronel João Sá protected him" (Antônio da Silva 1999).

The historical facts that Pedro Batista ended his penitential mission in the

Elderly baiano who in 1945 welcomed Pedro Batista to Santa Brígida. Photo by the author.

Colonel Jõao Sá, the political leader of Jeremoabo. Photo from author's personal archive, photographer unknown.

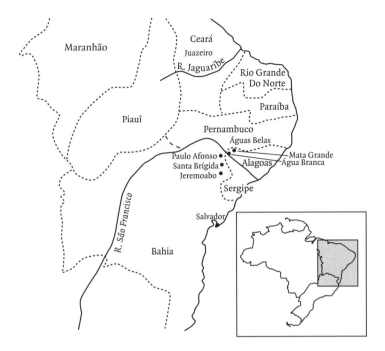

Northeast Brazil with sites most relevant to the history of Santa Brígida.

summer of 1945 and proceeded to invite his followers to settle with him suggest two compelling questions about motivation and agency. First, why did
Coronel João Sá, who controlled affairs in Santa Brígida and its environs, grant
Batista permission to settle?[5] And second, why did approximately 2,000 romeiros choose to leave their communities of origin over the course of the late
1940s and 1950s to relocate in Santa Brígida? Politics is central to the answers
to both questions. In the first case, however, this was in the form of coronelismo and party politics. In the other, it was in the form of popular resistance
against those elite actors representing the church and state who punished backlanders for pursuing their alternative religious beliefs and for accompanying a
popular santo.

The Sá Family and the Early Career of Coronel João Sá

Pedro Batista and his romeiros might never have managed to settle in Santa
Brígida free of fear of harassment had it not been for Coronel Sá's strong support. By tracing the coronel's family history, political socialization, and early

career, one gains insight into those elements that likely contributed to Sá's later endorsement of Batista and his followers.

João Sá's paternal grandfather and the founding member of the Jeremoabo branch of the Sá family relocated as a young man from his native Água Branca (Alagoas) in the mid-1800s. Shortly thereafter, the young man married into one of Jeremoabo's most powerful families, the Martins. They were relatives of Cícero Dantas Martins, the baron of Jeremoabo, who was born in Jeremoabo and rose to be not only the most powerful leader in northern Bahia but also one of Antônio Conselheiro's greatest nemeses. One of the Sá couple's children was Jesuíno Martins de Sá, father of Colonel João Sá. The latter's leadership style, as well as his early treatment of Pedro Batista, were foreshadowed in some intriguing ways by his own father's career as a merchant and politician.

Jesuíno, like his father, managed to marry into a family possessing wealth and power. His wife Emiliana was raised by a paternal grandmother who was the widow of an affluent sugar planter. Emiliana's father, himself a local politician, encouraged his son-in-law Jesuíno to enter politics, and he supported his efforts (João Gonçalves de Carvalho Sá 2000). Jesuíno became the first mayor elected in Jeremoabo after the transition from empire to republic, serving from 1889 to 1894. He distinguished himself, too, as a successful merchant, and it was said of him that "among the merchants in [the state capital of] Salvador, his word was money" (Lima 1953, 38). While the following description of Jesuíno, penned by one of his sons, is obviously colored by filial pride, the laudatory discourse does provide some insight into the kind of exemplary figure Jesuíno's offspring, including João Sá, sought to emulate: "In all aspects of life, he left a mark of honor; in commerce he left his credit, in politics his firmness, in society his example as a head of a family. In all of these fields he made more friends than adversaries" (ibid., 39). Perhaps it was just such a family legacy of actively pursuing allies that inclined João Sá to look more toward the potential benefits than the risks when he assessed early on what Pedro Batista and his romeiros might mean for Sá's considerable political ambitions.

Interestingly, João Sá was not the first in his family to reach an understanding with a "suspect" beato. Apparently, half a century earlier his father, elder brothers, and a few of Jeremoabo's other leading merchants and civil authorities journeyed north to visit Antônio Conselheiro and his followers. Angry words were exchanged over the merits of the republic and its policies (such as civil marriage). At that time Jesuíno was wrongfully accused of being a post-office official and a government spy. Family lore has it that Jesuíno defused this tense situation by insisting on his position as a businessman "who provided services to the community" (ibid.). Moreover, he was able to convince a rapt Conselheiro, "who was sitting with his legs together and tucked in, in a Buddha-like position," to accept "the money offered by that honorable orator" (ibid.: 40–41). Unfortunately, it is unclear whether Jesuíno emerged from this encounter having brokered a commercial deal or whether he served, in any way, as a conduit between Conselheiro and Sá's kinsman, the baron of Jeremoabo. What is clear, however, is that João grew up with knowledge of this dramatic encounter between his father and Conselheiro. Perhaps it served as an example when his turn came to negotiate with yet another beato who had entered into his family's political sphere of influence.

João Sá was raised with his three elder brothers and younger sister on the Caritá farm in Jeremoabo. The largest holding in the town, it had been the birthplace and ancestral home of the baron of Jeremoabo, and its subsequent sale to Coronel Jesuíno demonstrates the Sá family's economic and political ascendancy within the town and region. In one history of the town of Jeremoabo, Caritá is described as having long been "the center of high-order political decision making for the northeast of Bahia" (Almeida 1998, 13). While João's brothers pursued careers in business, medicine, and engineering, respectively, and his sister married a man who preceded João as mayor of Jeremoabo, the youngest of the Sá boys set his sights on politics. In this he was to prove highly successful, serving as mayor of Jeremoabo twice, as senator in the Bahia state legislature six times, and as the state leader of the powerful Partido Social Democratico (PSD) for many years (João Gonçalves de Carvalho Sá 1999, 2000).

When people conjure up images of the Brazilian backlands, three social types come to mind: the coronel, the bandit (*cangaceiro*), and the beato. João Sá as the inveterate backlands coronel had his own significant relations with the other two dominant types. In Sá's case the bandit was none other than Lampião. In August 1928, after years of involvement in bloody clan feuding and banditry, Lampião crossed the Rio São Francisco into Bahia, claiming to be in pursuit of refuge and a second chance at a peaceful life. Shortly thereafter he had what appeared to be a chance meeting with Coronel João Sá, who was by then "northeastern Bahia's most important politician [and] a man with whom [Lampião] needed to reach an understanding" (Chandler 1978, 116). Chandler's account of this initial meeting offers insights into this astute and flexible politician, a man clearly able to reach amicable agreements with the most "infamous" of the Northeast's social pariahs: first the cangaceiro and later the beato.

> Once their identities were established, Lampião invited Sá and his party to drink with him. In the ensuing conversation, he gave the assurance once

again that he bore no ill will toward Bahia, saying that he had come there
only to rest. As long as he had money for his expenses, he said, he would
inconvenience no one, but once his money ran out he would be compelled
to request aid from citizens of means. The two men talked for two hours
or more and, since a part of their conversation was away from the ears of
others, it presumably included matters they preferred to keep confiden-
tial. It was the beginning of a relationship between the two men that was
to be long lasting and mutually satisfactory. Sá apparently became one
of Lampião's most trustworthy protectors in Bahia; in return, Lampião
always respected Sá's twenty or more ranches. (ibid., 116–17)

Chandler goes on to say that Sá's friends claim that he was never a willing
coiteiro (protector of bandits) but was forced to act to protect his property. While
this may be true, more critical observers note that Sá enriched himself by en-
gaging in a game common to political bosses at the time, that is, playing off
both sides. As a local historian expressed it,

> Coronel João Sá gained a lot of strength during the time of Lampião.
> People say he transacted economically both with Lampião and with the
> police who were chasing him. So he got very rich during this period. He
> provided all the logistical support for the police and all the logistical sup-
> port for the bandits. (Marco Antônio Dantas de Almeida 1999)

Allegedly with Sá's blessing, the bandits would occupy choice property and
tell the owners, "Either you sell the land [to Sá or other coronéis] or your wife
will be a widow." There are also claims that Sá instructed the bandits to torch
the registry offices of neighboring towns so that deeds to property might be
contested and lands subsequently appropriated by Sá and his allies (ibid.).
Finally, the police who fought Lampião often complained that he and his band
possessed newer and more improved issues of ammunition than were available to his pursuers. Such ammunition had to have been provided to Lampião
by influential friends who had powerful contacts in the south of Brazil. Coronel João Sá was identified as one of these suppliers by one of Lampião's bandit
confidants who later turned government informer (Chandler 1978).

Challengers and Foes

Thus, in the late spring of 1945, when Pedro Batista was first introduced to
Coronel João Sá and requested his permission to settle in Santa Brígida, the
beato stood before a seasoned backland politician. Fortunately for Batista, the

coronel was a man already comfortable with augmenting his power and wealth by positioning himself, if necessary, well beyond the fringes of official politics and "cultured" Brazilian society.

Although Sá was prepared to support Batista and his followers, he confronted obstacles. First, only seven years before Batista's arrival, a millenarian community established in nearby Pau de Colher had collapsed violently. Local Bahian police and soldiers were called into action there and more than 400 people were killed (Estrela 1997). In fact, Major Felipe, the high-ranking police official who was opposed to Batista's settlement in Santa Brígida, had fought the millenarianists of Pau de Colher. Second, memories of Canudos remained very much alive in the region. Jeremoabo is less than forty miles from Canudos, and its militia had joined the forces that defeated Antônio Conselheiro. In the mid-1940s elderly residents still proudly recalled their days of service. Finally, politicians representing the União Democrática Nacional (UDN), a rival political party associated nationally with liberal professionals (*bacharéis*), were more than willing to raise the specter of Pau de Colher and Canudos in their bids to keep Sá from permanently settling Batista in Santa Brígida and profiting from romeiro votes and labor.

Not surprisingly, the first official challenge to Sá's support for Batista came from Major Felipe Borges de Castro, the regional sheriff. Among other things it was his job to keep the countryside quiescent while the central government under Vargas's lead concentrated on urban industrialization and building a corporatist political structure tied securely to the state. According to ex-mayor and local historian Luís da Silva (1999), the regional sheriff "was a hard liner.... He knew the story of Canudos well [and] Pau de Colher, and he was afraid that if too many people gathered [around Batista] it would cause trouble for the government." In his early denunciation of Batista, the regional sheriff also made reference to the matter of vagrancy—a modernist shibboleth that had plagued Batista earlier in his religious mission. As one baiano observer of these events noted, "No one knew where he was from, so people [including the sheriff] were suspicious of him" (Antônio da Silva 1999). Warning that Batista's seemingly innocent move "to build small houses for prayer [was really intended] to take over the city," Borges de Castro soon ordered Batista and the head of Santa Brígida's Marques da Silva family to meet with him in Jeremoabo (ibid., 1999). Coronel João Sá and the town's judge, Dr. Antônio Oliveira de Brito, also attended the meeting.

Borges de Castro and Oliveira de Brito were both Sá appointees. As such, either or both could have easily been removed from office had they strayed too far afield from the coronel's objectives. It may well have been the case, then, that Sá actually colluded with the "good cop–bad cop" brand of interrogation that was initially employed. He may have sought to communicate to Batista right from the start that as the region's leading politician he had the power either to monitor and thwart the beato or to protect him if a mutually satisfying agreement could be brokered.

The story of this eventful meeting has been passed on to Marques da Silva's grandson Luís da Silva (1999), who recounted:

> Felipe Borges de Castro said to Pedro Batista that he was going to get a document for him to sign. Whoever committed a mistake in the romaria, Pedro Batista would pay the price. Seu [Mr.] Pedro said, "Look, I can't. Whoever commits an error I'll hand over to justice, to the authorities." Seu Pedro was very respectful of authorities. . . . João Sá knew that the Vargas dictatorship was going to end and that Seu Pedro was going to get a lot of people, and they would all be his voters. So João Sá said that it [the sheriff's proposal] was against the law, that he could not do that. Felipe would have to come up with another argument to take Seu Pedro away.

When local leaders from Santa Brígida went before Felipe Borges de Castro to defend Batista's settlement, they pointedly avoided references to his status as a beato, pressing their argument instead on the grounds of population scarcity and the need for more inhabitants to ensure the town's future economic growth and progress (João da Silva 1999). Theirs was a discourse in step with the Vargas regime's larger national agenda, which was committed to the dissemination of progress and modernity throughout Brazil. They also, wisely, adopted a strategy that sidestepped then current state policies aimed at harrassing and punishing leaders of unorthodox religious groups and practices, such as Umbanda and Kardecism (Brown 1994).

Of course local officials of the UDN party were disturbed by the prospect of hundreds of additional votes being cast for Sá and his candidates.[6] Accordingly, General Liberato de Carvalho, a key figure in the apprehension of Lampião, and the brother of José Maria, UDN's political boss in the region, tried unsuccessfully to remove Batista from Santa Brígida.

It is also likely that some in Sá's own party objected to the taint of fanaticism and backwardness associated with a figure like Batista, to Sá increasing his political leverage within the party once he controlled the romeiros' votes, or to both. Whatever the case, Sá early on consulted with the state's governor and likely with other party leaders. Referring to that time, Pereira de Queiroz states, "The Coronel took responsibility for him [Batista], vouching that he would comport himself as a good and tranquil person, and would not be a new Antônio Conselheiro" (Queiroz 1973, 111). Apparently, as the most powerful political figure in northeast Bahia at that time and as a highly influential leader of the state's ruling party, Sá's endorsement of the beato held.

The Political Pact between Coronel Sá and Pedro Batista

The founding of the romaria in Santa Brígida must be contextualized within not only the locality but also the nation. The year of Batista's arrival in Santa Brígida marked a transition in national politics. In 1945 President Vargas was forced to relinquish power in the face of widespread public demand for elections and an end to arbitrary rule.[7] The new constitution of 1945 formally established a liberal democracy with a federated republican system. Nonetheless, as had also occurred in the revolution of 1930, which had brought Vargas to power, this latest change in regime occasioned no significant modification either in the role of the state or in the social and economic structures supporting it.

Superficially, the multiparty electoral system that operated from 1946 to 1964 and the expansion of suffrage to all literate persons over the age of eighteen appeared to be a genuine response to popular demands for a more representative and responsive political system. In practice, however, these initiatives neither rationalized nor democratized Brazilian politics. In fact, two of the most important parties active during this period, PSD and Partido Trabalhista Brasileiro (PTB), were created by Vargas himself. Consequently, in 1945 when Vargas supporter and seasoned politician Coronel Sá chose to back Pedro Batista and to facilitate the settlement of his romeiros, he must have been aware that, at least in the short run, open elections would mean little more than a continuation of the existing pattern of collaboration between the central government and rural coronéis. In fact, elections sweetened the pot as successful candidates for federal and state office repaid their local power brokers with an increasing number of public-service posts and revenues.

Among the most important political understandings Pedro Batista and João Sá reached involved the beato's agreement to repay the coronel's protection with a pledge to deliver most, if not all, of the romeiro votes for Sá's designated candidates. While few of Batista's adult followers were literate and thus formally eligible to vote, in practice only a scrawled signature was required to cast a ballot, and most could manage this prerequisite. For the most part, the electoral pact between the coronel and the beato operated smoothly and in accordance with the electoral practices of the time, as exemplified in a letter from Sá to Batista: "I want to communicate that our candidate for President of the Re-

public is D. Juscelino [Kubitschek] and Jango [João Belchior Marques Goulart]
for Vice President, men who were connected to the late D. Getúlio Vargas; you
should start making your arrangements with your people" (10 September 1955,
Pedro Batista da Silva Papers).[8]

Tall, lean, and weathered by decades of exposure to the unrelenting rays of
the Northeastern sun, romeiro Fernando Reis (1999) took pleasure in recalling
earlier times, including the conduct of politics in the 1940s and 1950s. "There
were no politics, no nothing," he assured me. "We already knew who to vote
for; we had a fixed candidate, that was [the candidate of] Coronel João Sá.
The whole thing was arranged before the election." Reis further explained that
Batista ensured that his promise to Sá, or to any other vote seeker, was fully
honored by instructing the local election supervisors to place a given number
of ballots in the boxes of particular candidates (ibid.). It was in this way that
Batista directed a modest number of votes to Sá's UDN rivals, a practice that
helped to keep UDN's local band of bandit enforcers at bay.

As the number of romeiros settling in Santa Brígida grew over the course of
the early 1950s and Getúlio Vargas returned to office (1951–1954), Batista began
to request that Sá provide additional services and amenities for his prospering
community. Some of these, such as teachers and a post office were ultimately
forthcoming, but apparently the beato chafed at the slowness with which these
benefits arrived. It was this dissatisfaction, and the fact that the beato was both
courted and intimidated by rival politicians, that led him to seek greater independence from Sá. Such independence was in evidence when, in the 1954
elections, Batista instructed his romeiros to divide their votes evenly between
Sá and the rival party. That this was a message to the Sá family to cease taking
Pedro Batista's support for granted could hardly have been missed, since João
Sá's son, João Carvalho Sá, was the PSD candidate for state senator.

Thus, the millenarian leader was not only able to effectively negotiate an accommodation with local political figures but also to do so at a date well beyond
the period in which the literature has typically addressed such matters. Moreover, it was Batista himself who invited the state in when he demanded such
public institutions as state-funded schools and a post office. Furthermore, the
Pedro Batista movement exemplified how the dominant discourse constructing a messianic figure could turn around dramatically once the religious leader
was accepted as a client of powerful politicians. After all, just a decade earlier,
the press had maligned him as an ignorant and dangerous drifter. Local political chiefs and policemen in Alagoas and Pernambuco had humiliated and jailed
him. Similarly Bahian state authorities who sought to banish him had com-

pared Batista to the "notorious" leaders of Canudos and Pau de Colher. These powerholders thus disciplined and labeled the beato in a manner that, from the perspective of contemporary scholars, exemplified the response of the dominant classes to acts of popular resistance. In this instance, Batista was viewed as a threat to church hierarchy, to political stability, and to the unitary modernizing project of the Brazilian bourgeoisie. While overblown, such concerns on the part of elite Brazilians did have some validity, as evidenced in Batista's repudiation of church reforms (e.g., his claim that the Vatican's endorsement of Christ the King was satanic) and in his apocalyptic discourse. Although Batista was an admirer of Vargas, the beato's teachings implicitly pointed to the inadequacy of national leaders and awakened the hopes among the rural poor for divine retribution against the immoral rich and powerful.

In light of the initial parrying between Batista and his rivals, it is remarkable that a mere decade later the most powerful leader of the UDN in Bahia, Juracy Magalhães, sent a telegram to Batista in which he wrote, "I come to solicit, *illustrious patrician,* your valuable and decisive support for my victory in the campaign for Governor of the state" (15 September 1950 or 1958, Pedro Batista da Silva Papers; emphasis added). Moreover, some years later Batista was included among the local dignitaries invited to the neighboring city of Paulo Afonso to meet personally with presidential candidate Marechal (Marshal) Henrique Teixeira Lott. One factor that loomed large in this metamorphosis was the ability of Batista, local politicians, and government authorities—with both the witting and unwitting aid of the media and the academy—to obscure the popular resistance and apocalyptic beliefs that drew so many to Santa Brígida and that characterized much of the life of its romaria.

Folk Catholicism, Lay Religious Orders, and Resistance

Pedro Batista and his romeiros sought a safe haven where they might socialize their children in accordance with the antiga lei and engage in religious practices denigrated and at times even outlawed by powerful segments of the church and state. For the backlanders who relocated to Santa Brígida, it was a site pulsating with biblical significance. It was also a setting where collective resistance might be mounted more concertedly against the almost century-long practices of attacking and suppressing folk Catholicism. The forms of resistance and cultural production engaged in by Batista and his followers belong to a lineage of alternative beliefs and practices that includes Padre Ibiapina and his beatos/beatas as well as Padre Cícero and Juazeiro.

POPULAR RESISTANCE AND THE LINK BETWEEN
PADRE CÍCERO AND PEDRO BATISTA

As a historical actor Padre Cícero challenged his ecclesiastical superiors regarding matters of control over the divine, the enforcement of church policy,
and demonstrations of faith. A parting of the ways was apparent when, despite
his knowledge of the disciplining measures the bishops had earlier directed
against Padre Ibiapina, a youthful Padre Cícero chose to respond to the general lack of institutional support for backland clergy by himself instituting a
lay order of beatas in Juazeiro. His defiance—along with his willingness to embrace such humble backlanders as the poor, dark-skinned, and female Maria
Araújo—was equally evident when Padre Cícero refused to renounce his claim
that the host he had administered to the beata had miraculously transformed
into Christ's body. He held fast to his convictions and to his support for Araújo
and her sisterhood of beatas despite both his subsequent suspension from the
priesthood and the subjection of the women to a humiliating inquisition and
denunciation by church patriarchs. Indeed, when faced with these tribulations
the cleric explained that although he would like to obey the church hierarchy,
his main bond was with God (Paz 1998, 47). Moreover, he responded equivo-
cally to such "heresies" as claims of his divinity and of Juazeiro being the future
site of Judgment Day and Heaven on Earth (ibid.; Della Cava 1970).

During the priest's lifetime and years after his death, the bishops and other
high-ranking church authorities sought to punish "fanatical" devotees and to
stifle their beliefs and practices. They did so, for example, by refusing to fill the
vacant post in Padre Cícero's church (and main chapel in Juazeiro) between the
years 1885 and 1916, by threatening with excommunication pilgrims who journeyed to Juazeiro, and by refusing to baptize children whose chosen name was
Cícero or Cícera. They also redoubled their practice of removing support from
lay orders and confraternities in an attempt to replace them with the organization, rituals, and doctrine of the orthodox church (Paz 1998).

As Renata Marinho Paz (1998) observes, these punitive actions backfired.
The masses only intensified their devotion to Padre Cícero, whom they came to
revere as one of their own: a victim of the elite and a persecuted santo. Moreover, vindictive church leaders deprived believers of more sympathetic priests
who might (as has been the case more recently) have abided their congregation's unorthodox enthusiasms while patiently channeling these into more official expressions of faith. As noted in the last chapter, many backlanders grew
increasingly fearful of God's wrath against what they viewed as an immoral and
treacherous clique of ecclesiastical and secular leaders. From the perspective

of many sertanejos, these leaders were bent on punishing the most religiously committed and thus jeopardizing all Brazilians' salvation. Under these fearful circumstances, such believers turned ever more intensely to their folk practices and lay practitioners. Consequently, the very lay beatas and beatos the church sought to delegitimate and marginalize grew in importance and stature.

The resistance surrounding Padre Cícero proved particularly attractive to his female beatas. Although generally accepting of orthodox Catholicism's patriarchal belief system and hierarchy, beatas were nonetheless able to expand their spheres of operation and influence. With few clergy willing, or perhaps able, to defend the events in Juazeiro, the beatas entered the breach. They acted to keep Padre Cícero's legacy as a santo alive and, more generally, to sustain folk Catholic practices and apocalyptic beliefs. If there were any doubts about the beatas' resolve or capacity to keep the torch burning, consider this: bloodstained altar cloths linked to the miracle, which the bishop had demanded with threats of excommunication after they had become objects of veneration, managed to be sequestered and guarded by beatas for some fifty-five years—reappearing in 1988 at a symposium held in Juazeiro! (Paz 1998, 100).

Pedro Batista made his entrance into the countryside only a few years after Padre Cícero had "moved on" (*se mudou*). One popular bendito prophesied the priest's resurrection.

> I am going, but I will return
> Follow my commandments
> With faith recite your rosaries
> So that you will recognize me.

That Pedro Batista profited from such prophecies and from the religious practices associated with devotion to Padre Cícero is apparent in the fact that the beato drew the bulk of his followers from places like Água Branca and Águas Belas—prominent sites for pilgrimages to Juazeiro.[9]

Moreover, in Água Branca, home of the largest concentration of romeiros to resettle in Santa Brígida, the link is especially clear between the beatas devoted to Padre Cícero, on the one hand, and the great enthusiasm generated for Pedro Batista, on the other. Água Branca's sisterhood of beatas represents this important link because the second most important figure in the romaria, Dona Dodô, spent her formative years with this lay order. Moreover, once she relocated to Santa Brígida, Dona Dodô introduced many of the teachings and religious practices she had learned from the beatas of Água Branca. In according Dona Dodô prominence in this account, I seek to reverse that tendency in

Maria das Dores dos
Santos, circa 1950. Photo
from author's personal
archive, photographer
unknown.

Brazilian millenarian studies to focus almost exclusively on male leaders (see
Paz 1998 for a notable exception).

THE BEATAS OF ÁGUA BRANCA AND DONA DODÔ

The lay Order of the Sisters of St. Francis, or the beatas of Água Branca as they
are popularly known, was founded in 1890 by Padre Cícero Joaquim de Siqueira
Torres, a devotee of Padre Ibiapina and a colleague and early supporter of Padre
Cícero of Juazeiro. Água Branca's lay sisters dedicated themselves to God, to
the education of abandoned children, to the preparation of young women for
matrimony, to social work for the community, and to the maintenance of the
community's churches (Torres 1990).

   While the beatas' main building was in the town of Água Branca, smaller
branches were established in more remote rural hamlets throughout the municipality. The existence of these outposts proved fortuitous, since following
the untimely death of Padre Torres in 1898, a more orthodox priest was appointed, and he cracked down on the town's beatas. For almost two decades the

beatas' alternative religious devotions were practiced secretly in rural hamlets, such as the one in which Dona Dodô was born in 1903. Theirs was a form of Catholicism in which prayers directed to the saints were believed to be miraculous, where folk healing occurred, and in which persons with special divine gifts might be possessed with spirits in order to perform good acts and speak in God's name (Riedl n.d.).

It did not take long before the young Maria das Dores caught the attention of the beatas. They marveled at the youngster who knelt in prayer for hours on end before church altars and who politely rejected their suggestions that she join the other children in play. As she herself explained with a mixture of pride and awed humility, "I don't know what it is, ever since the time I was a little girl, even without education, I was always able to respond to the hardest theological questions. And this amazed everyone, the priests included" (Maria das Dores 1974). One of the favorite stories told by those who knew her in Água Branca involves her precocious commitment to the poor. As a young child, Dodô's father had asked her to mind his small store while he left on a short trip. While he was away she distributed most of his food among the poor.

Dona Dodô was thirteen years old when Água Branca's hard-liner was replaced by Padre José Nicodemus. Fortunately for her and the other beatas, the new priest, who presided from 1916 to 1932, was sympathetic to the women's calling. Moreover, unlike his predecessor he did not oppose pilgrimages by his parishioners to Juazeiro. Under the tutelage of Padre Nicodemus and the beatas, the young Dodô discarded her everyday dress for the sisterhood's brown robe, rope sash, and veil. She dedicated herself to the study of the principal novenas, prayers, hymns, and penitential acts that the faithful termed a antiga lei to distinguish it from, in their view, the less efficacious modern church liturgy and practice. Moreover, with the authorization and assistance of Padre Nicodemus, Dodô founded a small, secret sisterhood devoted to Nossa Senhora da Boa Morte (Our Lady of the Good Death), which she later took with her to Santa Brígida. Dona Dodô was also introduced to moral and spiritual precepts that would forever guide her life and that she would pass on to others in Santa Brígida. These included living a life dedicated to penitence and poverty, ever vigilant in the knowledge that the Antichrist was present and the Day of Judgment near. What she referred to as her mandamentos (commandments), also included instructing people in the teachings of the antiga lei (e.g., special rosaries and novenas dedicated to popular saints), caring for the sick and destitute, and ensuring that even the poorest soul was provided with a decent burial accompanied by prayer.

Dona Dodô's early participation in Água Branca's sisterhood of beatas helped to ignite and sustain her contacts with Padre Cícero and Juazeiro. It was a lifelong relationship that saw her embark at the age of twelve on her first pilgrimage on foot to the holy city. Although too modest to comment in any detail, Dona Dodô clearly gained Padre Cícero's attention early on. As a teenager she was already leading pilgrimages on foot from Água Branca to Juazeiro, serving as a messenger between the religious authorities and politicians of the two towns, and occasionally providing domestic service within Padre Cícero's own residence. At that time the young woman perceived herself to be in the service of, in her own words, "two saintly men": Padre Nicodemus and Padre Cícero (ibid.). Later, she would add Pedro Batista to that vaunted list.

It is true that she, like other beatas, often accepted a subordinated status within the male-dominated ecclesiastical hierarchy. Moreover, she very consciously sought to model her behavior on the Virgin Mary. As a consequence, she emulated the feminine "ideals" of virtue, purity, self-abnegation, and service to others. Nonetheless, insofar as she and other beatas challenged the official church by continuing to support popular practices and alternative practitioners, they insisted on an empowered and empowering role for women.[10] Accordingly, Dodô enjoyed a degree of autonomy highly unusual for any woman, let alone one so young and poor. She proved herself to be brave and highly independent when she crossed mountains inhabited by wild mountain lions while guiding pilgrims to Juazeiro; when she left her home late at night, traveling on foot to minister to the sick and dying; and when she stood undaunted before and bettered bandits who had come to assassinate a political chief in Água Branca. She also explicitly refused the more conventional roles of wife and mother. Instead, she later assumed the revered status of godmother (*madrinha*) of the entire romaria.

The early 1930s proved particularly trying for Dona Dodô. In 1932 Padre Nicodemus, whose practices were considered decidedly unorthodox by his superiors, was transferred from Água Branca; Padre Cícero died two years later. Padre Nicodemus's replacement proved hostile to the beatas and their *antiga lei*. He tried to force them into convents and threatened those who refused, like Dona Dodô, with excommunication (Reidl n.d.). Reflecting on those difficult times, Água Branca's current priest, Padre Rosevaldo (2000), is far more generous in his assessment of Dona Dodô, and he takes care to place her within a historical moment characterized by tensions between the church and its rural practitioners: "Dona Dodô went to Santa Brígida and created her group of beatas. Her religious experience was that of a person who saw herself as someone sent by God, a missionary who had a gift. She had her own prayers. Their religion was based on the structure of the Catholic Church, but deep down they had their secrets, which the priests did not know. This caused a certain conflict over power."

To remove herself from the harassment directed against her and the other beatas, Dona Dodô elected to spend long periods of time in Juazeiro, and it is there, in 1940, where she first encountered Pedro Batista. As she expressed it, "The minute I saw him I knew my mission and his would be one" (1974). Later when the beato made his way to the municipality of Água Branca, Dona Dodô left Juazeiro to join him there. And when Batista ended his penitential mission and settled in Santa Brígida, he called on her to help him set the romeiros on the path to salvation.

ROMEIROS' MOTIVES FOR SETTLING IN SANTA BRÍGIDA

The motives of the few thousand romeiros who along with Dona Dodô chose to relocate to Santa Brígida were no doubt multiple and mixed. Nonetheless, the accounts I have been able to collect that speak to motivation turn out to be remarkably uniform. For a romeiro the act of publicly discussing his or her decision to relocate amounts to a testimony of faith — a faith made all the more virtuous by its refusal to bend before the objections and ostracism of skeptical peers and more powerful foes. Consequently, a move to air additional motives, such as a desire for economic improvement, might from the romeiro narrator's point of view unnecessarily complicate or undermine the purity of the testimony. To at once acknowledge this rhetorical fact yet also try to open the lines of analysis a bit further, I will present both a insider's ("emic") and an outsider/analyst's ("etic") portrayal of motivation.

The three testimonies that follow are fairly typical. They tell of pilgrims who were secure in their convictions that Pedro Batista was, at the very least, a messenger of God, if not, more portentously, the promised reincarnation of Padre Cícero. As is captured in the second account, many romeiros insisted that their ability to perceive Batista's divine mission came from God and was a gift he bestowed in recognition of the individual's extraordinary piety and faith. Along with this gift came a capacity to comprehend the truth and an obligation to act in accordance with this knowledge, that is, to accompany Batista on his divine mission to save as many souls as possible before the impending apocalypse. Poor and illiterate romeiros referred proudly to their divine gift of enlightenment. Challenging such elite descriptions of millenarianists' intelligence as "degenerate," "insane," "psycho-erotic and infantile" (cited in Levine 1992, 206–8), romeiros often deemed their own comprehension of spiritual matters far superior to that possessed by formally educated and, by and large, skeptical and belittling patrons and professionals. In short, my romeiro informants

attributed their willingness to support Pedro Batista to divine intercession. By
contrast, as an outside analyst, I am more apt to attribute their agency to a
form of popular religious consciousness that endured in certain backland communities, which remained sites for the maintenance of alternative notions of
knowledge/comprehension, power, human initiative, and the nature of a just
and moral order.

I learned about Antônia da Cunha's call to accompany Pedro Batista one late
afternoon after she and I had finished decorating an altar in her home. It was
soon to be the site of a novena in honor of São Antônio whose festivities Dona
Antônia helped to sponsor yearly. As I placed the last flower around an old picture of Pedro Batista, I took the opportunity to ask her if I might one day record
her recollections about the first time she met her Padrinho. She jumped at my
request and instructed me to get my tape recorder right away. As I depressed
the record button, she took a deep breath and commenced.

> I long desired to visit my Padrinho Cícero in Juazeiro, but I was poor and
> never could. [Toward the end of his life] they limited the number of people
> who could visit him. Then people began to say that we need not worry,
> because beginning in 1940, my Padrinho Cícero would travel freely and
> openly in the world.
>
> And this was the time that my Padrinho Pedro Batista began to travel
> through the world. But I did not know at first if my Padrinho was Padrinho
> Cícero. I knew that Padrinho Cícero had one finger with part of a nail miss-
> ing. When I entered the room where my Padrinho [Pedro] was resting on
> a hammock, I looked down at his hands. But his fingers were bent about
> his knees. When I approached him for a blessing, he put out his hand and
> smiled. I saw the finger with the partial nail! And instantly he entered my
> heart. With joy I repeated to myself, I have met my Padrinho Cícero and
> have received his blessing. . . . From that day on I vowed to follow him.
> His mission was *fina* [precious, extraordinary].
>
> So when we learned in 1945 that my Padrinho had settled in Santa Brí-
> gida, we were overjoyed. My husband and I didn't think twice. We com-
> pleted our obligations [as tenant farmers in Mata Grande], packed our
> few belongings, and left for Santa Brígida. . . . We left as poor country folk
> and arrived to a place of suffering. My Padrinho always said, "Don't come
> to Santa Brígida if you want to get rich. Come if you are willing to suffer;
> it is better to bring six sacks of patience than six sacks of gold." (1973)

Unsolicited, I first heard about Ana Rodrigues's initial encounter with Pedro
Batista as I traveled with her and several other romeiros to the patron's day fes-

tivities for Our Lady of the Immaculate Conception in her native community of
Água Branca. Familiar sights and sounds seemed to jog her memory. Shortly
afterward she agreed to allow me to record her recollections.

> The sheriff threatened to jail people if they visited my Padrinho. Many
> called him a charlatan, and I was uncertain and afraid [of being jailed].
> My mother was always sickly and she insisted that we travel to see my
> Padrinho at the ranch where he was staying. When we got there a large
> crowd was waiting, but my Padrinho looked up and his eyes met mine.
> "I know there is one among you who is afraid and uncertain. Do not be
> afraid, my mission comes from Our Father and it is to warn you about
> the great agonies that are drawing near." I felt my body turn cold. I knew
> from that day on that I would follow him anywhere and obey his com-
> mandments. . . . It was not anything that came from me; it came from Our
> Father, and no one could dissuade me—not even my Godfather [a mem-
> ber of Água Branca's powerful Torres family], who was opposed to my
> leaving. I remembered that a good priest used to say, "Some people study
> and gain knowledge; others become even dumber." I who don't know any-
> thing, who can't even sign my name, know when a *história* [story, mission]
> is linked to Our Father. Many others, who had attended school, tried to
> stop me, but I knew my understanding came from the Lord and was far
> superior to theirs. (1973)

Finally, Paulo Duarte (1974) explained to me that he had lived most of
his young adult life suffering from debilitating headaches. Despite this he
struggled to maintain his wife and young children modestly by working as a
cobbler and farmer in a small town in Sergipe. As he recollected,

> I lived twelve years so sick that many thought my wife would be a young
> widow any day. One day a relative, who knew of my suffering and the
> money I had wasted on doctors, told me about this curer, Pedro Batista.
> He urged me to visit him. After my Padrinho cured me with prayer and
> holy water, he explained how the spirits of those seeking comfort and
> grace had sought me out, and how they were causing my suffering. He
> removed those spirits and told me to never again smoke, drink, or use
> profanities. . . .
> I tried so hard to follow my Padrinho's orders. I remembered that he
> had said that if Our Father smells the slightest trace of cigarette smoke on
> a poor soul after he has died, the person is hung up feet first and burned
> until his spirit is cleansed! My friends in Sergipe couldn't understand this,

and they tried to get me to smoke and drink with them. One day I did, and I was back in bed for weeks with terrible headaches and my children hungry. Another time I was helping a friend on his farm. He offered me a swig of *pinga* [alcohol], which I couldn't refuse. But then he gave me another. I said, "Sorry, compadre, I can't drink anymore." He got angry and threw the pinga in my face! People began to think that I was trying to act better than they, and they began to avoid me. Others said that I was learning *feitiçaria* [witchcraft]. . . . One day I asked a neighbor if he would loan me a sack of farinha because we were low on money. "Get farinha from your Padre Cícero," he shouted. Well, I decided I could no longer live there.

I made three pilgrimages to Santa Brígida. On the first trip my Padrinho asked, "How are things in Sergipe, my *caboclo* [Indian/backwoodsman, an affectionate name Batista often used when addressing his followers]?"

"Not well, my Padrinho. Land is tight and we have to pay the owners a lot of money."

"Well, my caboclo, the world is big. There are other opportunities."

On my third trip, my Padrinho asked, "My caboclo, how do you like Santa Brígida?"

I said, "It's like this, my Padrinho, I have friends and family in Sergipe, but they've all turned their backs on me."

"Wait until next year, until the drought passes, and bring the others."

I didn't know what he meant about the others, but to my surprise, my mother and father-in-law decided to relocate as well.

As it turned out, at first the conditions in Sergipe were much better; the land was more fertile and we had more rain. But we did not come to live better [materially]; we came so that I might remain healthy and obey my Padrinho's commandments. . . . We came for the penitence. . . . All acts of penitence done in the name of my Padrinho and Madrinha Dodô will be repaid tenfold on the Day of Judgment.

My own attempts to comprehend and gauge the range of motives leading individual romeiros to spurn the counsel of priests and patrons, as well as dissenting family members and friends, and to pull up stakes to follow Pedro Batista to Santa Brígida does not diverge greatly from my informants' explanations. I believe they were motivated foremost by spiritual concerns, so much so that they were willing to endure the condemnation and ostracism of their patrons and neighbors. Where we diverge slightly is in my insistence on situating these concerns within the broader context of ultramontane church reforms and the backland elite's modernizing project, on the one hand, and on the resistance and accommodation by a segment of the rural poor to these initiatives, on the other. Santa Brígida represented a setting where people were encouraged to maintain their devotion to a spiritual leader believed to be the incarnation of Padre Cícero. It was also a site where backlanders were free to collectively practice religious rites that were denigrated or outlawed in their communities of origin despite popular concerns over salvation and the feared apocalypse.

Earlier millenarianists were motivated not only by spiritual concerns but also by deeply unsettling political and economic changes. These threatened the very security and subsistence of many backlanders and further fueled apprehension about divine punishment. They also exposed the contingencies and cruelties of patronage. Was there a similar lack of confidence in national politicians and local patrons in the Pedro Batista movement? Here the evidence is more ambiguous and generally less compelling.[11]

In marked contrast to earlier santos and their followers, who dubbed republican leaders Antichrists, Pedro Batista and his romeiros had nothing but praise for President Getúlio Vargas. One popular vignette recounted by older romeiros illustrates the very intimate way in which romeiros engaged Vargas and how they embroidered him into their own life histories; the story alleges that Vargas visited Dona Dodô when she lived in Água Branca, praising her for her service to the poor and elderly and promising that one day soon the government would assume far more responsibility for these much-needed services (Alzira Bezerra 1974). In contrast to how they received earlier republican leaders, many backlanders had faith in Vargas's ability to create social conditions conducive to their salvation. In fact, elderly romeiros went so far as to claim that unlike other presidents Vargas actually possessed divine powers. For Batista and his followers, then, it was not Vargas who represented a danger to the larger moral/spiritual order, but those within the president's inner circle who championed such "dangerous" practices as individualism, capital accumulation, and conspicuous consumption.

The seeming abandonment of patronage in the backlands had also contributed to the emergence of the earlier turn-of-the century movements. Did patronage as a cultural construct and set of practices continue to play a role in the creation of the later Pedro Batista movement? It is first necessary to consider how members of the backland elite were able to recoup some of their previously lost power. By the 1930s and 1940s many elite backland families had managed to reach an understanding with state authorities. The latter required agricultural profits to help finance urban industrialization, and they sought quiescence in the countryside during a turbulent period of rapid urbanization.

President Vargas and his agents rewarded accommodating coronéis and large landholders with continued access to federal power and with patronage and minimum interference in the countryside. From the perspective of the agrarian elite, then, the Vargas years constituted the initial phase of a long-term trend that, while subordinating the rural power structure to the state, assured its continued viability and reaffirmed its importance within the larger political order (Cehelsky 1979). This meant that the deteriorating material conditions and strains on patronage ties that helped to galvanize earlier episodes of millenarian protest were far less in evidence, on the one hand, and that mechanisms to redress local grievances were more likely in place, on the other.

Like their millenarian predecessors, Batista's followers belonged to the humble ranks of rural dwellers dependent on the goodwill of local patrons. The romeiros were predominantly mestizos (referred to colloquially as *morenos/coboclos*), who prior to resettling in Santa Brígida eked out livelihoods as small farmers/ranchers, tenant farmers, artisans, or petty merchants. As I learned while recording life histories, these families had little or no financial cushion with which to manage such reccurring hardships as serious illness or crop failure. This vulnerability elevated the pursuit of a bom patrão (good patron/boss) to the top of their survival strategies. By the 1930s and 1940s my romeiro informants enjoyed access to a wider and larger array of potential patrons (e.g., landowners, merchants, professionals, state bureaucrats) than had their parents. This reflected the greater socioeconomic differentiation in the countryside in the wake of republicanism and intensified agrarian capitalism. Although this expanded "patronage market" made it somewhat easier than in the past to line up potential "benefactors" and to cast off excessively exploitative ones, the bargain remained bleak. As Nancy Scheper-Hughes (1992) notes, "This is a vicious cycle and a relationship in which both parties can feel themselves ill-served and exploited, for what is being hidden in this 'bad faith' economy (Bourdieu 1977, 176) is the true nature of the relations governing the transactions, where desperation can be called loyalty and exploitation can masquerade as care and nurturance" (111–12).

On the one hand, an earlier generation of backlanders—including thousands of millenarianists—saw the hegemonic niceties of a purportedly moral economy stripped away and unmasked in all its bad faith violence. On the other hand, neither this older generation nor their progeny possessed the political and economic resources to dismantle such an oppressive system. Although the raw desperation behind the search for a good patron may have eased for some after the dark days of the dawning republic, the pursuit still endured. Early in his career Pedro Batista had all the trappings of not just a bom patrão but an ideal one. This promise materialized fully once he settled in Santa Brígida. Moreover, Pedro Batista's patronage became even more necessary and valuable for those backlanders like Paulo Duarte who were ostracized by their former patrons and friends due to their devotion to the beato.

However, while many romeiros were quite frank both in discussing their past and present needs for a good patron and in praising Batista as the ideal patron, very few claimed to have been drawn to the beato on material/ instrumental grounds. Duarte, for instance, clearly corrects any impression that, despite inadequate land and expensive rents, he was drawn to Santa Brígida on largely economic grounds, stating, "We didn't come to live better materially. We came so I might remain healthy. . . . We came for the penitence."

In fact, those who had arrived in Santa Brígida in the 1940s and 1950s asserted that the social and economic rewards that ultimately followed from relocating proved wholly unexpected. To what extent these assertions are conditioned rhetorically by romeiros' "higher truth claims" to faith and spiritual calling remain unknowable at this time. Nonetheless, based on her 1950s ethnography, Pereira de Queiroz noted that while "many relied on [Batista's] properties to cultivate their own small plots; others, and in no small quantities, brought their own money to buy or rent land" (Queiroz 1965a, 274). Along similar lines an early romeiro settler from Águas Belas assured me, "It was easier to live there. It was much better. Águas Belas had already been a city for almost one hundred years. When I arrived Santa Brígida had nothing really" (Geraldo Ferreira 1999).[12]

Another motivating factor promoting relocation to Santa Brígida was family reunification. The highly devout Lopes family of Água Branca, for example, boasted several hundred in their ranks, and most of them settled together on the outskirts of Santa Brígida. As Paulo Duarte's earlier testimony intimates, family reunification may have been motivated not only by feelings of solidarity and affection but also by deprivations caused by worsening social isolation in communities of origin once kin relocated to Santa Brígida.

Family dynamics operated in a different fashion for the sizable number of abandoned women with children and unmarried women who elected to settle in Santa Brígida.[13] They sought the protection and communion the romaria afforded. They were also the most vulnerable to the social isolation some experienced once their devotion to Batista became known among their neighbors. Sitting by her handcrafted clay cooking pots during a slow morning at Santa Brígida's weekly market, Raimunda de Lima (1977) recounted, "My husband left me with three young children. This one here was an infant. I was struggling to manage with the help of my brothers. . . . We were orphaned without a mother and father. When I first visited my Padrinho and Madrinha Dodô [in Santa Brígida], I realized I had once again found my mother and father. . . . I guess I should have realized that many who did not have the merit to understand their mistério would turn their backs on me. It was hard, but it only made me stronger in my resolve to leave as soon as I could. . . . Like a good father, my Padrinho furnished me and my children with a home, with food, and with work on his farm."

Finally, in light of the generally unflattering way in which many romeiras described (nonromeiro) rural men, it may well have been the case that certain women were attracted to Batista for his strong hand in condemning adultery as well as such vices as drinking and gambling whose expenditures cost poor households dearly. Batista was extremely profamily, arguing that it was a divine and socially stabilizing institution. As such he personally arranged many unions and conducted nuptials between abandoned or single romeiras and unattached romeiros—sometimes in collective weddings. Recalling her sadness some thirty years earlier, Renata Torres (1977) reminisced, "For his romeiros, the most important thing was to obey. Nobody refused what he ordered. Eight of us were married at the same time. I was fourteen, and I cried so much. But it didn't change things. His decision held." [14]

"Normalizing" Santa Brígida

Given the divergent politics behind Coronel Sá's acceptance of Batista and his romeiros, on the one hand, and the latter's decision to resettle in Santa Brígida, on the other, how did Sá manage to bridge the divide between his respected status as a contemporary mid-twentieth-century politician in times that demanded "order and progress" and his romeiro clients' beliefs and practices, which most outside observers would have branded as backward and fanatical? Foremost, the coronel required "mainstream" performances from Batista and his followers when they were under the scrutiny of outsiders. Other concessions to mid-twentieth-century rationality and modernity Sá demanded included Batista's agreement to cut his long beard, to desist from curing, and to discipline his romeiros from pursuing such "fanatical" actions as ingesting his hair clippings or bathwater for medicinal purposes.

Coronel Sá was not alone in attempting to normalize Pedro Batista and his romeiros. Members of the scholarly community also became implicated through their representations of Santa Brígida. Foremost among them were sociologist Maria Isaura Pereira de Queiroz, who conducted many months of fieldwork in Santa Brígida over the course of the 1950s, and her junior colleagues and students who engaged in briefer stints of research in the 1960s. These scholars produced books, articles, and even a documentary about Santa Brígida (see Queiroz 1958, 1965a, 1965b, 1973; Lima 1968; Fukui 1979; Muniz 1967).

Her training in functionalist sociology made Pereira de Queiroz particularly attentive to exploring the ways in which religious practices, such as the romeiros' Dance of São Gonçalo, reduced anomie and fostered social solidarity in the otherwise (allegedly) disorganized Brazilian countryside. As a pioneer in the development of Brazilian rural sociology Pereira de Queiroz, with the help of her collaborators, pursued another agenda as well. While her early writings contributed to that intellectual tradition that envisioned the existence of "two Brazils"(Queiroz 1958), she and her students later attempted to bridge such difference and supposed disarticulation between the two Brazils. They did so by rendering the rural hinterlands "legible" to more educated and powerful Brazilians. Indeed, by the mid-1960s the explicit and politically progressive aim of these scholars was to convince urban professionals that "remote" and "exotic" locales like Santa Brígida were really neither. Rather, they were very much part and parcel of Brazilian society and the nation (Sérgio Muniz, personal communication, 2000).

Although no one can dispute the merits of such a project of inclusivity, at the time it had the unintended consequence of muting difference. Consider the 1967 documentary on Santa Brígida, *O povo do velho Pedro*, produced and directed by Sérgio Muniz in collaboration with a team of young scholars trained by Pereira de Queiroz. The film adeptly portrays a slice of life in the backland community: it shows romeiros struggling to eke out a livelihood despite primitive technology (e.g., ox-drawn plows and archaic manioc presses); it contains footage of the aftermath of a killing, which serves to underscore Pereira de Queiroz's (Queiroz 1958) convictions about "antisocial" baianos living side by side with the orderly and peaceful romeiros; and it includes shots of religious processions, a curing ritual, and romeiros requesting blessings from their Padrinho. Yet, in seeking to avoid "excessive" othering, Muniz unfortunately misses the opportunity to highlight how the beliefs and practices of his romeiro subjects revolve around millennial expectations.

This reluctance to grant millenarianism the privileged place it merits is most explicitly captured in two segments of the film. First, the narrator (Muniz) claims that the romeiros settled in Santa Brígida to live close to Pedro Batista mainly because of the drought and political persecution. Left unstated is the nature of those messianic and apocalyptic beliefs that may have provoked political persecution in the first place.[15] Moreover, neither in this film nor in the

works of Pereira de Queiroz and her students is it clear that the numerous rituals and processions performed in this community are directed to Pedro Batista
and God to ensure the salvation of as many souls as possible before the imminent Day of Judgment. Another opportunity to bring apocalyptic sentiments
more fully into the film was squandered when an infirm Batista surrounded by
his devotees looks directly into the camera and taps his own arm saying, "All of
us have to pass through this hand; you don't believe this, do you? Here the rich
and the poor and the priest, all have to come here." For romeiros with whom I
have watched the video and discussed its content, this image of their deceased
Padrinho and his proclamation are clearly the most powerful segment of the
entire film. For them it confirms their ardent belief that he is that divine figure
who will judge the living and the dead on Judgment Day. Yet this highly dramatic
moment goes by without follow-up or commentary by the filmmaker/narrator.

Recently, when I asked Muniz how he interprets Batista's statement, he
claimed that he thought Batista was referring to his role as a political boss
(chefe político), a leader who controlled all political affairs within Santa Brígida.
That Muniz could have reached this erroneous conclusion is not surprising.
Not only did the highly urbane and politically savvy Muniz seek to find a kindred
spirit—rather than a religious zealot—in the rural other, but also, in preparing to film the documentary, he consulted works prior to filming that left him
unprepared to appreciate the intensity of the religious devotion, cultural creativity, and popular resistance operating in Santa Brígida. Instead, he turned
to works in which religion is largely reduced to its social functions of reducing
anomie and building social solidarity (Queiroz 1958, 1965a, 1965b).

Other studies by certain University of São Paulo scholars also promoted the
larger project of leveling difference, to this end following the conventional
community-study format of depicting the community's kinship organization,
economy, and party politics (Queiroz 1973; Fukui 1979). Yet in neglecting to
situate their analysis of the romaria within a framework in which religion, cultural creativity, and political-economic forces are all in play and mutually con-
stitutive, these scholars failed to grapple with important features of romeiro
resistance. Instead, depending on the particular author and the time the work
was produced, the romeiros are portrayed as either the victims or beneficiaries
of an inevitable historical march toward modernity and national integration.
Missing from such a unitary narrative is the romeiros' impressive accomplishment in successfully negotiating a space for cultural pluralism and an alternative modernity.

As I prepared myself in the early 1970s for fieldwork in Santa Brígida, I considered myself fortunate because my own training in symbolic anthropology

and my mentoring by Victor Turner, a brilliant analyst of religion and ritual practices, positioned me to examine what I understood to be an insufficiently explored dimension of romeiro life. Although epistemological differences are certainly crucial to the contrasting ways in which my predecessors and I have interpreted religion in Santa Brígida, I want to add another element that also accounts for the lesser treatment of religious ideology and practice in Pereira de Queiroz's work than mine. It has to do with the dialogical and rhetorical nature of fieldwork and the very different "politics" operating during the moments my predecessor and I were engaged in research.

The Dialogical Nature of Fieldwork

During the years 1954, 1955, and 1958, when Pereira de Queiroz conducted research in Santa Brígida, Pedro Batista was seriously engaged with politicians and government officials at the local, state, and federal levels. For this reason alone, it is understandable that the Pedro Batista refracted through the sociologist's writings is far more the patron and political boss than the prophet. However, that was exactly the public persona Batista was encouraged (if not disciplined) by his political superiors to evince when he confronted influential outsiders like University of São Paulo professor Pereira de Queiroz. Indeed older romeiros concurred with Fernando Reis (1999) when he informed me, "My Padrinho asked us not to do certain things that outsiders would not understand, like drink my Padrinho's bathwater and ask him for a cure when the professor was around."

Revealingly, a teacher who was working in Santa Brígida during the sociologist's two initial stints of research and who accompanied her during her visits to Batista's home had this to say when asked whether Batista and his followers discussed religious matters during her and Pereira de Queiroz's visits: "No, never. I would go there with Isaura [Pereira de Queiroz] and spend hours talking, but he didn't talk about religion" (Maria Rodrigues 2000). When asked whether she recalled if Pereira de Queiroz inquired about religion, the former schoolteacher continued, "No, she would hope that he would say something. We heard a lot of nonsense from the romeiros about how he performed miracles. . . . I don't know if he was putting on an act for me, but when I was around he never talked about religious things or prayed or anything like that. . . . He never said, 'I am going to cure someone,' when I was around. But I heard he cured people. The baianos would tell me. They would say, 'He does those things. He doesn't do them around you because you are not a romeira' " (ibid.).

What may also be gleaned from Maria Rodrigues's comments is that it was

Batista, most particularly, who "scripted" the discourse and practices when outsiders were present; were his followers' commentaries and practices to go unrestrained, he might well have been placed in a compromised position with respect to his political patrons. This is a very different figure than the Pedro Batista who but a few years earlier had freely informed his interrogators—be they sheriffs or priests—that the apocalypse was imminent and that he was a crusader against the satanical Cristo Rei ("O beato 'autorizado' a fazer propoganda contra Cristo-Rei," *Jornal de Alagoas*, 22 February 1942, p. 6). This was a man who now recognized that, in the proximity of influential outsiders, measured and secularized discourse and practices were necessary to best protect that semiautonomous space he had secured for himself as a leader and for his romaria.[16]

Of course, when I arrived in the mid-1970s at the height of a repressive military dictatorship, the romeiros hardly felt free from external scrutiny or fully at liberty to discuss transgressive beliefs and practices with outsiders. Nevertheless, by the late 1960s the romeiros had come to fear that their spiritual mission was being severely compromised and jeopardized far more by forces *internal* to the romaria than by the external ones. Critics pointed the finger of blame at those who refused to follow their deceased leader's teachings and to increasing socioeconomic stratification within the romaria. Confronting such distressing times, the highly mystical Dona Dodô prophesied that a dark-haired woman who was a messenger of God would soon arrive from across the seas to take stock of the community and to report back to God. It was my unusual "fortune" to show up in Santa Brígida with long dark hair, pens, notebooks, and a tape recorder just a few months after Dona Dodô had delivered this prophecy. And if it is the case that Pereira de Queiroz's training at the Sorbonne had left her primed to find anomie, my training with Victor Turner predisposed me to jump right in and ask people about their religious beliefs and practices.

Since I am dealing with dialogical matters, I should make it clear that I did not learn of Dona Dodô's prophecy until ten months into my initial fifteen-month stint of field research. It was shared with me by a close informant who made it clear that most romeiros had by then come to believe that I was very pious and serious but not divine. His disclosure managed to clarify certain previously puzzling matters, such as the request by several romeiros to have me pray over them. Fortunately this request was met by Dona Dodô's retort that I had the power but was as yet too young to harness my gifts. I should add that I suspect that Dona Dodô and several elderly romeiros believed back then, and continue to believe today, that I possess certain mystical powers.

The professional ethics of handling such an attribution are both daunting and complicated. While I certainly did nothing to encourage this ascribed identity, I appreciated that to strongly repudiate it would have been to challenge the legitimacy of the author of the prophecy, Dona Dodô, which was decidedly not my aim. Moreover, by then I knew that most romeiros expected divine beings to deny their special status. Nonetheless, to say nothing after the information had been shared with me would have been disingenuous and unethical. What I elected to do was to reiterate, whenever appropriate, that I was a student at a university in the United States and was in Santa Brígida to research and write a scholarly book, as Pereira de Queiroz had done before me.

While I assume that Dona Dodô's prophecy initially made certain romeiros more receptive to speaking about their religious beliefs and to including me in their practices, I believe that over time another motivation came strongly into play: my own willingness to partake in religious practices and to learn about beliefs that many romeiros of my generation had come to reject. By the mid-1970s ardent romeiros were eager to have the value of their practices affirmed and recorded by a young stranger, whatever the true purpose of her mission might be.[17] The dialogical universe in which I operated and to which I contributed had its disciplining features, however. I learned from Dona Dodô that Pedro Batista had ultimately failed in his spiritual mission because he "turned too much to politics and therefore sacrificed his divine calling" (174). She, on the other hand, made it clear to me and to others that she disliked and feared politics. So, at her gentle urging, I turned from inquiring too persistently about the larger political contexts in which Santa Brígida had evolved and was then embedded. Consequently, I became a regular fixture in the church, not the mayor's office, and I participated in scores of religious processions and pilgrimages.

I raise this matter because in my first scholarly representations of Santa Brígida, I created narratives that privileged symbolism and that provided a much-needed window into certain Northeasterners' worldviews (Pessar 1976, 1982). My early writings were, admittedly, far less attentive to the larger political-economic contexts in which the movement developed and interacted.[18] Consequently, based on my initial fieldwork, the Pedro Batista I presented to my readers was far more the prophet than the worldly politician. My oversights led to a host of surprises when in the summer of 1999 my two research assistants and I embarked on archival research in Santa Brígida and in the state capital of Salvador. At that time, we found several pieces of correspondence between regional politicians and Pedro Batista, as well as campaign fliers with Pedro Batista's picture alongside local and state politicians. In light of this material I now feel both obligated and empowered to craft a revised narrative of Pedro Batista: one that is truer to his multifaceted leadership style and that places his movement within a fuller range of cultural meanings, social institutions, and historical processes.

Conclusion

Accounts that have situated Brazilian millenarian movements within their larger political-economic contexts have tended to cover an earlier historical period and have treated the more dramatic movements of Juazeiro, Canudos, and Contestado. The Pedro Batista movement offers an opportunity to broaden understandings of the engagement among millenarianists, state authorities, and other elite actors for the period that commenced with the Vargas Revolution of 1930 and that continues to this day. Such a treatment permits a much-needed revision of those teleological arguments that quite prematurely deliver a eulogy for millenarianism once the modern state comes into being. Modernity did not make millenarian movements obsolete; the process proved far more complex and reciprocal in nature. As both sides accommodated the other, the romeiros achieved enough autonomy to maintain and elaborate unconventional beliefs and practices. Santa Brígida became a site amenable to alternative readings of the times, competing understandings of power and knowledge, and communal forms of social organization. For their part, local and national authorities were mollified by assurances of nonaggression on the part of Batista and his followers. They were also heartened by the romeiros' general willingness to permit those agents charged with disseminating dominant ideologies and practices of modernity and centralization to operate relatively unencumbered within Santa Brígida. The potential friction between popular and elite political agendas was greatly reduced by the ability of political boss Coronel João Sá and Pedro Batista to mask those particularly transgressive and challenging elements of the romeiros' religious ideology and ways of life. In this masking, they were abetted by the first wave of scholars to study Santa Brígida.

"WORK LIKE YOU'RE GOING TO LIVE FOREVER AND PRAY LIKE YOU'RE GOING TO DIE TODAY"

In the latter half of the 1940s with many backlanders highly motivated to join their Padrinho in Santa Brígida and with Colonel João Sá willing to receive them, Pedro Batista, Dona Dodô, and their romeiros faced the challenge of creating a new community modeled strictly on their religious beliefs and millennial expectations and on their alternative engagements with modernity. During the community-building years (1945–1965), the popular homily, "*Trabalhem como quem nunca há de morrer e rezem como quem vai morrer hoje*" (Work like you're going to live forever and pray like you're going to die today) proved emblematic (Elias dos Santos 1974).[1] The latter half of the trope fixed the romeiros' sights on salvation, and it also captured the belief that the apocalypse was drawing near. With this preoccupation in mind, the romeiros mobilized to craft a physical environment worthy of this cosmic drama. This meant converting Santa Brígida into a new Jerusalem and second Juazeiro. The romeiros also introduced penitential practices to better their own and many others' chances for attaining salvation. On the other hand, the admonition to work like you are going to live forever exhorted the pilgrims to engage in hard work so that their material security and well-being were also guaranteed.

How were the romeiros able to attend simultaneously to both demands? After all, it might be argued that the emphasis on hard work and material security undermined older Christian tenets encapsulated in the second half of the refrain, those teachings that posit the transitory nature of material existence and the dangers of becoming overly attached to this life. It is also true that an emphasis on concerted work and the material rewards it facilitated was a message wholly consistent with the state's project to produce modern subjects suited to the demands of expanding national labor and consumer markets. While these latter objectives were most assuredly not goals Batista valued or pursued, in the early years of community formation he was able to manage such tensions.

Once settled in Santa Brígida, the romeiros interacted with institutions and authorities that in the past had made the practice of folk Catholicism so difficult. Local clerics maintained the policy of opposing and denigrating these adherents of the antiga lei, while politicians and journalists chose to strategically overlook millenarian beliefs and practices. Instead, they turned their sights to the first part of the popular refrain and accordingly praised the hardworking romeiros as modernizing and highly productive compatriots, fully in step with Vargas's national slogan of "Order and Progress."

The Romeiros Build a New Jerusalem and a Second Juazeiro

Placemaking entails cultural claims and social acts by which a population calls a location their own and infuses it with an appropriate past and future (Appadurai 1995). Before describing in some detail the romeiros' acts of placemaking, it must be noted that Santa Brígida's baianos had their own, competing set of narratives. A much-faded title and accompanying oral history instructed the baianos that their community had been founded in 1816 by Joaquim Marques da Silva, who received a royal grant of approximately four leagues square (Lindoaldo Alves de Oliveira Papers). It is said that the community was renamed Santa Brígida from its original Fazenda Itapicuru de Cima when Joaquim's young wife, Brígida, died while on a trip to Portugal. The bereaved widower chose to remain in Portugal and deeded his property to his father-in-law.

If the baianos based their understandings of entitlement and belonging on legal documents and ancestral ties, the romeiros chose to stake their claims to Santa Brígida on religious grounds. Theirs was a form of entitlement informed by folk Catholic tenets, biblical scriptures, and a conviction that it was Santa Brígida's destiny to replace Juazeiro as "the new Jerusalem."

Romeiros smile when they recall that many tried to dissuade Batista from settling in such a violent and infamous locale; what these naysayers failed to see was the powerful beacon of light drawing Batista to Santa Brígida. In recounting this narrative of discovery, romeiros often added that in the past many backland hillsides had been ablaze with magical lights, which slowly disappeared as "the times worsened and people disregarded the antiga lei" (Raimundo da Silva 1974). Pedro Batista was sufficiently worthy and spiritual, his romeiros add, to be able to perceive and appreciate Santa Brígida's unique enchantment. Indeed, he named one of the hills Encantada (Enchanted) and the hillside Serra do Galeão (hills of Galilee). Batista and his followers accepted the mission to acknowledge and further develop Santa Brígida's extraordinary mistério. In doing so, they determined that Santa Brígida had earlier been the site of the Garden of Eden, Gethsemane, and the Calvary. To commemorate this sacred history, they constructed the twelve Stations of the Cross along the Serra do Galeão.

These acts not only reclaimed the town's past glory but also challenged Juazeiro—with its own sacred hillside and Stations of the Cross—as the most holy, and apposite, home for God's chosen. The romeiros insisted that with their help the entire cosmic cycle would be completed shortly in Santa Brígida. It, not Juazeiro, would be the new Jerusalem and the Kingdom of God. Chapbook author João Oliveira nicely captured Pedro Batista's teachings about this new Juazeiro when he wrote,

> Let us work with faith
> For here, God willing,
> We will create a Juazeiro.
>
> Juazeiro in respect,
> Juazeiro in religion,
> Juazeiro in counsel,
> Juazeiro in unity,
> Juazeiro of Our Mother of Suffering,
> Juazeiro of those with love for
> Padre Cícero Romão. (n.d., 11–12)

This change in venue was necessary, Batista counseled, because Juazeiro had become sullied. It had fallen victim to misguided clergy who persecuted devout followers of Padre Cícero and to avaricious merchants who exploited resident and visiting pilgrims.[2]

Juazeiro had an important, albeit secondary, role to play in the ensuing cosmic drama. Raimundo da Silva, a romeiro curer, sat down with me in 1974, and his eyes took on a sparkling clarity common to older romeiros who were intent on telling me something they considered especially miraculous and profound. He instructed me to turn on my tape recorder and recounted:

Romeiros in an Easter procession praying before a Station of the Cross in the Serra do Galeão, 1974. Photo by the author.

You see those hills behind us. Long, long ago they were the Garden of Eden, a place of abundant food, water, and gold. Back then the people did not know sin, suffering, or death. But slowly the people began to disobey the law which God had given them; they began to think that they were better than the Lord. So Our Father condemned them to know death and suffering. And he scattered them to the Four Corners. Their perfect city was transformed into the infertile rock and bush you see here today. God declared that the people had sinned so much that they would have no chance for eternal forgiveness and rest until the coming of the Savior.

In Santa Brígida when my Padrinho arrived, there were bandits, and among the baianos, brothers killed brothers. It was Sodom and Gomorrah. But it all changed with my Padrinho; he saw a beacon of light drawing him here. With the coming of the new inhabitants, my Padrinho, Madrinha Dodô, and their romeiros, God has given a second chance for us all: souls condemned to hell and purgatory and their descendants now living on earth, the living and the dead, the rich and the poor, all will have to pass through my Padrinho's hands on that day. . . .

There will be a great procession. All will participate, the living on earth, with the spirits, saints, and angels traveling above them. First we will stop at Água Branca. It is there where we will find the throne of the Holy Ghost. Then the procession will continue on to the Hills of Arraripe [outside of Juazeiro] where the throne of Our Father is to be found. After the Day of Judgment, which will take place in the Hills of Arraripe, all those who have been saved will return to Santa Brígida where Jesus' throne will be found. His Kingdom on Earth will dwell there forever.

Pedro Batista prophesied that the Day of Judgment would arrive in the year 1950. When that did not occur, he revised the date to 1960.[3] An excerpt from a romeiro's letter to his parents, dated 26 December 1959, provides a window into this moment of millennial anticipation: "Look, Mother, the era that has been spoken about has arrived and I plan to go home in 1960, if we are alive. Look, my Padrinho Cícero used to say that the ramp to 1960 was hard to climb; look at the difficulties we are already seeing. I only want to go home when Pedro Batista makes his declaration of what we will know about 1960. I've been here for eight years and everything he said I'm seeing. I see crazy people arrive and he puts his hand on their heads and the people leave well, and it is with the word of God that those who don't know anything are quieted and comforted" (Pedro Batista da Silva Papers). According to romeiros who remember these ominous prophecies, when the apocalypse failed to materialize, Batista rededi-

Pedro Batista's home, 1974. Photo by the author.

cated himself to improving the material lives of his romeiros while exhorting them to remain vigilant.

Romeiros perceive and treat Santa Brígida, in its entirety, as a numinous and highly prophetic place. Nonetheless, certain sites, like the hills of Galilee and Batista's home, are considered to be especially holy.

During his lifetime, Batista's residence stood out as one of the largest and best-appointed homes in the community (Queiroz 1965b). Yet more impressive is what its adornments and decor communicate about its owner's spiritual stature and political standing. As the visitor approaches the bright turquoise house, he or she observes the "Trinity" guarding its exterior: on the front gables are a white dove, representing the Holy Ghost; a bust of Pedro Batista, which alludes to the fact that Batista is considered the Son; and the figure of Padre Cícero as the Father. Batista often welcomed his romeiros and guests on the front veranda. Greeting them were also *pés de mamona* plants, known to ward off the evil eye and to bring good luck. Nonetheless, most romeiros preferred to receive Batista's blessing inside the house, where they would find him seated upon a large wooden armchair surrounded by pictures of saints and politicians. This is a setting that many associate with heaven and God's throne.

Romeiro visiting Pedro Batista's home, 1974. Photo by the author.

The pictures that flank the "throne" include large photographs of other beloved leaders like Emperor Pedro II and Getúlio Vargas, as well as campaign photos of politicians who had visited Batista in search of votes. These photographs remind the observer of Batista's extraordinary power. As romeiro Zé Albino Sousa proudly informed me in 1974 after I had inquired about the identities of some of the individuals pictured on the walls, "Politicians, doctors, very influential and cultured men, they all came to see my Padrinho. He never sought them out. Such was the mystery of my Padrinho. He would say, 'All these great men come before me. The day you see Pedro Batista take a blessing from any man you will know he has met his superior.' And up to the very day that he 'moved on,' it never happened, not even once!"

In addition to and far more plentiful than the photographs of politicians, are statues and portraits of saints, many of which were given to Batista by visiting romeiros and other guests. There are also photos of deceased romeiros and individuals who had beseeched the beato for a cure or help and whose petitions had been subsequently granted. During Batista's lifetime visitors beheld the beato surrounded by the sacred and profane, by celestial power and mundane power, by the living and the dead. In short, the house showcased Batista as an exceptional figure who belonged to and mediated between and among multiple realms.[4]

The beato's home also served as the social locus of the community. Romeiros would congregate there after long hours in the fields, asking for a blessing or cure, listening to his *palavras santas* (sainted/sacred words), bringing children for baptism, and seeking advice on personal matters. The tremendous importance his counsel assumed came to trouble otherwise sympathetic non-romeiros: "The people gave him all this power. Even to take medicine they would go and ask him. If they were going to Paulo Afonso they would go ask him if they could go. If they were going to sell flour they would ask him whether the sale would work out. He was given too much power. Maybe he did not even want all this power over daily events" (Maria Rodrigues 2000).

Batista's house became associated with *movimento* (movement, activity), as well. "Every day new cars pulled up in front of my Padrinho's house. Some days there were so many new faces, so much movimento, that it was a holiday!" (Zé Albino Sousa 1974). *Movimento* is a term associated in Brazil with urbanization and increased activity and vitality. Marvin Harris writes of a Bahian town in the 1950s, "The people of Minas Velhas are, in fact, passionately fond of the quality of life called movimento. At the fair or a religious *festa* [festival], the movimento is at its best—a combination of shuffling feet, voices in debate, church bells ringing, a band playing, firecrackers going off, and people milling about in their best clothes. The average level of movimento is the factor which most distinguishes the city from the country and a good city from a mediocre one in the eyes of the people" (1955, 32).

Without a doubt for the romeiros, the marked increase in movimento in Santa Brígida over the course of the forties and fifties reinforced the charisma of their leader and convictions about the growing vibrancy of their community. In their view the humble and mighty were drawn to the community, having recognized the true significance of Pedro Batista and Santa Brígida. Jumping up from his wooden bench as he often did when he wanted to emphasize a particularly noteworthy point, Augustino Veloso (1973) exclaimed, "I tell you, Santa Brígida was a backwater. Ask any baiano; they'll admit it. Then my Padrinho came and there was more movimento in one day than there had been in one year before his coming! This was the mystery of my Padrinho." Such movimento and its associated trope of *progresso* (progress) could easily have been interpreted ominously by Batista and his romeiros as satanic temptations aimed at leading people away from the vaunted pursuit of God and salvation. Instead, these experiences were ingeniously folded into the larger romeiro narrative of the imminent Day of Judgment and Heaven on Earth.

While the movimento in Santa Brígida was certainly impressive by local standards, it was paltry in comparison to what was occurring in neighboring Paulo Afonso, some forty-plus kilometers to the north. Moreover, while the romeiros turned to the Bible to gain a sense of entitlement to and purpose within their new surroundings, they did so in the shadows of Paulo Afonso. There federal dollars were being pumped in to create a state-of-the art hydroelectric company. National and international scientists and engineers worked in concert with Brazilian manual laborers to harness the waters of the Rio São Francisco and deliver energy and water to the blighted Northeast. Desire for a long-awaited future was palpable in the two communities. However, in Paulo Afonso the narratives and acts of placemaking were highly public and were featured frequently in the regional and national press, whereas in Santa Brígida the romeiros' millennial dreams remained largely hidden from public view. Over time the appeal of places like Paulo Afonso were to exert a strong pull on the imaginations of romeiro youth.

Lives Dedicated to Penitence

Through elaborate acts of placemaking the pilgrims of Santa Brígida fashioned their new home in the *caatinga* (scrub, forest land) into a setting fit for the conclusion of a great cosmic drama and worthy of Heaven on Earth. What remained was for the romeiros to receive proper instruction regarding the actions needed to ensure that when the apocalypse did arrive, they and as many sinners as possible would merit salvation and reside forever in Heaven on Earth. It is here where the division of labor and complementarity between Pedro Batista and Dona Dodô became most pronounced. He was the author of the master narrative, which combined folk Catholic and spiritist teachings. These warned of the impending apocalypse, explained that spirits of the dead were entering the bodies of devout Catholics to benefit from their piety before Judgment Day, and instructed the romeiros to practice penitence to save themselves and others. In the tradition of the backland conselheiro, Batista also instructed people about the specific behaviors needed to better ensure their salvation. As Antônio Conselheiro and Padre Cícero had done before him (Otten 1994), Batista insisted that his romeiros refrain from smoking, drinking, gambling, fighting, adultery, usury, and wearing unkempt or immodest clothing.

Once a romeiro had managed to discipline his or her body in accordance with these strict norms, the individual was ready to participate in the romaria's lay orders, confraternities, and collective rituals. It was then that Dona Dodô assumed primary responsibility. Although she consulted with Batista, she took

Members of Os Penitentes pray at night in Santa Brígida's São Pedro church, 1974. Photo by the author.

the lead both in instituting many of the religious organizations and in supervising the nightly prayers, myriad saint's day celebrations, and a host of other penitential rituals. By dint of her leadership and teachings, centuries' old institutions and practices remained vital in Santa Brígida. Thus, while in other rural communities the inhabitants increasingly bowed to the pressures exerted by modernizing church officials and other professionals, at least for a while the romeiros of Santa Brígida successfully resisted.

Dona Dodô and others realized that their beliefs and practices were considered transgressive, and they recognized they might be punished for them. Consequently, in the first few years of the romaria, Dona Dodô taught the special rosaries, hymns, and penitential acts she had learned as a child in Água Branca only to those romeiros whom she deemed sufficiently pious and trustworthy. Behind bolted doors in select homes, she led her flock in nightly prayer. Dina de Lima attended these prayers as a young child, and she was later trained by Dona Dodô to memorize hundreds of hymns and numerous rosaries so that she might help lead the romeiros in prayer. As she reminisced about her early childhood and worried about her own children, who showed no inclination to follow in their mother's footsteps, Dina observed, "We prayed locked in a

São Pedro church, 1974. Photo by the author.

house. I think Madrinha Dodô was afraid of the police or something—she had no official documents" (1999).

Significantly, a few years later the heads of two religious confraternities, the Men's Penitent Society and São Gonçalo, did officially register with government officials in Jeremoabo and Salvador. This suggests that by that time certain romeiros felt sufficiently versed in and comfortable with governmental regulations, as well as confident about the support of political allies, to take such steps. Further proof of this greater confidence lies in the fact that by the early 1950s the romeiros had moved beyond private homes and locked doors. They were by then holding nightly prayers at the base of several large crosses they had planted throughout the community.[5] In 1958 the romeiros built their own church and dedicated it to both Pedro Batista and São Pedro. The church became the setting of nightly prayers and religious festivals directed by Dona Dodô and other lay leaders.

Dona Dodô also went about recruiting several unmarried romeiras into her own lay order of beatas, *as beatinhas* (the little beatas). It is likely that when she took this step she was mindful of Padre Ibiapina's prophecy that as long as one charity house survived, God would bring no harm to his people (Della

Cava 1970, 22). She also took care to reconstitute the sisterhood she had created years before in Água Branca, Nossa Senhora da Boa Morte. This group was charged with holding vigil over the saint's image during the entire month of August. Each day of the week a different woman and her family were responsible for guarding the saint; each night all members of the sisterhood were obligated to assemble to recite in unison the saint's highly demanding rosary. This involved kneeling and rising one hundred times while praying, "In the camp of Josafa, I will encounter Satan; I will say, Go away, Satan, with me you have no power; not with me nor with my family, because we have the penitence of Our Lady of August. One hundred times I kneel, one hundred times I rise, one hundred Ave Marias I pray, one hundred times in the evening, one hundred times during the day. Bless me, Virgin Mary, Amen" (Dina de Lima 1999).

As Dona Dodô went about teaching the new rosaries (one for each day of the week, as well as others for additional saints) and introducing new penitential rituals, she cautioned that if even one among an entire group of penitents had previously disobeyed the romeiro mandates, all would suffer equally from this failure.[6] None would receive the benefit of the prayers toward their own salvation. This was one of many tenets intended to subordinate the individual to the collective good.

In the early years of the romaria, enthusiasm was high, dread of an impending apocalypse real, and pride paramount in being chosen by God to save so many throughout the world. The romeiros proved themselves avid disciples. Many hundreds attended nightly prayers led by Dona Dodô and her *rezadores* (prayer leaders), and they dutifully participated in the many saint's day festivals held throughout the year. The religious holidays they observed included:

— January: Festa dos Reis (Festival of the Kings), São Gonçalo, São Vicente, São Sebastião, Nossa Senhora da Solidade
— February: Nossa Senhora da Saúde, Nossa Senhora das Candeias, Quaresma (Lent)
— March: São José, Padre Cícero, Semana Santa (Easter)
— April: Bom Jesus, São Jorge, Santa Joana D'Arc
— May: Nossa Senhora do Socorro, Nossa Senhora da Assunção
— June: Corpo de Cristo, Santo Antônio, Santo Enofre, Coração de Jesus, São João, São Pedro
— July: Coração Imaculada de Maria, Nossa Senhora do Carmo, Senhora Santana
— August: Nossa Senhora da Boa Morte

Members of Nossa Senhora da Boa Morte praying over the saint's image, circa 1970. Photo from author's personal archive, photographer unknown.

Leader of the religious group São Gonçalo, 1999. Photo by the author.

An elderly Pedro Batista surrounded by members of the Sacred Heart of Jesus, 1967. Photo by Sérgio Muniz.

A member of the Santa Joana performs in the church, 1967. Photo by Sérgio Muniz.

— September: Nossa Senhora das Dores, Santa Quitéria
— October: Santa Brígida, Nossa Senhora da Aparecida, São Francisco
— November: Dia de finados (All Souls' Day), Todos os Santos (All Saints)
— December: Natal (Christmas), Nossa Senhora da Conceição

Dona Dodô and Pedro Batista also selected certain individuals to lead an ever-increasing number of lay religious confraternities charged with praying for the salvation of the dead and honoring particular saints. These included Os Penitentes (Men's Penitent Society), Nossa Senhora da Boa Morte, Coração de Jesus, São Francisco, São Vicente, São Gonçalo, Santa Joana, and São Jorge. In some instances, as with Os Penitentes and São Jorge, romeiros brought organizations and practices from their communities of origin and requested permission from Batista to reestablish them in Santa Brígida.

Although all the confraternities were perceived to be penitential and all required absolute obedience to the antiga lei, some were considered to be more fina (pure and spiritually demanding) than others. For example, groups like São Jorge and Santa Joana were understood to be *brincadeiras*; that is, although they involved devotion to a saint, they also furnished entertainment for the participants and their audience. Other groups like Os Penitentes, Nossa Senhora da Boa Morte, and São Francisco were acknowledged to be particularly demanding spiritually and physically, as well as highly efficacious.

For romeiros, the sense of sanctity ascribed to Os Penitentes was exemplified by the fact that the members' identities were not to be revealed, even to their own wives.[7] Indeed, their prayers and penitence were too holy to be viewed by women and children.[8] Hence the men dressed in long blue robes with appliquéd white crosses and hoods that covered their faces. Lounging comfortably on the eve of the new millennium in his well-appointed home with its VCR and wet bar, a man who had been a member of the society in his youth explained,

> We would meet in the cemetery at 7:00 P.M. after everyone else had returned to their homes for the night. When we were ten or twelve years old we entered the Men's Penitent Society. When I was part of the penitence there were more than one hundred people; now there are a handful. But at those times it was very beautiful. We had a lot of faith. We would meet in the cemetery and put on our uniforms. Then we would go up to the hills [of Galilee] to pray at the Stations of the Cross, come back to the town, visit my Padrinho's house, and finish up in the cemetery. By then it would be past midnight. . . . On special occasions like Holy Week we would flagellate ourselves with whips. It was to remove our sins. The whips had small

zinc pieces attached at the end and they were sharp like a knife. As you beat yourself, it lacerated your back and you bled. (Francisco Sousa 1999)

The confraternity of São Francisco was another highly rigorous organization. During the month of October the members were expected to dress in long brown robes tied at the waist with a white cord; they were to don the robes on awakening in the morning and wear them until they returned from nightly prayer. For the duration of each day, the members were not permitted to sit or recline lest they desecrate the robes and jeopardize the collective acts of penitence. Apparently by the mid-1960s Dona Dodô had become concerned that many romeiros were continuing to wear the robes without fully adhering to the confraternity's exacting regulations. She came to fear for the spiritual health of those who were insulting the powerful saint. Accordingly, she ordered all the members of the confraternity to travel with her to the pilgrimage shrine of São Francisco de Canindé, where the robes were deposited for good. That was the first time, to my knowledge, that Dona Dodô insisted on diminishing the penitential rigor of a set of ritual practices in order to better protect her charges. In so doing, however, she also reduced their capacities to save needy souls. That early intervention marked the first in a series of actions on her part and those of other romeiro leaders aimed to reduce the demands and, consequently, the spiritual efficacy of certain confraternities and penitential rituals.

Local Priests Struggle with Santa Brígida's "Fanatics"

Turning back in time to an evening in 1947, one might well imagine Dona Dodô gazing contentedly at a long procession of men, women, and children dressed in starched white clothing and engaged in fervent prayer. She would have had reason to feel satisfied at having maintained her pledges to the two priests she called santos, Padre Nicodemus and Padre Cícero, to keep the antiga lei alive.

There was another priest, however, who had a stake in Santa Brígida at that time, and he would have been far from pleased. Padre Magalhães, a native of Portugal, had been the resident priest in Jeremoabo since 1928. To the priest's discomfort, his local benefactors, the Sá family, had been willing to endorse Batista and his "fanatical" followers after insisting on modest concessions aimed at moderating the romeiros' religious "excesses." Padre Magalhães could not be so accommodating. As the head of one of Brazil's oldest parishes (created in 1718), he was committed to enforcing the church's teachings. These included the subordination, if not the total eradication, of those lay practitioners and lay orders that challenged ecclesiastic authority. That on his yearly or biannual

Gathering of three clergymen, a lay romeiro church leader, Maria das Dores, and Santa Brígida's first mayor, Zenor Pereira Teixeira, circa 1970 (Mayor Pereira Teixeira and Monsenhor Francisco José de Oliveira flank Maria das Dores). Photo from author's personal archive, photographer unknown.

visits to Santa Brígida he found it necessary to travel with armed guards attests to the fact that he had made no headway in convincing the romeiros to accept the teachings and practices of the orthodox church.

Unfortunately I have been unable to uncover in ecclesiastic archives any correspondence between Padre Malgalhães and his superiors concerning Santa Brígida. Nonetheless, material from interviews with Monsenhor Francisco José de Oliveira—Magalhães's replacement as of 1959, and a man with equally strong views—provides rich insights into the controversies surrounding the church and the romaria. It appears that up until Batista's death in 1967 church officials pursued a policy toward the "heresy" they found in Santa Brígida similar to the one they had adopted earlier in Juazeiro. That is, they refused to budge in their conviction that the type of popular Catholicism practiced in Santa Brígida was wrong and the practitioners disobedient. Or, as Água Branca's Padre Rosevaldo (2000) succinctly put it, it was "a conflict of power."

As the romeiros tell the story, it was not always thus. They insist that when Padre Magalhães first arrived in Santa Brígida to celebrate mass, both Pedro

Batista and Dona Dodô were present, and they urged all romeiros to attend. Apparently the situation deteriorated quickly when the priest proceeded to lambaste the beato for baptizing children, for prohibiting his followers from marrying in the church, and for counseling them against confession. Incensed, Batista stormed out of the church with his flock in tow. One gains a perspective on the priest's position by considering the strong views his successor, Monsenhor Francisco José de Oliveira, still holds today, years after the official church has made concessions to the more fervent beliefs of many of its rural parishioners. As he and I sat in his residence beside Jeremoabo's main cathedral, Monsenhor Francisco (1999) described his predecessor as a "saintly man, a hero. He did not tolerate fanaticism, and he dove in and didn't fare well." Having been asked to clarify what he meant by the term *fanaticism*, the monsignor paused for a moment and then continued, "Fanaticism here for us is when a person, a religious person, Catholic or not, has *despreparo cultural*, a lack of culture that leads a person to believe any message of any adventurer that arrives. For example, [take the case of] Canudos, which was the largest war that Brazil had. . . . [Fanaticism] occurs in all of Brazil, [but it] especially [affects] the Northeasterner. He is dominated by fanaticism."

It is sobering to reflect that this pronouncement by Jeremoabo's fair-skinned monsignor was offered more than a century after Euclídes da Cunha had concluded that the mestizo backwoodsmen's "crude religious practices . . . reveal all the stigmata of their underdeveloped mentality" (1944, 112). According to the monsignor, Batista "was not a bad man, but he had a distorted faith, an altered faith." As for the romeiros, he noted, "They were very religious. They prayed even excessively." [9]

The monsignor's interpretation of the true cause of the tension between the beato and Padre Magalhães is intriguing. For Monsenhor Francisco, Batista was a man who thrived on power and controlling others; consequently, another powerful religious figure, like the parish priest, represented a threat that had to be dismissed by the beato. Perhaps Monsenhor Francisco was only returning the favor when in our interview he chose to forcefully debunk popular claims about Batista's spiritual powers and to replace them with a far more Machiavellian portrayal: "Pedro Batista came to enjoy such prestige that he saw that it was advantageous for him [to claim that he had divine powers]. He was not dumb; he was not educated, but he was smart. . . . He tried to impress the public with his convictions."

The priests' disciplining attitudes, their disrespect for Pedro Batista, and their disdain for the romeiros' faith and intelligence caused the romeiros to redouble their resistance. Largely disregarding Dona Dodô's appeals for patience and tolerance, and rejecting her suggestions that they attend mass when the priests appeared, most romeiros voted with their feet. For his part, Batista refused to attend another mass, and he continued to inveigh against ecclesiastical "innovations" such as Cristo Rei, whom he dubbed the Antichrist. Moreover, he angrily decried priests whom he claimed insisted on baptizing babies only so that they might enrich the church coffers. He countered that God's work should never have a dollar sign attached to it, and he used his own example as an unpaid counselor and curer. His romeiros, not surprisingly, saw no problem in the beato's having assumed control over sacramental rites the church reserved only for ordained clergy. They defended, for example, his practice of baptizing his followers, recalling that the missionaries had instructed lay religious leaders to do so, since in the past so many young children had died without benefit of this sacrament.

On a more charitable note, Monsenhor Francisco described Batista as "a pragmatic man who put people to work, set up grain depositories, planted food, [and] distributed food." As Monsenhor Francisco's comments partially capture, by the mid-1950s Batista had emerged as a powerful and gifted landowner, patron, entrepreneur, and politician. Moreover, within the larger municipality of Jeremoabo, it was Santa Brígida that was publicly celebrated as an oasis of prosperity, hard work, and modernity.

That line of modernist thinking that insists on viewing religion—especially as practiced by rural people—as somehow backward and traditional may make it hard for some to grasp how a beato like Pedro Batista and his devout romeiros could manage such a feat. Of course, Batista and his romeiros hardly orchestrated these gains alone but participated in larger regional and national trends. Nonetheless, the initial incentives for growth and innovation originated within the romaria.

An Alternative Modernity: Prophecy, Penitence, and Progress

Both Pedro Batista and Dona Dodô were tied to those religious traditions that originated in Brazil with the early missionaries and have been elaborated ever since by folk practitioners. While they articulated prophetic themes and apocalyptic warnings introduced by the Jesuits and Capuchins, they also propounded a popular Oratorian theology, as exemplified by the sermons and acts of Padre Ibiapina, who championed "practical charity." Such charity extended not only to repairing run-down rural churches and cemeteries but also to constructing public works. For Batista, practical charity was the religious tradition that inspired and legitimated his very intense involvement in the material well-being of his followers. What Hoornaert writes about earlier religious leaders, whom he calls "frontiersmen," is apposite to Batista as well: "We find ourselves before a generation of leaders (Padre Ibiapina, Padre Cícero, Antônio Conselheiro) who, on one hand, identified with the problem of the sertanejo and, on the other, were modernizers who impelled the sertão in the direction of the modern world" (1997, 120).[10]

Oratorian theology's practicality and pragmatism encouraged and legitimated both Batista's embrace of certain modern institutions and his willingness to take up select modern teachings and technologies. Yet Batista was not only a frontiersman eager to blaze new trails into modernity; he was also a resident of the "border." His was a border zone where visions of and dispositions toward the benefits of modernity were balanced against and tempered by an equally strong awareness of the dangers of becoming overly attached to one's fleeting life on earth, especially in light of the impending apocalypse. Hence the homily "Work like you're going to live forever and pray like you're going to die today." Similarly, Batista's hybridized vision of modernity caused him to urge followers to move beyond mere subsistence, and he provided them with the tools to do so. Yet he also exhorted them to remain "wholesome" farmers and to refrain from the vices of commercial avarice and exploitation. As Fernando Reis (2000) explained, "My Padrinho wanted us to be farmers not merchants, because merchants always charged for everything and often too much. He said that if ten or twenty people came to the home of a farmer, he would have food for everyone for free. If the same thing happened with a merchant, the merchant would charge everyone for food. He use to say, 'A farmer negotiates with God, and the person who negotiates with God always wins.' "

In Batista's statements are echoes of the same general distrust and disdain for those impersonal and potentially exploitative new technologies that decades earlier had incited backlanders to smash merchants' and tax collectors' scales. Nonetheless, living more than a half century after the Quebra Quilo movement, Pedro Batista was forced to acknowledge the inevitability of these technologies, along with advising fairness and moderation. "In business he didn't want people to measure or weigh something falsely, or to charge too much. He didn't like it when people lived only off business and commerce, because he said merchants always lied and stole. He preferred it if one also worked in the fields" (ibid.).

Another feature found in the teachings of religious leaders, like Padre Cícero, Antônio Conselheiro, and Pedro Batista also merits attention. Inasmuch as their brand of practical and pragmatic Catholicism insisted on the dignity and piety of hard work, it proved a useful foil to that brand of elite thinking that blamed the poverty in the sertão on its inhabitants' "inherent" laziness (Greenfield 1999). Gerald Greenfield notes that by the turn of the twentieth century, the South and the "new" North (the Amazon region) were associated with modernity and progress in the national imaginary. This was very much in contradistinction to the older Northeast, which was perceived as still largely wedded to its colonial economy of sugar and hides. "Coinciding as it did with the pattern of droughts, millenarianism, and banditry, the relative economic decline of the Northeast suggested an obvious link between regional backwardness and the inherent qualities of the land and its people. Who would anticipate anything other than decline from a primitive, ignorant, tradition-bound people who lived in an almost barbarous fashion?" (ibid., 102). The newspaper articles published in 1942 on Pedro Batista and other beatos provided a forum to discuss this "unfortunate" legacy. Elite Brazilians, it will be recalled, had clear plans for redressing through education the Northeasterners' primitiveness and fanaticism and for using the law to eradicate their fanatical ringleaders.

Under these circumstances there was little, if any, place for the "strange" mix of prophecies, miracles, and apocalyptic expectations that Batista brought to his own modernizing project for Santa Brígida and its romeiros. At best bourgeois modernizers viewed orthodox Catholicism as peripheral to modernity and folk Catholicism as antithetical to the norms and goals of a modern nation. As a consequence, once Batista emerged as the poster child of a regional and national elite determined to bring the Northeast into the fold of the modernizing nation, all allusions to Batista's status as a beato and to the millenarian beliefs and practices of his romeiros were erased from official correspondence to him and from journalistic accounts about him. This form of representation apparently eased the problem of dissonance his elite and professional supporters might have faced and made it possible to treat him like any other political boss.

The problem was that this realpolitik stance was hardly one shared by Batista's romeiros. If the discursive repertoire available to powerful Brazilians would not allow for a messianic modernizer, neither would most romeiros entertain the existence of a santo who, in practice, became beholden to and at times "bettered" by politicians and technocrats whose morality and power were profoundly suspect. It is exactly this conundrum that years later occasioned Dona Dodô to lower her gaze and tell me with a voice tinged with sorrow that Batista, "had entered the world of politics and sacrificed his divine mission" (1974).

This critical assessment, however, was based on problems and disappointments that emerged late in Batista's life, once the romaria was securely on "the road to modernity." Over the course of the late 1940s and 1950s—the community-building years—there was little to indicate that Batista was not, from the perspective of his romeiros, seamlessly combining prophecy, penitence, and progress.

Santa Brígida: The Granary of Jeremoabo

If the romeiros were to progress in Santa Brígida, they needed land on which to build their homes and create their farms. In Santa Brígida, like the rest of the Northeast during the 1940s, political power and large landholdings continued to go hand in hand. Over the course of the Estado Novo and the Second Republic (1945–1964), national leaders generally refrained from disturbing the traditional social organization of rural areas and the local control of the landed elite to ensure both the latter's continuing support and general political stability. As Monsenhor Francisco tells the story, Coronel Sá initially feared vagrancy and unrest among a large group of unemployed romeiros. He summoned Batista to Jeremoabo and ordered, "Put these people to work" (1999). To facilitate this he rented land to the beato in Santa Brígida. The romeiros place a slightly different spin on the same story: "My Padrinho had very many people in this region, really a lot of people, and he didn't have land. So he said, 'Coronel Sá, sell me that land, Gameleira, so that I can give my people land to work.' Santa Brígida was not a place of hardworking people. . . . Those that came here to be with my Padrinho from Alagoas, Pernambuco, and Sergipe were all hard workers. So they wanted to work. So my Padrinho said, 'Coronel, sell me that land.' At that time, Coronel João Sá said he would give that land to my Padrinho for a hundred million. My Padrinho said, 'I can't afford that.' Then the Coronel said, 'Let's do the following. I'll rent the land to you cheaply, and then you can rent it to your romeiros' " (Mariano Alves 2000).

At first, such an arrangement seemed to satisfy all concerned. Yet after a short while Batista and his romeiros recognized the severe constraints entailed in renting land from Sá and other baiano landowners, constraints especially galling for a population that was eager to improve its property and overall productivity. As his usually measured tone filled with indignation, Mariano Alves recalled, "When my Padrinho first arrived here, the people would rent land to outsiders, and then when the harvest was almost ready, they would take back the land with the crops. . . . The romeiros would lose all their crops. When one had to rely on the justice system, it was controlled by Coronel João Sá, the father of the baianos. [The sheriff, too, was a baiano]. When someone said, 'You can't go back to that plot to work on it anymore,' then you didn't go, because otherwise they'd kill you. So my Padrinho said, 'Let me get some land for my people to work' " (ibid.).

In addition to Sá's land, Batista also initially rented land from the head of Santa Brígida's Marques da Silva family. A wry smile emerged as Luís da Silva (1999) recalled just how astute Batista was and how hardworking and obedient his romeiros proved to be. Apparently Batista approached da Silva's grandfather Jacob requesting permission to clear some ground for a small farm. Batista allegedly stated, "I just want to work for one day, to show these people how one works." An accord was easily reached, and then the beato proceeded to assemble several hundred romeiros. Clearly savoring the tale, da Silva continued, "So he went there to clear the land, some people dug, some collected the wood, others carried it on their backs. When the day was over he said, 'Let's measure how many *tarefas* we have worked. . . . So we measured and it was sixty-four tarefas and twenty-seven *varas*, more than twenty hectares, in one day only, carried on their backs!" [11]

By 1952 Batista had managed to purchase four sizable tracts of land, thus successfully extricating himself and many of his romeiros from the burdens of renting land from their baiano neighbors. He did so by combining the funds he had received in charity with the profits made in sales of his own livestock and harvested crops and those donated by his grateful romeiros. By far the largest holding was Gameleira, measuring 5,112 hectares, which Batista purchased at a very modest price from João Sá. In that case, four years of rental fees went toward the downpayment on the property.

As the ledgers meticulously kept by Batista's literate overseers show, by the early 1950s Batista had become the town's largest employer and benefactor. His four farms, Gameleira, Batoque (500 hectares), Minuim (100 hectares), and Oliveira (70 hectares) provided the bulk of the local population—in which romeiros now outnumbered baianos—with permanent and seasonal employment, as well as access to land as tenants or sharecroppers. Moreover, homes had to be built for the newcomers, and Batista often served as a contractor of sorts. He assigned men to various tasks and arranged fair remuneration for their services. In a pattern typical of any backland's patron, the Sunday evening before the town's weekly market found romeiros lined up before a table set up by Batista's overseer. There they received their week's wages or obtained an advance on the anticipated sales of their harvested crops. Where the situation differed in Santa Brígida, however, was in the fact that many romeiros sought to donate their labor to Batista. "He would say, 'My caboclo, come and pick up your money.' 'No, I don't want to take any of your money.' 'You worked, didn't you? So you must pick up your money.' 'But I don't want to, my Padrinho. All I

Romeiros working collectively to harvest crops, 1974. Photo by the author.

want is that you ask God to give us good health. If we have health, we have everything.' Many people did not want to be paid. But on Sunday everyone would go and pick up his money" (Geraldo Ferreira 2000).

In describing the dramatic changes in the residents' standards of living once Batista settled and turned his own and his romeiros' hands to farming, Fernando Reis (2000) reminisced, "The situation here started through a miracle. There was nothing here, only poverty." Reis can be allowed a certain amount of hyperbole when describing what was by any estimation a tremendous increase in the quantities of crops produced locally and marketed regionally. Among other initiatives that helped to spur production was Batista's move to introduce drought-resistant crops, such as cotton and palm. He also addressed problems of labor shortages and of insufficient income to pay needed workers. To do so he bucked national labor trends and revitalized the practice of (unpaid) labor exchange (*batalhão*) among his romeiros.

So impressive was the growth in agricultural production and sales in Santa Brígida that it caught the attention of a journalist who wrote a featured column on noteworthy Bahians in the leading state newspaper, *Estado da Bahia*. In place of Reis's reference to a miracle, the more secular journalist likens Batista to a "modern *bandeirante*." In doing so he alludes not only to the original bandeirantes—the bold colonial explorers who ventured into the Brazilian interior in search of gold and indigenous slaves—but also to their latter-day successors. In this way, he includes Batista among those modernizing bandeirantes who patriotically accepted Vargas's challenge to carry progress into the interior by embracing his "March to the West" policy (Levine 1998). Thus, in little more than a decade, Batista had been refashioned in leading regional newspapers from a beato—and hence a retrograde and dangerous religious fanatic—to "old Pedro Batista," a contemporary bandeirante and *getulista* modernizer. The July 1954 article states, "The cultivated areas, in the entire zone of Santa Brígida, which [once] did not exceed two thousand tarefas, today have no less than twelve thousand, revealing the entrepreneurial spirit of old Pedro Batista, a true modern bandeirante of the abandoned town of Jeremoabo. In order to have an idea of the agricultural progress of Santa Brígida after the arrival of old Pedro Batista, suffice it to say that the production of manioc flour, beans, and corn is now superior to the consumption of the entire municipality of Jeremoabo" ("Homenagens," *Estado da Bahia*, 10 July 1954, p. 5).

For those eager to increase agricultural production and domestic consumption without resorting to "disruptive" programs of land redistribution and rural labor organizing, old Pedro Batista must have seemed a figure eminently worthy of praise. Articles such as the one above, which appeared in the commemoration (*homenagens*) section of one of Bahia's leading newspapers, gained him this recognition.

As the agricultural surplus produced on Batista's lands and on those of his romeiros grew, the leader searched for new and better outlets beyond the confines of Santa Brígida and Jeremoabo to market the romaria's crops. In taking steps to link Santa Brígida to larger regional markets, Batista availed himself of and contributed to those efforts afoot on the federal and state levels to better integrate the nation and foster industrialization. For example, he purchased two used trucks in Paulo Afonso and used them to transport romeiro produce to larger cities and to carry goods into the community. In this way he avoided the middlemen who traveled periodically to Santa Brígida intent on purchasing locally grown crops at much reduced prices and on selling commodities to romeiros at inflated costs. Now Batista was able to assemble his romeiros' surplus in bulk and to have his overseer negotiate far more advantageous prices from large wholesalers and textile factory owners in major Northeastern cities. He also acquired advances from factory owners, which he distributed among his romeiros to help defray costs for the next year's planting.

Unfortunately, in the sertão economic fortune can be fickle. The years 1954,

1955, and 1956 brought devastating droughts to the region. As far as his followers were concerned, it was in these years that Batista revealed himself to
be, very much, a santo. Perhaps reflecting that dimension of his religious formation that anticipated times of divine punishment and suffering, Batista was
careful to deposit and store large quantities of his own harvested crops permitting their sale only when the next year's rains had begun. He advised his
romeiros to do the same. This proved to be an exceedingly wise strategy when
in the mid-1950s the anticipated rains never came. Almost a half-century later
Mariano Alves (1999) looked out on his own fields where the crops stood
stunted due to lack of rain and recalled, "Look, I don't know how many thousands of sacks he had stored away. There were those three years of drought . . .
where he gave his thousands of sacks away to the people. He did not sell one
liter of grain to the people. . . . He was the only one who did that in this entire
region. Coronel Sá told him he was crazy, that he could make lots of money.
But gaining wealth while others suffered, that was not for my Padrinho."

Recalling the same incident, Fernando Reis (2000) added that among the
produce Batista was able to distribute were sacks of seed and food crops that
romeiros had earlier donated to their Padrinho. "Some would give one bag of
produce; another would give two. Some would give five kilos and another ten,
depending on how much each person could afford. . . . He would add that
produce to his own stock. He would store it and keep it for when there was a
drought. Once there was a drought, he would give it away to those who could
not afford to buy any. At that time, everyone lived off and depended on what
God gave them."

Yet as the drought wore on, increasing numbers of romeiro men chafed at
being a burden, and they petitioned Batista to allow them to migrate to such
cities as São Paulo and Brasília in search of employment. Geraldo de Lima
(1999), a romeiro now in his early seventies recalled that Batista was generally
opposed to the idea of outmigration but at times relented, as he did in Geraldo's
case: "People who could would ask his permission to go to work in Brasília.
Brasília started during the time of drought. He didn't like it when people asked
to leave. He did not want people to leave Santa Brígida. But many people asked,
and he would let them go, though he did not like it. He wanted the person to
be patient and wait. He would say, 'No one dies of hunger here.' . . . For the
most part, the men who went earned some money and returned."

Perhaps it was his own experiences in Southern Brazil that motivated Batista to oppose his romeiros' wishes to migrate. He appears to have feared a
change in mentality and in lifestyle among the migrants—perhaps especially
among romeiro sons who migrated with their fathers. His concerns proved

well-founded. Whether Batista liked it or not, his absent romeiros were being exposed to patterns of modernity and consumption unfathomable from the margins of the sertão. Indeed, one enthusiastic romeiro migrant, no doubt wrapped up in the excitement and grandeur associated with the construction of the new capital of Brasília, sent his Padrinho an invitation to its inauguration. The fact that Batista kept the invitation (it was found almost a half-century later among the beato's possessions stored by Dona Dodô) seems to indicate that despite his reservations about his romeiros' desire to work temporarily in Brasília, he, too, was intrigued by the millennial-like plans of Vargas's successor, Juscelino Kubitschek. A secular prophet, Kubitschek promised to accelerate history and Brazil's destiny of greatness by delivering "Fifty Years of Progress in Five."

The Creation of Colônia

No doubt Batista's most decisive and impressive move to align himself with and benefit from certain national efforts to modernize Brazil was his 1953 decision to donate Gameleira to the federal government so that it might be converted into a *núcleo colonial*: an agricultural cooperative (henceforth referred to as *colônia*).[12] Geraldo Portela (2000), the son of the second administrator of Santa Brígida's colônia and himself an official of the government's land reform agency, noted: "The colonization program began during the government of Getúlio Vargas with the objective of occupying the agricultural frontiers, expanding these frontiers. The state would acquire land, create all the infrastructure of the núcleos, and then settle the colonists. They would provide, among other things, technicians, credit for plantings, and seeds." In step with Vargas's overall strategy of noninterference in the rural social structure, the president *encouraged*, rather than legislated, modern methods of colonization, agricultural production, and crop diversification (Cehelsky 1979).

It is unclear when and how Batista first learned of this ambitious federal program. Some suggest that he learned of the program through government agricultural officials who first worked with him in the early 1950s to arrange the transfer to Santa Brígida of seeds, powdered milk, and farming implements from a federally funded program. Others claim that he spoke of such programs existing in Southern Brazil at the time he was a farmer there. And one man observed that word of the government program was being regularly aired on the radio and that Batista might well have learned of the program, or gained more specific details, through this venue.

More intriguing still is the matter of Batista's motivation. In this regard, it should be noted that, according to several romeiros, Coronel João Sá (Gameleira's original owner) was not at all pleased with the initiative. Mariano Alves (2000), himself a member of the colônia, recalled, "When he donated it and Coronel Sá found out, he said 'Seu Pedro, you donated the land to the federal government?' My Padrinho replied, 'Yes, I donated it.' Coronel Sá said, 'If I were you I would not have done that. The federal government is going to create a real mess for your people here.' "

Although João Gonçalves de Carvalho Sá (2000) disagrees with this claim and argues that his father was always supportive of the plan, there are several reasons to question his assertion. First, there was the Coronel's apparent refusal to furnish Batista with a title to Gameleira several years after the actual sale had occurred. Antônio da Silva (1999), a native son of Santa Brígida and contemporary of João Sá observed, "Coronel João Sá sold the land to Pedro Batista and then didn't want to hand over the title to Pedro Batista. . . . Because Pedro Batista did not have family . . . [and was] an old man of seventy or eighty years, [Sá] thought, tomorrow he will die and I can keep the land. . . . Pedro Batista had more experienced people with him who said, 'In order to not lose the land fully, give it to the federal government.' So he gave it to the federal government. . . . When he gave the land to the federal government, Sá had to hand over the title."

Second, by the 1950s national and regional leaders confronted the dilemma of how best to modernize an inefficient and exploitative agricultural sector and integrate it into the rest of the economy *with a minimum of disruption*. Despite their continued collaboration with powerful national leaders, members of the rural oligarchy, like the Sá family, recognized that their ability to define in their favor the terms of lower-class incorporation had been compromised from 1945 to 1964 by the existence of a competitive, populist democratic system. Indeed, the very functioning of that system sometimes encouraged rural mobilization and introduced radical ideologies challenging the hegemony of the landed elite. It is likely that Coronel Sá feared that at the heart of rational economic arguments and policies for agrarian reform, such as the núcleos coloniais, lay a far more daunting challenge to the existing rural political order and its traditional distribution of power and status (Cehelsky 1979).

Third and relatedly, by the mid-1950s Batista was seeking to strengthen and diversify his political alliances. He hoped to use this greater political leverage to convince Coronel Sá not to take the romeiros' loyalties and votes for granted. Batista sought expanded government services for Santa Brígida, defending his position by pointing to the town's impressive growth and prosperity and its comparatively large contributions to Jeremoabo's tax base. Moreover, he hinted at the merits of Santa Brígida's eventual emancipation from Jeremoabo to become its own freestanding municipality. Consequently, by donating Gameleira to the federal government, and thereby inviting federal officials into the community, Batista adeptly pursued his goals of increasing his visibility as a leader and broadening his political base.

He proved successful on both fronts. For example, he came to the attention of a high-ranking official of the federal agency National Institute of Immigration and Colonization (INIC) shortly after donating his property. The official wrote, "I am aware of and appreciate your highly patriotic work helping the colonization of our state. I want to thank you greatly for such worthy work" (Pedro C. M. Peixoto, 16 December 1955, Pedro Batista da Silva Papers). Furthermore, the universe of politicians Batista might forseeably call on expanded as colônia's administrators introduced him to their own candidates for state and federal offices. One even brought Batista with him to Paulo Afonso to meet presidential candidate Marechal (Marshal) Henrique Teixeira Lott. The colônia's first administrator, José Dortas Montargil, urged Batista in 1954 to instruct his romeiros to vote for different candidates than the Sá family supported. Dortas Montargil took up the cudgel for his candidate for federal deputy, Dr. Renato Martins, who was a figure already familiar to Batista. While serving as a senior official of the federal colonization program, Martins had visited Santa Brígida to ensure that the beato legally owned Gameleira.

> With this messenger I am sending you the publicity for our chief, which will provide you with a better opportunity to learn about our candidate for federal deputy. Please accept with an open heart this material from your loyal friend and be assured that in the national congress, Santa Brígida will have a constant and fearless defender. . . . Every time he speaks of Santa Brígida, he never ceases to speak with admiration and respect for you, thus revealing how much he wants for that good and dynamic little land. Tell all the people of Santa Brígida, and most particularly your voters, that Dr. Renato is worthy of their vote because they can anticipate many good things for all those people who struggle for a better old age and more rest. (José Dortas Montargil, 3 September 1954, Pedro Batista da Silva Papers)

Several weeks later this letter was followed by another from Dortas, who enclosed ballots for Batista to distribute among his voters (28 September 1954, Pedro Batista da Silva Papers). This time the person Dortas endorsed was a candidate for state deputy. As it happened, Dorta's choice was running against Colonel João Sá's son. Batista apparently decided to play both sides, with the result being that in the 1954 election all of the Sá family's candidates lost in Santa Brígida.

An additional motive for Batista's donation of his land was his great admiration for Getúlio Vargas, who was again in power. The beato was apparently quite aware of his own finite resources and believed that, with Vargas at the helm, his romeiros would be well taken care of as beneficiaries of a federally supervised colonization project. These sentiments, as well as the very paternalistic/personalistic manner in which older romeiros perceived politics and power, are captured in the following statement.

> When my Padrinho saw how the people were suffering [through the droughts] he decided to donate [his property] to the federal government. He sent a letter to Getúlio Vargas saying he wanted to donate [several thousand hectares of] land to the federal government so that they would open a colônia in order to provide for his people during hard times. Soon Getúlio Vargas sent a government official. Renato Martins came. He was the head of the federal colonization project. . . . When he arrived here and my Padrinho showed him the land title, he said, "OK, Seu Pedro, I'll take it and show it to the president." Within a few days machines and tools started arriving. (Geraldo Ferreira 2000)

Fernando Reis (1999) added, "People here thought the project would be very good; and it did help a lot at first. What got in the way was the death of Getúlio Vargas. After his death a lot of things went downhill. Getúlio had more interest in helping others."

Finally, most romeiros agree that Batista was motivated by a concern for his romeiros after his death. Her eyes suddenly brimming with tears, Alcira Bezerra (1974), herself a great grandmother many times over, recalled: "My Padrinho was always a good father to us all. He realized that when he moved on there might not be enough land to go around for all his romeiros and they might fight among themselves. He decided to leave the land and the care of his romeiros to another good father, the president of Brazil."

Once the colônia in Santa Brígida was officially approved, Batista encouraged his romeiros to sign up for plots of land. The attraction was clear as Fernando Reis (2000) noted, "Many people had never had their own land and [with the colonization program] they got twenty-five to thirty hectares of land."[13] Reflecting back on those early years when the channels of communication and cooperation between officials of the federal government and Batista were open and "respectful," one romeiro recalled that the members of colônia found themselves "protected by God and the government" (quoted in Muniz 1967).

Ultimately 160 tracts, each measuring on the average of twenty-five to thirty hectares, were distributed among romeiros and a few baianos. There were modest fees involved. Although most colonists believed that these were intended to pay for the land, they were actually used to subsidize such expenses as technicians' salaries, machinery and tools, the construction of private homes, and community structures such as a school, church, clinic, mother's club, and small airstrip. Although the colonists were given five years of grace, they were expected to pay their fees in installments over the span of the first ten years, at which point they would receive title to their land.

In 1974, some twenty years after the project had begun, I found that very few colonists had been able to successfully cover their fees, and many were extremely demoralized. A large part of their frustration and anger centered around how the second administrator had treated them — and by extension how he had treated their Padrinho. They were also disturbed by a government bureaucracy that had, at various times, seemingly abandoned them, making payment of their fees and the acquisition of land titles extremely difficult. In the mid-1980s the federal government ceased to assume any official responsibility for its colônias, since all had been declared "self-sufficient" and "emancipated" (according to official parlance). When I last returned, in 1999, I found that all of the original colonists who had chosen to continue to struggle for ownership of their properties had managed to acquire titles to their plots. However, more than one half of these individuals had elected subsequently to sell their property and relocate either within the municipality or elsewhere in Brazil (Mariano Alves 1999).

All one has to do is look over the original maps of colônia with its uniform grid of 160 farms grouped into four agglomerations and its impressive design for an urban center complete with larger homes for the administrators and technocrats, a school with a playground, church, clinic, cinema, and airstrip to realize that this was a modernist project wholly distinct from the more conventional rural lifestyle and conception of space the romeiros were accustomed to. What initially eased the dissonance and raised the colonists' comfort level was their conviction that Batista endorsed the plan. Referring to a period in the mid-1950s when she was conducting research in Santa Brígida, Pereira de Queiroz writes, "Pedro Batista goes to Gameleira weekly to inspect the works; he is the owner, once again in that he still thinks of Gameliera as his. The engineer explains to him the plans, and seeks his approval. When he returns, the romeiros go at dusk to ask about the progress of the work. The old man explains" (Queiroz 1965b, 283).

Occasionally bureaucratic sensibility and empirical science had to bend and accommodate the beato. As the son of the second administrator recalled, "The doctor and dentist came once a week to see patients. And there is a very interesting issue here. The doctor prescribed the medicine, but Pedro Batista had to approve it. . . . You put a doctor there and he said, 'You take this medicine or you will die.' [But] Pedro Batista had to be consulted. He was heard" (Geraldo Portela 1999).

Finally, with respect to the regulations and new procedures the bureaucrats and technocrats introduced, colonist Geraldo Ferreira (2000) explained, "Anything the government ordered us to do, we would do, because a person is small when compared to the government. But they were educated people. They did not teach us wrong things. They knew how to teach well. They taught us how to plant, to run a small farm."

Despite such testaments to cooperation and consensus between Batista and colônia officials, there were clear difficulties and ultimately a sense of betrayal on the beato's part. Perhaps the first stirring of discontent emerged over Batista's unflattering comparison between the first administrator, whom he praised for his dedication to farming, and the second, whom he found overly committed to flashy public works. The following account of a pointed exchange between Batista and Portela is telling in this regard.

> One day Portela arrived and my Padrinho was in his chair. My Padrinho said, "Seu Portela, you will have to pardon me for what I'm going to say. You learned how to construct things, how to build, but you don't know how to plant crops. Aren't you an agricultural engineer?"
>
> "Yes, I am."
>
> "Well what kind of assistance have you been giving to the colonists?" Portela replied in that smooth talking way of his.
>
> My Padrinho said, "You know about construction, but you do not know anything about agriculture. If you did you would get everyone to plant and would provide assistance." . . . [My Padrinho tried to change the way Portela was doing things,] but Portela was in control of the colônia. (Geraldo Ferreira 2000)

What Batista apparently failed to grasp was that in introducing into the desolate Brazilian backlands "flashy" public works, Portela was acting in the service of a government pursuing a First World status. Through impressive public works the elites' millennial vision of a modern Brazil destined for greatness was staged and new modern subjectivities and subjects fashioned. Moreover, these acts contributed to the increasingly hegemonic notion of the state as *the patron* par excellence.

Letters Batista received over the years from colônia's first administrator, Dortas, reveal Batista's growing disaffection. In a 1962 letter rich in pastoral imagery (in contrast to Portela's modernist discourse and practice), Dortas praised the romeiros and vilified his successor: "When I read your letter, my old and loyal friend, I sensed that same Santa Brígida, with her orderly folk, her days of sun and nights of stars, her people, and why not just say it, her poetry, that not even the lack of human solidarity on the part of Mr. Portela has been able to destroy" (1 August 1962, Pedro Batista da Silva Papers).

After inquiring about the state of repair of an electrical generator and whether Batista still controlled it (or, as implied, whether Portela had appropriated it), Dortas went on to advise the leader about the political candidates he was supporting in the upcoming election. He followed this by inquiring about the number of votes he could count on from Batista, asking, rhetorically, "What have the politicians of your municipality done for our Santa Brígida in exchange for your political support? From your card, I know they have done almost nothing" (1 August 1962, Pedro Batista da Silva Papers). As if responding to Batista's earlier written grievances about Portela, Dortas concluded with word that he would request a transfer to Santa Brígida when his current tour of duty in another colônia ended. He added, "We will finish that work which we began and that constituted the dream of your life as a generous man and a saintly soul, who only wanted to see your people assisted and following on a path of hard work and prosperity" (1 August 1962, Pedro Batista da Silva Papers).

Although Portela did have some local champions both in 1973/1974 and again in 1999/2000, I found that his critics far outnumbered his defenders. By far the strongest criticism leveled against Portela were accusations of corruption. Geraldo Ferreira (2000) explained.

> He got very rich, but he left the colonists with nothing. He stole. The flour would come in trucks for all the colonists. He would go to Paulo Afonso and have four or five sacks baked into loaves of bread for the colonists, so that each family shared one or two loaves. The rest he sold to the owner of the bakery. The colonists were naive; they did not know how to hold a meeting or draw up a petition.
>
> He was very clever. When government officials came to check on the colônia, he would put his arm around them and take them on a walk. The official would ask, "What is lacking for the colonists?" Portela would reply, "We don't need anything. Everything is going well." It was a big lie.

As I learned from my discussions in the mid-1970s, not only did most romeiros blame Portela for what they perceived as the demise of colônia, but they also hinted at their Padrinho's seeming inability to end Portela's humiliation of colonists and to stop his blatant corruption. This pointed ominously to a general weakening in the beato's spiritual and secular powers over the course of the 1960s. Whereas in the early years the colônia had seemed to embody, as Fernando Reis (1999) put it, the perfect balance between "God's protection" and "the government's protection," later the government seemed to have bypassed the beato altogether, leaving the romeiro colonists exploited and vulnerable. Under these changed circumstances, the romeiros were left to compare their recollections of a once seemingly invincible leader who miraculously punished his oppressors during the thaumaturgical years and was soon after praised by high-ranking government officials as a patriot against later, far-less-flattering images. For example, an elderly and infirm Batista found himself uninformed about the visits of federal officials who had come to inspect colônia in search of possible corruption.

While over the course of the 1960s and 70s the romeiros developed their own increasingly dismal and dark narrative of colônia and its impact on themselves and their Padrinho, government officials blithely neglected to consider such an account. Rather, they placed their own spin on the Santa Brígida colony. The way in which it was portrayed in a federally sponsored documentary provides yet another potent illustration of the fact that the "spiritual enchantment" of Santa Brígida and its romeiros' millennial hopes were phenomena that modernizing politicians and technocrats refused to see and/or share with the public at large. These failed to conform to their own, more secular narrative of Brazil's millennial-like mission to become a fully modern nation and First World power.

A Corner of Hope

During the early 1960s with the national economy deteriorating and then president João Goulart moving increasingly to the left, powerful segments of the military and of the middle and upper classes united and orchestrated a coup. The first military president selected was Humberto Castelo Branco. Early in his administration, the native of Ceará sought to design a modest plan for land reform within an explicitly capitalist framework.[14] As Castelo Branco turned his hand to this matter, he was surprised to learn that a government-sponsored colonization program already existed. Consequently, he decided to finance a documentary on a successful project with the aim of showing the film around the country to persuade large landowners to donate unused land. The Santa

Brígida colony was selected, and Portela hired the publicist Oscar Santana to write and produce the documentary, *A Corner of Hope*.

Santana (2000) set out to create a realistic portrait of his subject matter. He envisioned that the highlight of his "true-to-life" documentary would be a planned visit by Castelo Branco to Santa Brígida. At that time the president would personally present the keys to a new home in colônia to the protagonist of the film, Jacob Duarte. Insisting that the film be as realistic as possible, Santana arranged for Jacob to be moved to the top of the list of recipients. Santana trusted that this intervention would ensure that the heightened emotions Jacob and his family projected on receiving the keys and entering their new home would strike the audience as both moving and authentic. In light of the filmmaker's efforts to create a true-to-life documentary, it is ironic that, according to Santana, he was never briefed by Portela on the distinctive history of Santa Brígida's colônia and its members. Moreover, despite spending almost three weeks in the colônia, Santana reported that he simply assumed that the land had been donated by an elite backlands family that sought anonymity. As a consequence, the true history of what drew the colonists to that specific locale is totally absent from the film's narration, as are shots of colônia's benefactor, Pedro Batista. Rather, the film presents an essentialized narrative of poor sertanejos fleeing drought, then being "rescued" and led into the modern age by agents of a generous and forward-looking state.

The film opens with a flashback of the Duarte family who are walking single file along a dusty dirt road. They carry simple farming implements, and their meager household and personal possessions are tied up in bundles attached to a pole that each supports on his or her shoulder. The film's narrator states that the Duartes are on their way to an already overpopulated city, like so many other desperate, landless Northeasterners before them. Fortune smiles on them, however, when they are spotted by a friendly agent of the federal colonization program. Exiting from his modern jeep, he persuades them to reconsider their plans, and they proceed together to Santa Brígida's colônia. Through the film's narration one gains an appreciation for elite views about the "backward" rural poor. The audience is also privy to paternal notions regarding the government's beneficence in bestowing modernity on their subaltern charges. The filmmaker pans in on the Santa Brígida colônia and the Duarte family while the narrator states, "We are going to tell the story of this family, which is the same story of the more than 138 families that arrived here. They are now living here with a fervent desire to make up *for the time they have lost*. There are one thousand caboclos up until now who have come from several Northeastern states and who, with good orientation, will become excellent farmers. They live on and off their own land, producing for the great urban centers of the country. It is the harmonious process of fastening the rural man to this rural area, where he can produce so much better than anyone else" (Santana 1965; emphasis added).

By referring to the colonists as caboclos and showcasing the tan-skinned, straight-haired, and angular-featured members of the Duarte family, the film's producers also advanced a larger proposition about race, region, national belonging, and progress. At the time of the filming, caboclos were understood to be mixed-race individuals of mostly European and indigenous ancestry who typified the nordestino. In a move to modulate the racism and classism of previous generations, scholars and technocrats allowed that despite past defects, like excessive traditionalism and religious fanaticism, "nearly white" caboclos, like Jacob Duarte, were authentically Brazilian (Blake 2001). With instruction, they were capable of modernizing their ways of life and of contributing to the Brazilian "miracle" of unprecedented economic growth.

Amid images of tastefully handcrafted objects displayed on store shelves and of romeiros laboring together in the construction of large buildings and in the clearing of carefully engineered roads and fields, the narrator states, "The time available to the colonists is almost always taken up in the study of different forms of manual labor. In this way, one can observe the use of raw materials from the region to create [marketable] handicrafts" (ibid.). Totally missing from this discourse is the "dissonant" fact that much of the romeiro colonists' time was actually devoted to prayer, penitence, and visits to their Padrinho (of whose identity and importance neither the filmmaker nor the audience ever learn). Instead, the narrator reduces the romeiros to modernizing national subjects eager to learn to labor more scientifically and productively. Although a blatant distortion of the actual romeiro colonists' aspirations and agency, such a tale no doubt appealed to the film's sponsors: members of a military dictatorship that sought to convert Brazil into a world power through pursuing capitalism within a technocratic framework.

The film also references the modernist triumph of man and machine over nature. This sensibility had earlier inspired the building of Brasília (Holston 1989), the "opening" of the Amazon, and the construction of the hydroelectric company in neighboring Paulo Afonso, and it continued to embolden the imaginations of Brazil's newest leaders. Over images of huge bulldozers cutting through earth and brush, the narrator proclaims, "Men and machines work side by side in the construction of a landing strip for medium-sized airplanes. It is the road to emancipation!" (Santana 1965).

The climax of the film shows a smiling, though clearly deferential Jacob, who receives the key to his new home from the president of the colonization program, who pats the willowy farmer on the back. (Castelo Branco had been delayed in Paulo Afonso and could not make the engagement in Santa Brígida.) For a viewer who is familiar with the true history of Santa Brígida and its colô-nia and who is cognizant of the ways in which Pedro Batista had been eased out of his leadership responsibilities there, it is at once disturbing, yet inevitable, to hear the federal government being trumpeted as Jacob's benefactor and the author of his new status as a member of a cohesive community: "Like so many others, he received from the hands of the president of INDA the key to his own home.[15] It was the transformation of an old dream into tangible reality. . . . Today he receives the blessed harvest. Taking the produce that was planted by his own hands to the cooperative, he is now a part of the community. It is every-thing he ever wished to have. He has control over his own means of survival, so that he can guarantee brighter days in the future of this huge country for his children" (ibid.).

In light of this last reference to Jacob's children, it should be noted that at several junctures in the film there are shots of young children lined up in orderly fashion in crisp school uniforms. Lest the audience miss the nationalistic de-sires affixed to these well-scrubbed, uniformed youth, the filmmaker makes sure always to have them framed against a Brazilian flag waving somewhere in the distance. The suggestion that these youngsters represent a brighter future for the Northeast is also intimated as Jacob's young son looks longingly at them when the family first arrives in colônia.

The film concludes with footage of the region's jewel in the crown, the hydroelectric plant in Paulo Afonso, and with a promise: "The Brazilian agricul-ture of this important nation will one day show the same progress as is shown in the production of energy" (ibid.). The final shot is of a large Brazilian flag.

The film provides a modernist and markedly nationalistic portrayal of a seg-ment of Santa Brígida's romaria. It is clear that the local colônia officials who colluded in keeping Batista hidden throughout the filming had determined that state officials would be incapable of imagining or condoning the pairing of a "progressive" colonizing project with an "old-fashioned" (if forward-looking) beato with apocalyptic leanings. Consequently, although romeiros are featured throughout the documentary, their very history and beliefs are erased. They are fashioned into the type of modernizing rural subjects imagined and desired by agents of a military government that operated, for the most part, on uni-tary and totalizing understandings of modernity and of Brazil's "millennial" destiny of greatness among the nations of the world.

A Routinized Santo

The first ten years of settlement and community building in Santa Brígida clearly added to Pedro Batista's status as a charismatic leader. In those years he managed the inevitable strains Weber (1947) addressed in his work on charismatic authority and its routinization. By contrast, the last twelve years of Batista's leadership proved far less kind. Under the best of circumstances he faced an uphill battle to maintain an antiquated, patriarchal form of patronage. He also struggled to balance values and norms associated with the antiga lei with those of mid-twentieth-century modernity. To further complicate matters, by the late 1950s local political bosses, Bahian state politicians, and officials of the federal government had Batista where they wanted him: he was understandable within their own categories of personhood and politics. The rub for Batista was that once the politicians and technocrats situated him within their system of political patronage and hierarchy and insisted that he play by their rules, he became a minor player. This, in turn, contributed to his ultimately becoming a fallible leader, a definite liability for a santo who earlier in his career had demonstrated his invincibility before secular authority. Indeed, Batista's weakness led some romeiros to question his adequacy as leader of the romaria.

CHAPTER FIVE

PEDRO BATISTA "MOVES ON" AND THE KING ATTEMPTS TO CLAIM THE THRONE

Romeiros still marvel at the fact that in the early years, the spiritual purity of life in Santa Brígida stripped years off "old Pedro." Yet as the years progressed and their leader experienced deceit and disappointment from both within and without the romaria, he showed obvious signs of physical decline. Following a debilitating illness that left him partially paralyzed, the romeiros came to fear that, like Padre Cícero, Batista too might "move on." Although the beato made it clear that Dona Dodô was to replace him, during his declining years and shortly after his death certain romeiros disputed not only his legitimacy to lead but also the wisdom of his choice of successor. Such challenges offer further insight into popular charismatic authority by offering an opportunity to explore the tensions that controversial bids for charismatic leadership fomented within the romaria as well as between the romeiros and representatives of the state. These challenges also reveal the dialectic between popular millenarian action and Brazilian state formation that emerged during the military dictatorship of the 1960s and 1970s.

A Prophecy Is Realized: Santa Brígida Becomes a Municipality

In the early 1950s, when Santa Brígida was still a backwater, Pedro Batista had confidently proclaimed that someday the town would be emancipated from

Jeremoabo and elevated to the status of municipality. Some ten years later town councilman Joaquim Teixeira stood on a platform before a group of romeiros and baianos and read a proclamation demarcating the boundaries of the new municipality of Santa Brígida. Although Pedro Batista was too ill to attend the ceremonies and had in fact left the town earlier in the day for medical treatment in Água Branca, this political achievement represented the beato's last hurrah. Due to its nesting within the romaria's prophetic tradition and because it apparently represented the last episode of Batista's strength and singularity as a leader, the emancipation of Santa Brígida in 1962 is inscribed in romeiro social memory as an eminently *local* affair—one in which the beato is featured as the only significant protagonist. What local accounts fail to capture is that Santa Brígida's emancipation was actually part of a far larger political drama occurring at the national and state levels.

In September 1961 the Brazilian constitution was amended to change the form of governance from a presidential to a parliamentary system. Conservative political forces authored this change to curtail the executive powers of the progressive president, João Goulart. Under the newly instituted system a given state's representation in the parliament, and thus its influence in national politics, was very much dependent on its total number of municipalities. Consequently, in a race to expand their power base, the political elite of Bahia, including the Sá family, moved to create additional municipalities by subdividing large political units like Jeremoabo. On the same day that Santa Brígida was emancipated and romeiros were basking in their leader's unique power and his capacity to prophesize, two other districts of Jeremoabo were similarly decreed free-standing municipalities. Jeremoabo's local historian, recalls, "João Goulart was sympathetic to the communists. [His rivals] tried to orchestrate a military coup [in 1962], but Rio Grande do Sul stood up to them. The people here were afraid of losing control of everything. The Northeast was controlled by the coronéis. . . . So they started emancipating towns. . . . There are people who say that it [the emancipation of Santa Brígida] all started because Pedro Batista wanted it. But on the same date practically sixty towns were emancipated. If it were something [just about] Pedro Batista it would not have been like that. It was something political, at the federal level, to mitigate communism" (Marco Antônio Dantas de Almeida 1999).

It is instructive to compare Almeida's account of the larger events surrounding Santa Brígida's emancipation to the one offered by Fernando Reis (1999): "My Padrinho only got involved in politics so he could see this place emancipated. He forced himself to do all that. Because if he had not entered politics, this place would still not be emancipated." Reis's statement not only credits Batista alone with the accomplishment, but it also hints at the uneasiness some romeiros experienced on seeing their santo truck with mundane politics.

A Leader in Decline

In the social memory of the romaria Santa Brígida's emancipation is understandably recalled as a high point in the community's history and in their leader's career. By contrast, the micropolitics of the actual event and Batista's subsequent, unsuccessful attempts to establish a small military outpost in the new municipality reveal a picture of a leader already in physical and political decline. Yet even before Batista had departed for emergency medical treatment the town was buzzing with the news that Sá family rival and local head of the opposition UDN party, Coronel João Maria, was planning to disrupt the proceedings. This is not altogether surprising, since João Maria was the local representative of the national party in power, which opposition leaders like the Sá family sought to outmaneuver by creating additional PSD-affiliated municipalities. As the current leader of the romaria Zezé Ramos (1999) recalls, João Maria did not want his local PSD rival—and soon to be first mayor of Santa Brígida—Joaquim Teixeira to officiate the event.

> Joaquim asked permission of João Maria to read the new municipal boundaries. João Maria said he would not allow it.
> Joaquim said, "I'm sorry but I am going up [to the platform], even if it means I don't come down."
> João Maria said, "I'm going to kill you now," and he went to get his gun.
> I was with Joaquim when João Maria stepped off the platform to get his gun. I ran to Dona Dodô and said, "Coronel João Maria wants to kill Joaquim." . . . .
> João Maria came to his room to get his arms, and Dona Dodô [intercepted] him. [She said,] "Coronel, . . . what was it I said to you yesterday?" . . . He had a lot of respect for Madrinha Dodô, and she had said the day before, "I want peace during the political emancipation tomorrow."
> He said, "Dodô, pardon me."
> Dona Dodô said, "Drink this coffee." He sat down and drank the coffee. She whispered to me, "Tell Joaquim to get off the platform and go to Pedro Batista's house and only leave the house when this man leaves." Joaquim went to the house of my Padrinho and João Maria left. Madrinha Dodô took charge of the situation.

It could hardly have escaped the romeiros' attention — and had to be a matter of concern — that the person who "took charge of the situation" in Batista's absence was Dona Dodô. All insisted that she was an individual wholly above and inimical to politics. As Fernando Reis (1999) put it when contrasting Batista's willingness to engage in politics with her stance, "Dona Dodô had a different story. Dona Dodô did not get involved with this business. Dona Dodô's mission was only penitence." Yet with Batista gravely ill and absent from the proceedings, it fell to her to enter into the political fray and to broker an uneasy peace.

Actually, that was the second time that Dona Dodô had involved herself directly in local politics. Two years earlier João Maria had allegedly threatened to unleash the gang of bandits he protected in Santa Brígida if his party failed to win the next presidential election. Without informing Pedro Batista, a frightened Dona Dodô instructed more than half of the romeiro electorate to cast their votes for UDN candidate Janio Quadros. This marked the first and only time that party won a national election in the town. When many years later I questioned why she would have acted behind Batista's back and what his reaction was, Alzira Bezerra (1974) commented, "I can only imagine that he was not pleased, but it was already done. She acted like a good mother; she was afraid her children would be harmed by the bandits. In earlier years before my Padrinho took sick he would not have tolerated this; he would have acted promptly to stop João Maria from making such threats. But by then he was sick and I imagine Comadre Dodô wanted to keep it from him, to keep him from getting upset." Certainly, João Maria's threats in 1960 and again in 1962 were hardly idle ones — the former had strong ties to the local bandit Pedro Grande, whose band was involved in extortions and numerous killings — and Dona Dodô's attempts to appease him were understandable.

Shortly after the 1964 military coup, martial law was declared in Santa Brígida. Locals claim this dramatic step was taken to facilitate the apprehension of Pedro Grande and his gang. Yet in light of the military's crackdown on all popular organizing, it is likely that marshal law was also instituted to afford closer military surveillance over the romaria. While earlier religious leaders like Antônio Conselheiro and José Maria reacted defensively to even the suggestion of military intervention, Pedro Batista roundly welcomed this new development. In fact Batista upped the ante when he proposed to military officials that he leave all his inheritance to them in exchange for a permanent military post in Santa Brígida. In this spirit, a copy of Batista's will with the military featured as his sole beneficiary was sent to the army's sixth regional office in Salvador. Soon after, representatives of the local armed forces in Paulo Afonso were told to void the will since only the minister of war in Brasília had the authority to relocate a military post to Santa Brígida, and he had no intention of doing so. There is no reason to doubt Batista's sincerity on the matter, but it is also true that his overture followed that time-honored pattern wherein the beato accommodated to powerful authorities and implicated them in the continuing viability of the romaria.

Although military authorities rejected Batista's proposal, they were none-theless mindful and concerned about mounting challenges to his authority within the romaria. Recollecting with evident pride his many years as a local military informer, Luís da Silva (1999) reported that during the late 1960s he was in weekly contact with army officials in their Paulo Afonso headquarters, and they told him in no uncertain terms, "If there is a problem, you come look for us, they might want to take advantage of . . . the old man."

There were unsettling incidents emerging on the economic front as well, and their management provides further proof of both heightened state/military surveillance in Santa Brígida and a general slippage in Batista's authority. For example, by the mid-1960s several romeiro cowboys were apparently openly flaunting the norm of giving the herd's owner (in this case Batista) the pick of the calves. Instead, they were bypassing their Padrinho and selecting the best animals for themselves, a move that resulted in mounting debts on Ba-tista's ranch. To make matters worse, the highly ethical and efficient former ro-meiro overseer had been pressured by several unscrupulous workers to leave his post. To salvage a deteriorating situation, Luís da Silva decided to consult with the government's special military sheriff stationed in Santa Brígida. Having secured his support, da Silva traveled to the town where the previous overseer was living and explained that the military wanted him to reassume his post. This was, no doubt, a request the overseer dared not refuse.

That interventions to blunt challenges to Pedro Batista's political leadership and economic well-being were necessary at all reveals a weakening in Batista's standing as political boss and patron. The João Gustavo affair indexed a differ-ent, though related, lapse; in this case the challenge involved Batista's stature as a spiritual leader and santo.

The Man Who Would Be King

In the late 1950s during a nightly prayer service in São Pedro church, João Gustavo suddenly became possessed by the spirit of Luíz Bell. At that time the spirit explained to all those assembled that Luíz Bell and Lucifer were one and the same. After spending almost two thousand years burning in hell, Luíz Bell had repented and had been pardoned by God. The spirit, continuing to speak through his host João Gustavo, concluded by stating that it was now Gustavo's sacred mission to preach the Word of God and to convince others to repent. Accordingly, he stationed himself in the church and prayed constantly for nine days. While there he verbally attacked and refused to let enter those romeiras and romeiros who adopted such "vanities" as dressing in short sleeves, using lipstick, and wearing wrist watches.

Shaking her head from side to side as if recalling the final tragedy, Alzira Bezerra (1974) said, "At first everyone paid attention to João Gustavo, because some of his words were good. He criticized the romeiros for caring more for comfort and vanity than penitence. . . . But, as the years went by, he began to say things that frightened us and that challenged my Padrinho. He said that Santa Brígida had become infiltrated by demons and that my Padrinho could no longer protect his romeiros from the evil forces! He said that if we did not accept him as our leader, God would soon build a guillotine and heads would roll in the streets. The streets would run with blood, that is what he preached."

In the face of such a bold challenge to his charismatic authority, Pedro Batista countered that Gustavo possessed the wrong kind of spiritual power. He charged that his rival was a devotee of Xangô, an Afro-Brazilian deity whom most romeiros associated with Satan. This denunciation caused many, but not all, romeiros to rebuke Gustavo. Although the numbers fluctuated over the years, Gustavo continued to attract to his home at least a handful of romeiros who participated in evening prayers, curing rituals, and séances.

In 1964 Gustavo and his family temporarily relocated to their former home in Mata Grande, Pernambuco. Gustavo continued to cure and hold religious services there. When he returned to Santa Brígida the following year, he brought several additional families from Mata Grande with him. Fearing trouble from the enlarged group, state authorities in Santa Brígida managed to convince Gustavo and his devotees to settle on colônia property in Quarenta.

Once settled in Quarenta, Gustavo ordered his followers to call him King Luíz Bell, and he stationed himself on a chair that he called his throne. Moreover, to complement his position as king, he appointed a neighboring woman queen, and other male and female suporters were appointed to the ranks of general, captain, and soldier. Both sexes dressed in all white with stripes placed on their shoulders indicating their rank. The new militancy in their dress matched Gustavo's heated denunciations of a spiritually weakened romaria. Many romeiros suspected that he was preparing to take over Batista's "throne" and home.

Not surprisingly, the police and local military informer in Santa Brígida also kept a close vigil to ensure that Gustavo's pronouncements that Santa Brígida would soon be purged in blood did not escalate beyond provocative discourse. According to Luís da Silva (1999), "I let them [the army] know everything. I was an informer, a secret agent. They had no doubt that I kept the house in order." These authorities braced themselves to defend Pedro Batista, Dona Dodô, and the romaria against an anticipated attack by João Gustavo and his devotees. They could hardly have expected that it would be them, rather than Gustavo, who would most immediately run afoul of Dona Dodô and the romaria—a turn of events occasioned by Batista's death and funeral. While the romeiros mourned Batista's passing and the authorities and Dona Dodô wrangled over Batista's remains, King Luíz Bell and his devotees waited in the wings.

Pedro Batista "Moves On"

As his debilitating illnesses advanced, Batista complained bitterly of the evil spirits sent by his enemies, which he claimed were attacking his body and racking him with pain. His sympathetic listeners were well aware that João Gustavo topped this list of enemies. Finally, on 11 November 1967 Pedro Batista died, or as his romeiros express it, "*ele se mudou*" (he moved on).

Although many romeiros claimed that Batista's passing took them totally unaware, he did signal his impending death. For example, Monsenhor Francisco claimed that a few months earlier a repentant Pedro Batista finally agreed to receive communion in secret from the priest. If true, this act marked yet another victory in the church's long crusade to subordinate lay religious figures to its authority. In a far more public gesture, Pedro Batista extended *perdão geral* (universal pardon) to all humankind shortly before his death. He also called Dona Dodô to his side and instructed, "Dodô, take care of my romeiros" (Samuel Rodrigues 1999). Some romeiros claim he added, "until my return" (Augusto Veloso 1974). This last phrase alluded to the belief that Padre Cícero is the Father, Pedro Batista the Son, and a soon-to-be-resurrected Batista the Holy Ghost. Thus, when Batista moved on, many anticipated his swift resurrection. They trusted that a younger and revitalized Batista would soon lead the pilgrimage he had prophesized: first to Água Branca, then to Juazeiro, and finally to Santa Brígida, the site of Heaven on Earth. If it were true—as João Gustavo and others had insisted—that religious fervor had waned in later years, the occasion of Pedro Batista's death served briefly to revitalize millennial expectations.

Anthropologists have long recognized that funerals are highly charged rites of passage in which underlying structural tensions may surface (Turner 1957; Geertz 1957). This was certainly the case in Santa Brígida. In her first decision as leader of the romaria, Dona Dodô instructed several trusted men to prepare Batista's body for viewing in his home. She is said to have counseled that either the beato would be resurrected or his body would remain wholly preserved, in other words, a *corpo santo*. Under no circumstances, she insisted, was he to be placed in a coffin or buried. The first person to dispute this plan publicly was Dr. Portela. He and his brother-in-law, ex-mayor Joaquim Texeira, countered that the body represented a health hazard and that a burial had to be promptly arranged.

Twenty-four hours into the romeiros' vigil and as a compromise awaiting Batista's resurrection, Dona Dodô instructed that the body be placed in a coffin. It was entirely sealed, save for an opening over the face. A member of Água Branca's Torres family recalled, "When we arrived there was such wailing. . . . I said to my companion, 'We have descended into hell. Now I know what it must be like there.' [When the authorities] insisted that they bury Pedro Batista many shouted in their grief that if he were to be buried, they wanted to be buried too" (América Torres 1973). Romeiros reported that only the fragrance of flowers wafted from the coffin, a clear sign of their Padrinho's mistério. Although he wasn't present at that time, Monsenhor Francisco (1999) told another tale, stating, "They thought he was a saint. . . . I heard that Pedro Batista had died and on the second and third day, there was that terrible stench. But the romeiros did not want to bury him."

By the second day, authorities from Santa Brígida and neighboring Jeremoabo and Paulo Afonso began pressuring Dona Dodô and other romeiro leaders to inter the body. Some also claim that there were threats of military intervention: "I also heard that members of the army stationed in Paulo Afonso were passing through Santa Brígida. The baianos told the romeiros that the army had arrived and were going to arrest those who were keeping Pedro Batista from being buried. They did it; they buried him right away" (Monsenhor Francisco 1999).[1] Ultimately, four days after Batista's passing, an extremely reluctant Dona Dodô agreed to a burial. Thousands attended the funeral. These included romeiros from all over the Northeast, local baianos, politicians, and friends of the deceased from many neighboring towns and cities. Monsenhor Francisco was absent, however, creating an opening for a more moderate priest to officiate.

For weeks after the burial, most romeiros eagerly awaited their Padrinho's resurrection. After two months Dona Dodô revised her opinion and concluded that the body was now a corpo santo. She accordingly militated to have the body disinterred. It is alleged that when news of this development reached Dr. Portela, he contacted one of the military commanders in Paulo Afonso who in turn instructed Dona Dodô that if she proceeded, she and her romeiros were liable to arrest and imprisonment. Disregarding this warning, a resolute Dona Dodô requested four trusted romeiros to accompany her secretly to the cemetery after midnight. Unearthing and opening the coffin, they claim to have found the body completely unaltered. The men were then ordered by Dona Dodô to re-seal the coffin and bury it again. They were also sworn to secrecy. Seven years later one of the men who was present that night explained, "It was a miracle. After two months under the earth any mortal would have begun to decay. But not my Padrinho. Such was his miracle that after all that time his body was per-fectly preserved. I think Dona Dodô removed the body just to see him again. She knew he would be perfect. She wanted to send his sainted body to the Vati-can or at least to return him to his house, but the government would not allow it. So she ordered us to cover the coffin and not to reveal our secret" (Zé Albino Sousa 1974).

Two years later Dona Dodô reassembled the men and ordered them to dig up the grave anew. Identical to the story told about his predecessor Padre Cícero, this time all that was found was a lone sock. The body had completely disap-peared. "When we opened the coffin, I almost fainted. Seu Fernando kept ex-claiming, 'Oh, my Padrinho, he has really been resurrected!' And Dona Dodô just stood off to the side, smiling peacefully, her head tilted slightly like the Virgin. It was a surprise to us, but not to her" (ibid.). Once again the men were pledged to secrecy.

Out of respect for Dona Dodô and mindful that she had subverted the law, I refrained from asking her why she had elected to disinter Pedro Batista. None-theless, when I questioned the man who shared the secret with me, he postu-lated that she viewed this act as a test of her faith and as a personal demon-stration of her obedience to a higher authority than the state. It is probably also significant that all of the men she invited to accompany her were actual or potential leaders of the romaria. Two of these had been quite forceful in advising her to obey the orders of government authorities during the burial controversy. By later openly defying secular authority, she communicated to these potential rivals that she was secure in her mandate and in her capacity to lead the romaria. Moreover, the exacting of a pledge of secrecy both bound the perpetrators as a select group and created a definite hierarchy with Dona Dodô as the superior who had pledged the others to silence. The fact that this secret was very publicly betrayed seven years later is indicative of the crisis of authority that the romaria experienced when I conducted my initial fieldwork in 1973/1974.

The "Official" Story

While most romeiros remained committed to the prospect of the beato's resurrection or of his becoming a corpo santo, outsiders charged with narrating and commemorating his death presented a starkly different version, one that totally elided the popular religiosity on which Batista's followers drew so liberally. For example, a short obituary published in a Bahian newspaper only mentioned his political and civic activities, such as having functioned as a local political boss and having donated 5,000 hectares of land for a núcleo colônial ("Sepultado Pedro Batista," *Diário de Notícias*, 19–20 November 1967, p. 6).

Moreover, despite having personally witnessed behavior at the time of Batista's funeral that local officials told me they viewed as ignorant and fanatical, they maintained their conventional discourse when preparing a motion to be approved in the Bahian state legislative assembly; thus, the man who was believed by his followers to be a santo, if not the actual messiah, was remembered in death by this governing body as "an old political boss and a generous benefactor of the Bahian people" (*Diário Oficial Estado*, 17 January 1968, pp. 35–36). Certainly these elite discourses do not capture the full range of Pedro Batista's gifted leadership. What they do capture is what politicians in the late 1960s were willing to entertain and publicly express about the type of leader the state was willing to endorse and commemorate. As "modern" leaders of a "developing" nation, they were anxious to celebrate Batista's patronage, generosity, and patriotism in helping the sertanejo poor become prosperous farmers. They were most certainly unwilling to complicate this image, and their own involvement with him, with dissonant images of Batista as beato, curer, conselheiro, and santo.

The King Attempts to Take the Throne

On 21 December, only five weeks after Pedro Batista's death, João Gustavo made his move. And, as many had predicted, his initiative ended in bloodshed. There are, of course, two sides to this story. Open to dispute is what motivated João Gustavo and his followers to leave their homes in Quarenta at midday on the 21st. One of Gustavo's followers insisted that they were merely engaged in an important act of penitence. She explained that Gustavo had long sought to dispel those rumors that he practiced macumba ("*se tratava de xangô*"). Consequently, with his followers in tow, he carried an extremely heavy Santa Cruz — a symbol of his Christian faith — from his home in Quarenta to Santa Brígida. On reaching the town, the entourage circled around the *cruzeiro* (large cross)

in front of São Pedro church, stopped before Pedro Batista's house, then proceeded en masse to Gustavo's home in Santa Brígida (Sônia Campos 1974).

Accusations about Gustavo's involvement with "the other side" had only intensified after his return from Pernambuco, although, ironically, this followed
from Gustavo's willingness to adhere to the law. While temporarily residing in
Mata Grande, Gustavo obeyed the sheriff and obtained a license that pemitted
him to hold "spiritist sessions" legally in his home. On returning to Santa Brígida, Gustavo attempted to reauthorize his license there. In contrast to Penam-
buco, where licensing was viewed by state authorities as a step necessary for
scrutinizing and disciplining practitioners of unorthodox beliefs, in Santa Brígida Gustavo's request only heightened the officials' and the larger community's concerns. At issue was the suggestion that Gustavo was inappropriately
seeking from the state and the public at large acceptance and affirmation of
his spiritual powers and authority.

A competing and widely endorsed interpretation of Gustavo's mission on
that eventful December day held that he and his followers were poised to take
over the romaria. Consequently, as Gustavo and his followers rested in his
home, word spread rapidly throughout the romaria that the next day was the appointed day. Recollecting that moment with great passion, Luís da Silva (1999)
asserted, "People were going to die; the majority of the romaria did not want
it. . . . They would have killed each other."

In hopes of avoiding a bloody melee, the sheriff, a soldier, and the police de-
partment's secretary decided to meet that evening with João Gustavo. Arriving
at the door of his home and having been (allegedly) informed by a voice inside
that the ensuing prayer service "was none of the [authorities'] business," the
sheriff retorted, "Well, I come as an authority to invite you to present yourself at
the police station. I'm going to ask some questions, and if you explain yourself
well, convincingly, your gathering can continue. If you don't explain yourself,
we'll see what we will do" (ibid., 1999). Another voice purportedly responded
that if they wanted Padrinho Luíz, the authorities would have to take them all.
And at that moment a piercing cry of "*berimba-pau*" went up, accompanied by
the loud tapping of clubs and sharply pointed wooden bayonets. The door flung
open and the three officials were pulled inside. In the words of one,

> All I could see around me were clubs. But I was lucky. Someone was hit-
> ting Oscar [the soldier] over the head with the large cross! We were totally
> surrounded and I was sure my time to die had come. But then in some way
> Mário [the sheriff] managed to extricate his gun. He fired three shots,
> and João Gustavo and his second in command were mortally wounded.

João Gustavo's son had been hit in the shoulder. In the sudden melee we managed to escape. . . . We gathered up some reinforcements and led João Gustavo's men to the jail. It was a night of torment. The women wept over the bodies of the slain, and begged the king to come back to life! The children cried for their mothers to feed them. Santa Brígida had turned into hell! (Eduardo de Farias 1974)

As soon as word spread in more elite circles about the killings, the measured and generally celebratory discourse about Pedro Batista and his romaria was replaced by long-submerged references to fanaticism and charlatanism. A sensational article published in the same newspaper that only months earlier had eulogized Pedro Batista as a backland politician and benefactor now employed a quite different discourse to characterize Batista and his followers. It is full of condescending imagery regarding "ignorant" backlanders and their "charlatan" leader—terms that had last been applied to Batista and his romeiros a quarter of a century earlier during the beato's thaumaturgical years.

A dispute between two groups of fanatics for the "throne" of the famed Pedro Batista, a type of "Antônio Conselheiro," who died ninety days ago in the city of Santa Brígida, culminated in the violent confrontation of 40 men commanded by the romeiro João Gustavo, known as Padrinho Luíz Bell, and . . . Sergeant Mário Francisco da Silva and soldier Oscar Santos. . . .

The curious history that culminated with Santa Brígida transformed into a war zone dates back many years when the individual Pedro Batista arrived in that locality, then much more backward[;] there he established a type of "reign," repeating [the pattern of] Antônio Conselheiro by recruiting around him a strong group of romeiros, fanatics who furnished him through their ignorance and credulity with all that the wily "beato" desired—properties, fortune, prestige, and above all, the authority of a demigod; he came even to possess a "throne," a simple chair that was converted into an enchanted place, where only he could sit. Absolute leader, adored by his followers, Batista also attracted enemies, among the least ingenuous who did not believe in his "virtues as a saint" who attempted to depose him from "the throne." One of these was "Padrinho Luíz Bell" who maintained his group around him, converting them into a constant threat. Both exercised total authority over their romeiros." ("Disputa para sucessão de Pedro Batista provoca conflitos com 2 mortos," *Diário de Notícias*, 28 December 1967, p. 6)

The fallout from the João Gustavo affair was not limited to bad press. There was a clear danger that the entire community might be forcibly disbanded by state authorities and some might even be put to death. As Luís da Silva (1999) explained, shortly after the incident he and the sheriff traveled to Salvador to meet with the secretary of public security. The latter allegedly asserted, "Now how many men do you want to end that romaria, tear everything up there, kill those people?" The mayor and sheriff respectfully declined the offer. They went on to explain that no state official had been killed or seriously injured, that the vast majority of the romaria represented no threat, and that the true instigator of the violence had been killed. The mayor also visited the office of *Diário de Notícias* to request that they publish a follow-up article based on an interview with him. One of its lines reads, "He said that the group directed by her [Dona Dodô] is orderly and quiet, and does not offer any threat to society, because 'if this weren't true, I would not permit them to stay in the city' " ("Prefeito de Santa Brígida acusa fanático Gustavo de haver praticado volência,"*Diário de Notícias*, 1 March 1967, p. 6). This statement was surely intended to calm official and public fears about the romaria and to emphasize that local authorities were fully in control of the situation.

At the same time Dona Dodô was summoned to appear before the head of police in Paulo Afonso where she was impressed with the gravity of the situation and instructed that she would be held personally responsible for any additional violence. Dona Dodô immediately traveled to Juazeiro to garner support there from influential politicians and citizens. They, in turn, informally contacted police officials in Paulo Afonso and Salvador, urging that no one be prosecuted (Maria das Dores 1974).

Excerpts from a letter written by romeiro leader João Oliveira Manuel Alves to former secretary for public security and longtime political ally of Pedro Batista, Dr. Antônio de Oliveira Brito, reflect two popular sentiments held by influential romeiros regarding the romaria's future during those perilous times.[2] On the one hand, there was clear apprehension as renewed charges of fanaticism and depictions of Santa Brígida as the "new Canudos" were aired by people in power. There was at the same time a keen awareness that, thanks to Batista's many accomplishments and accommodations as a political boss and benefactor, the romaria now found itself in a more favorable position vis-à-vis powerholders than it had in the early 1940s when the romeiros and their leader were branded as fanatics. Accordingly, Alves sought to accomplish several things when composing his letter; he endeavored to continue to position himself and the romaria as clients of Oliveira Brito, to pledge their continued respect for him and the state, and to persuade Brito to reciprocate with continued patronage and protection.

> Santa Brígida, 31 December 1967[3]
>
> Dear Secretary:
>
> You know very well, your Excellency, the consideration and respect that my Padrinho held for you; he always enunciated your name with satisfaction, and he would say that in the state of Bahia there was a man by the name of Dr. Oliveira Brito, who contributed so much to his being able to remain in Santa Brígida. . . . [This occurred] even against the expectations of a captain of the military police of this state, who at that time had the post of regional sheriff, a man by the name of Felipe; with your aid he [Felipe] was opposed and a form of suffering was ended [for my Padrinho.] It was one that had lasted more than ten years, and it had led to his imprisonment almost monthly without his being able to rest and call a place his own.
>
> At election times he would summon me as his most trusted aid and tell me to assemble the people and tell [them] that only through their votes cast for you might he possibly repay the past favor he had received.
>
> With the passing of the days and the accumulation of the years came that which I consider the most fatal blow I have received in my life, which was the loss forever of my Padrinho. But even with this sad separation, Dr. Oliveira Brito, I want to tell you that, in the name of the romeiros and myself, among all the good things my Padrinho told us, and we have maintained, one of them is the name of your Excellency. We are ready to follow your political orientation, to keep our ties to the government, society, and the constituted powers[;] for when they want to attack us, unjustly and without a reason, as was going to happen on December 22nd past, we would know earlier or later, your Excellency, that you will defend us like you always defended my Padrinho. (personal papers, Lindoaldo Alves de Oliveira, Santa Brígida, Bahia)

Batista's willingness to enter into patronage relationships with influential leaders like Oliveira Brito had its drawbacks as well as its virtues. On the one hand, such alliances ultimately caused Dona Dodô to lament the beato's having sacrificed his spiritual mission to more mundane affairs, and they later encouraged attacks on Batista's leadership by João Gustavo and his disciples. On the other hand, given the coincidence between the Gustavo affair and a period of intense state surveillance and military repression, it is likely that this bloody incident passed without reprisal because Batista had on behalf of the romaria cultivated good relations with local military officials and powerful figures in regional and national government.

Dona Dodô as Pedro Batista's Successor

With the horror of the João Gustavo episode behind her, Dona Dodô prepared to fulfill the mission that Batista had pressed on her: "to take care of [his] romeiros." In this spirit she hastened to remove Gustavo's Santa Cruz from the jail. It was a bold act that asserted the preeminence of divine power over evil and spiritual authority over more secular forms. In taking this step she lamented to her followers that a great affront and desecration had been perpetrated. The sacred object had first been used to venerate Xangô, then wielded as a weapon, and finally stored in a jail as police evidence. Dona Dodô's solution was to organize a procession of romeiros and to reclaim Gustavo's cross. While men customarily carry crosses and certainly one as heavy as this one, Dona Dodô reached for the Santa Cruz and settled it on her shoulder. She carried it unassisted to the São Pedro Church, where she placed it by the main altar.

Her courage and determination here and throughout the Gustavo tragedy, and her earlier resolve both to face down João Maria when he was intent on assassination and to negotiate additional time in anticipation of Batista's resurrection might well have proven to the majority of the romeiros that she was up to the task of replacing Batista. And perhaps she did not merely accede to, but actually encouraged, local officials to challenge and provoke Gustavo—a rival to her charismatic power.

Yet despite her leadership qualities and Batista's confidence in her as his successor, many romeiros remained uncertain. In the early years of the romaria the division of labor between Pedro Batista and Dona Dodô operated exceedingly well. She supervised all religious confraternities and rituals and cared for the elderly and destitute. He maintained an iron hand to ensure that the romeiros obeyed his teachings, and he attended to the security and material well-being of his followers. Just as Pedro Batista was believed by many to be the incarnation of Jesus, so, too, was Dona Dodô maintained by many romeiros to have received the spirit of Our Lady of Suffering. When the two combined forces to lead the romaria, it was by all accounts a fine union. It also was a pattern familiar and comfortable to Dona Dodô, who, as a beata first of Padre Nicodemus and then of Padre Cícero, was used to serving strong patriarchal figures. The problem arose when the patriarch Pedro Batista died and left her alone to lead the romaria.

In summing up the problems they saw in Dona Dodô's leadership, several romeiros referred me to the verses of the following bendito, which Dona Dodô composed soon after she arrived in Santa Brígida. Apparently she was sufficiently troubled by its content that she asked Batista whether she should share it with the others. Allegedly he assured her it was a divinely inspired hymn and needed to be disseminated.

> Praised be
> The powers of the Eternal Father
> Who gave us penitence
> To free us from hell.
>
> Penitence, my brothers,
> Performed with pain in the heart.
> Do not allow Our Lady
> To spill her tears upon the ground.
>
> The Virgin sheds tears
> For all we sinners.
> I am tired of advising
> Beware the Great Horror.
>
> Some desire and others do not
> The means of salvation
> On the Day of Judgment.
> There is no time for further reprimand.
>
> The Virgin looked over the world
> Little of worth has been accomplished.
> I give you all penitence
> For all to gain salvation.
>
> Make me worthy, Virgin Mary,
> Forgive my transgressions.
> He who forgets Jesus
> Passes to the left side [hell].
>
> Satan is smiling
> Cutting up and delivering great pain.
> As one of Mary's followers
> I want to gain salvation.
>
> Jesus Christ responded
> Little of worth has been accomplished.

The Virgin I left on earth
Is now tired of advising.

The Divine Holy Ghost
He descended to earth.
He came to advise us
Penitence or Hell.

After softly singing the bendito to me, prayer leader Josefa Gomes (1974) added, "As the bendito says, she [Dona Dodô] is tired of advising us sinners to keep practicing penitence. You have seen how often her tears have fallen because of our disobedience. She knows how tormenting and cruel the great horror will be and wants to protect her children. But who listens to her? It was different at the time of my Padrinho because he was forceful and demanded that people obey. . . . Now we are a divided people. Some think they can walk two paths simultaneously, but they are deceived. As the bendito says, 'He who forgets Jesus, passes to the left side and forfeits salvation.' "

Although fully respecting Dona Dodô and acknowledging her many virtues, most romeiros concluded that their leader should be male, as the following statement attests: "A woman is like all mothers. She is gentle and forgiving. A leader must be strong and punish his people when they are wrong. I ask you, is a father a good father when he leaves his misbehaving children unpunished? It is like Our Father; he does not like to punish his children, but we are sinners and as a good father he must punish our transgressions. Our Lady is different. She always takes pity on us. That is why when you have sinned you should always ask Our Lady to be your advocate before the Lord" (Alzira Bezerra 1973). And one of the leader's of the Os Penitentes commented, "A queen on the throne is fine. But how much better when she is at the side of a king" (José Alves 1974).

The Fragility of Charisma

The unraveling of many of Pedro Batista's earlier accomplishments exemplifies the well-known fallibility of charismatic authority (Weber 1947). Batista's downfall was occasioned by an inability to control those forces of bureaucratic authority he had welcomed and handled far more adeptly earlier in his career. Old age and ill health only exacerbated his difficulties. As a consequence he was outmaneuvered economically in his final years by unscrupulous employees and was challenged politically by a rival charismatic figure.

It was left to Dona Dodô to reconstitute the romeiros' slackening morale and assert her legitimacy as Batista's successor. This was a tall order, and one in which she would find herself once again pitted against a male rival for charismatic authority over the romaria. Gender undoubtedly contributed to the decisions of some to support her contender, O Velho (the Old One). Ultimately, however, the factors serving to galvanize and maintain this support had far more to do with each individual romeiro's socioeconomic standing and lifestyle than his or her views about gender and authority.

A ROMARIA SE ACABOU (THE ROMARIA IS OVER)

Although Pedro Batista had commenced with a plan to create a sacred community of equals under the authority of the beato and Dona Dodô, he unwittingly adopted measures that engendered difference and stratification within the romaria. These included such initiatives as the linkage of Santa Brígida to regional markets, the creation of colônia, and the acquisition of municipal status. Those who supported the Velho tended to be materially disadvantaged, and most lacked access to those forms of power attached to leadership positions in the romaria and municipal government. Their poverty, marginalization, and disappointment over millennial goals as yet unrealized made them highly receptive to the Velho and his insistence that he was Pedro Batista. In Brazil (and elsewhere) a highly elaborated millenarian tradition fosters the creation of new movements. What the Velho affair demonstrates, as well, is that once a millenarian movement becomes routinized and its most radical goals remain unfulfilled, the movements' disenfranchised may take up the tradition's symbols and institutions and fashion them into a new movement, with the marginalized featured as the elect and their former comrades as evil Antichrists.

A Stratified Romaria

When I first arrived in Santa Brígida in 1973, three groups of romeiros were easy to distinguish based on class position, authority within the larger community or the romaria, and lifestyle. While the romeiros did not assign specific names to the three groups I refer to here as "traditionalists," "moderates," and "modernists," they readily perceived the existence of three different, and sometimes, opposed segments among the romeiros. Moreover, they were generally in agreement as to who belonged in which of these three groups. Each group had a few memorable rituals or ceremonies, and its members either eagerly participated in or condemned these ceremonies. Such public acts served in the mid-1970s as venues for the expression of solidarity within the three groups and of struggles among them.

THE TRADITIONALISTS

Some two-thirds of the romeiro population belonged to the ranks of the "traditionalists" during the mid-1970s. Most of them belonged to the socioeconomic group referred to locally as *os pobres* (the poor). Many were members of colônia, persons who were barely eking out a livelihood on their plots of land. Only a few years earlier the federal government had terminated all activities in its numerous colônias and, consequently, Dr. Portela was relieved of his post in Santa Brígida. Many members of colônia felt themselves abandoned not only by their Padrinho but also by the very federal government he and they had fervently believed would protect them after his death.

Other traditionalists worked as tenant farmers or sharecroppers on the lands of more prosperous baianos and romeiros. In 1974 tenant farmers rented land at a few U.S. dollars per tarefa and provided their own seeds and labor. Sharecroppers, who tended to be poorer, worked the lands of larger farmers and received seeds and other inputs from the landowner. Depending on the land-tenure relationship, the yield from the sharecropped parcel would be divided either equally or in thirds with the sharecropper receiving the lion's share. As one traditionalist explained the logic of sharecropping to me, "This is the only way we poor folk can ensure that we do not fall too deeply into debt during a bad year. In a bad year we may have little or no crops to show, but we owe no rent, and the following year we can still get seeds and land from our patron without needing to beg" (Carlos Nascimento 1974).

Members of traditionalist farming households often needed to supplement their subsistence or near-subsistence income by selling goods in the weekly market, working in a trade or as an occasional farmhand, and laboring as domestic servants, laundresses, and so on. Farm hands earned between $1.50 to $2.50 per day, while domestic servants earned an average of $1.00 to $2.00.

Many of the traditionalists lived in rural satellites of Santa Brígida, such as the colônia settlements of Quarenta and Quarenta-e-dois and in Batoque, the location of one of Pedro Batista's farms. Their homes were typically con-

Traditionalist's home, 1974. Photo by the author.

structed of dry mud and thatch, and were furnished with simple wooden benches, a table, an altar, and hammocks.

While the traditionalists recognized Dona Dodô as the head of the romaria, many also considered another beato, José Vigário, to be their spiritual leader as well. Living in the hamlet of Batoque, José Vigário was a highly vocal critic of many of the moderates and modernists residing in Santa Brígida.[1] In the mid-1970s this man, whom many claimed possessed the spirit of the archangel Michael, did not mince words about the evil he contended now lurked in Santa Brígida due to the inhabitants' abandonment of the antiga lei and to their embrace of consumerism and modern, secular beliefs and practices.

At the height of the Velho controversy, I was invited to attend a curing ritual performed on a then very sick José Vigário. I was also requested to bring my tape recorder and to record the entire ritual. When I first arrived at his modest home José Vigário was slumped in a chair and could not even rouse himself to greet me. A worried throng of admirers hung close by his side as they listened to Maria Lopes's curative prayers. About an hour into her curing rite, Maria began to tremble, her voice turned hoarse, and her neck twisted in such a fashion that all understood she had received the (living) spirit of moderate leader Zé Albino Souza. Maria's voice began to hiss as she explained that she (i.e., Zé Albino) had contracted a *macumbeiro* (a ritual specialist of macumba) who recently had magically poisoned José Vigário. On hearing this confession Vigário began to cough uncontrollably and then expelled a small ball of string and matted feathers. Maria immediately cupped the offending ball in her hand and showed it to the distraught, though curious onlookers. Almost immediately, José Vigário rallied and delivered the following denunciation with surprising vigor and animus.

> I told Pedro Batista when he first asked me to settle in Santa Brígida that this is a caldron of macumba. He said, "Yes, but we will transform it into good." But I knew that the opposite would occur, especially when he allowed in those of the first deception: Zé Albino, Bárbara, and Zezé [all moderate leaders]. All the time they played up to Pedro Batista and Dodô, pretending to be model romeiros, while all the time they were planning for this—preparing to deliver the romaria to Satan. But I will tell you one thing, I am not soft like Dodô. This flesh may look feeble now, but this spirit has never been born and never will die! . . . Pedro Batista was wrong when he granted universal pardon. Not me, if it were not for that poor virgin, Dodô, the whole town of Santa Brígida would have long gone up in flames, such is my fury! That hellhole and its citizens may yet go up in flames, and Zé Albino, Bárbara, and Zezé will turn into serpents as the flames lap at their feet. You people gathered here in my home, you know who will be saved that day. And you must never forget why you will be saved. (José Vigário 1974)

For the most part traditionalists, like the ones who gathered around José Vigário during that highly dramatic curing ritual, formed the backbone of the romaria. Their continued commitment to practice the antiga lei ensured that their acts of penitence would be found meritorious by God and, it was hoped, benefit all humanity. Despite José Vigário's denunciation of moderate romeiro leaders, until the most difficult moment in the Velho controversy, most traditionalists continued to participate in the confraternities and prayer services led by these moderate figures. The only confraternity led and totally maintained by traditionalists was the Dance of São Gonçalo. In the mid-1950s Pereira de Queiroz praised this group as "an integrative and cohesive element, before all the different groups that compose the community, it functions as a symbol of it, not an element of distinction or division" (Queiroz 1958, 73). Yet some twenty years later it had assumed a wholly different character.[2]

THE MODERATES AND MODERNISTS

Approximately 28 percent of the romaria made up the ranks of the moderates in 1973/1974, while some 5 percent were modernists. The economic lives of members of both groups were similar. For the most part moderates and modernists earned their livelihoods as commercial farmers, merchants, truckers, and full-time municipal employees. These families were described locally as *rico* (the rich) and as *gente que vive tranquilo* (people who live comfortably). It was from their ranks that poorer romeiros commonly found employers, creditors, and patrons.

Such stratification and economic dependency did not sit well with a population that had until recently prided itself on its communalism and shared identity as poor farmers. Traditionalists fondly recalled Pedro Batista's patronage, and they contrasted it with the exploitative and self-aggrandizing ways of certain romeiro merchants, landowners, and government officials. This was clearly the position taken by Casimira Sousa, a traditionalist who supplemented her sharecropping family's meager earnings by selling fired clay pots in the weekly market. I encountered her one day as she was leaving the store of a romeiro merchant, who had just refused to extend her a loan. Visibly shaken, she stated that he grew rich on poor romeiros' crops, which he purchased cheaply and sold for sizable profits. "These [profits] keep his children in fancy clothes and his daughters caked in makeup, while I struggle simply to feed mine." Then in a voice loud enough for the merchant to hear, she continued, "My Padrinho always said, 'The rich only get rich on the backs of the poor'" (Pessar, field notes, 20 March 1974).

For their part, romeiro patrons expressed exasperation when speaking to me about their poorer "clients." The latter, they lamented, simply refused to understand or appreciate the risks involved in borrowing money from wealthier brokers and in agreeing to furnish loans, land, seeds, and so on to a highly vulnerable class of people. Several modernists proudly recounted work histories that clearly exemplified Pedro Batista's challenge "to work like you are going to live forever." Such work involved traveling at all hours throughout the countryside buying crops, then transporting them by foot or donkey to larger towns and cities. Although initially naive to the ways of business, these young men gradually accumulated skills and capital. For example, they negotiated credit with owners of agricultural warehouses and textile factories. With these funds in hand, they provided loans for their cash-poor romeiro clients who reciprocated at harvest time by selling their crops only to these romeiro patrons. (This relationship developed at a moment when Pedro Batista was cutting back on his middle-man activities, thereby ceding ground to the young entrepreneurs.) As this small group prospered, they invested profits locally in land, agricultural warehouses, stores, and trucks. They lived comfortably in homes with electricity, modern furnishings, stoves, refrigerators, and radios. In stark contrast

Modernists celebrating Brazilian national holiday, 1974. Photo from author's personal archive, photographer unknown.

to earlier years, many traditionalists felt uncomfortable entering the homes of these now prosperous romeiros. A young man summed up these changed circumstances by quipping, "Each pan has its own lid" (Jorge dos Santos 1974).

Although most of the people classified as ricos by their fellow romeiros belonged to the modernists, there were several notable exceptions. Moreover, many younger municipal workers, merchants, and tradespeople who earned only a modest wage (i.e., gente que vive tranquilo) were also recognized as modernists. What distinguished modernists from moderates, then, was not necessarily their respective standards of living but their contrasting orientations to the romeiro way of life. The modernists considered themselves to be "good Catholics" rather than "good romeiros." That is, they had abandoned the outward markers of membership in the romaria, such as wearing a rosary around their neck and dressing in distinctive clothing. Furthermore, they no longer adhered stringently to Pedro Batista's proscriptions against such "sinful" behaviors as smoking and drinking, and they only occasionally participated in romeiro rituals.

Many of the modernist males had come to adopt this new orientation following a stint of urban employment during one of the many periods of drought. These young men returned to Santa Brígida with some savings, and equally important, with a basic knowledge of urban ways and the larger market economy.

As he drove me and a few romeiro passengers in his new, bright-red pickup truck, modernist Nelson dos Santos (1974) confided that when he was doing business in Paulo Afonso and other cities, people would see his rosary and think he was a fanatic and ignorant. They would consequently try to take advantage of him; so, he stopped wearing the rosary. "It didn't make me less of a Catholic," he assured me (Pessar, fieldnotes, 13 February 1974). True to the nomenclature I have selected, these romeiros told me that they considered themselves to be "modern Brazilians" and that they had neither the time nor the inclination to pursue the rigorous penitential and charitable demands placed on a true romeiro.

The moderates, by contrast, considered themselves to be model romeiros. Several were leaders of the romaria's various irmandades. Moderates, who tended to have some formal education, compared themselves favorably to the traditionalists, some of whom they accused of fanaticism and of having misunderstood and misrepresented Pedro Batista's teachings. Moreover, unlike the traditionalists, some moderate leaders were quite willing to innovate in ways that blended romeiro beliefs and practices with discourses and values being disseminated more widely throughout the nation. The fact that in August 1974 two distinct commemorations for the elderly were held in Santa Brígida exemplifies this development.

Dona Dodô sponsored her own Festa dos Velhos (Festival of the Aged) to which she invited elderly romeiros from Bahia, Alagoas, and Pernambuco. She also contracted a priest from Água Branca to celebrate a mass in their honor. Traditional romeiro hymns accompanied the mass, and modest refreshments were served at Pedro Batista's home following the service. A few weeks prior to this festival moderate leader Zezé Ramos had surprised Dona Dodô by announcing that, as a public official (the municipal notary), he had decided to sponsor his own festival for all pensioners throughout the municipality.[3] Dona Dodô urged him to combine his celebration with hers, but he refused. Instead he invited an official of the national social-security program and an army general, both stationed in Paulo Afonso, to be his guests of honor.

At Zezé's event, both religious and national symbols were in evidence. For example, the national anthem was sung and the pensioners were given green and yellow sashes (Brazilian national colors) to wear. A mass was celebrated by Padre Mario Zenetta, the young resident priest in Paulo Afonso. He managed to tread a fine line between the precepts of Vatican II and Pope Paul VI's encyclical "Populorum Progressio," on the one hand, and a military dictatorship that declared itself friend of the church but staunch enemy of the "Communist Antichrists" who had infiltrated the church's ranks (Bruneau 1974). Gesturing toward the government official and the general, Padre Mario (1974) called the pension fund "a noble start with which to begin to minister to the great suffering and hunger that plague so many elderly Northeasterners in this great and growing nation." Lest there be any misunderstanding in the minds of the visiting government dignitaries where Santa Brígida and the romaria stood, Zezé (1974) ended the ceremonies by reminding his audience that Pedro Batista and Dona Dodô loved the poor. On the other hand, the two leaders reviled those who pretended to care about the old and destitute while they were really in league with Satan, "seeking to destroy the only true faith and Brazil's God-fearing president. The Communists tried to ruin it all. Thank God the army saved us from such evil."

This ceremony, and others like it, not only maintained the familiar strategy of seeking accommodation with political authorities, but it also represented attempts by the moderates to define a new middle ground for the romaria. Penitence and the legacy of moral concern for mankind would be sustained. Additionally, there would be greater leeway for embracing certain "exemplary" features of the dominant Brazilian ideology. For instance, in his speech Zezé expressed the revised, moderate position that *individual* upward mobility was not contrary to the teachings of Pedro Batista, as long as it was not flaunted and was accompanied by acts of charity. He also nested the romeiros' experiences within the larger context of the nation, a discursive move that in the past had typified outside observers rather than romeiro leaders. "Romeiros honor Pedro Batista when they work hard," Zezé exhorted his audience. "It is their faith and hard work that will build a great and strong nation" (ibid.).

Celebrations such as Zezé's modified the chain of command and symbolic template attached to ceremonies held in Santa Brígida and elsewhere in the nation. Increasingly, community festivals, like this one for Santa Brígida's elderly, were being organized and sponsored by the mayor's office and state officials, who stood in for more traditional patrons who were either physically absent or no longer cared to assume the sizable expenses involved in sponsoring community ceremonies (Zaluar 1983). Not uncommonly, this transition in sponsorship occasioned a change in the dominant symbols featured in the event; either religious and national symbols were combined, as in Zezé's commemoration for the elderly, or state discourse predominated. In this way, rural Brazilians were encouraged to identify nationally and in a more secular fashion than had been the case when saint's day festivals symbolized membership in and loyalty to an extremely localized community and power structure. That such patriotic and centralizing regimes of identity and power were so visible and proved so formative at this particular juncture in the romaria's history is a testament to the inroads made throughout Brazil by the highly nationalistic and authoritarian military dictatorship. Indeed the visiting general appeared quite at home in Santa Brígida, a fact wholly consistent with a regime that positioned itself squarely on the side of "Western Christian Civilization" and "old-fashioned virtues" (Bruneau 1974, 180).

With Pedro Batista gone and Dona Dodô pursuing a leadership style based more on compromise than authoritarianism, most moderates concluded that the romaria would never return to its past glory. They continued to lead and participate in romeiro confraternities and rituals to better ensure their own individual salvation and to honor Pedro Batista's memory. By the mid-1970s the cosmic narrative emphasizing Santa Brígida's future standing as Heaven on Earth had been dismissed by some moderate leaders as a distortion of Batista's teachings and by others as a missed opportunity. For their part, traditionalists tended to brand such positions as defeatist at best and as satanic at worse. Referring to the moderates' proclivity to blend aspects of the antiga lei with more contemporary practices, one traditionalist insisted, "There is only one path to God. You cannot travel on two paths at the same time. To think this is to fall into temptation" (Lenira Lopes 1976).

Finally, the younger generation and its socialization also served as grist for dissatisfaction and conflict within the romaria. By the 1970s romeiro youth were knowledgeable to varying degrees about national and mass cultures. They were exposed to these meanings and practices in the public school's curriculum and its celebration of national holidays; via the pop music and urbane banter of the town's modernist disc jockey, whose program was funded by the municipal government and aired most afternoons; and through the true confessions, movie, and fashion magazines modernist teenagers purchased in neighboring cities and then furtively shared with their friends.

Most of the traditionalist and many of the moderate parents I knew decried the modernists who imported such Trojan horses into the romaria. At best, such influences were perceived as distracting romeiro children from their far more virtuous religious obligations and, at worse, as seducing them into lives of materialism, promiscuity, and vice. These critics tried to separate their own children from "bad influences" among the community's youth and to emphasize religious over secular education. The parents seemed to be relatively successful back then, judging from the fact that most traditionalist and moderate teenagers I spoke to could reproduce benditos and saints' tales with far greater assurance and facility than they could sing contemporary rock songs, relate gossip about movie stars, or discuss past national heroes. But this was the last generation of romeiro parents who proved able to keep their offspring attentive, at least during their formative years, to the precepts and norms of the antiga lei.

Although the romaria was divided socioeconomically and ideologically into three segments, this triad actually folded into two over the thorny matter of the Velho. The majority of the traditionalists backed the Velho, while many moderates and all modernists opposed him. The controversy over his authenticity and legitimacy as the appropriate leader of the romaria is best understood within the contours of the divisions and trends of the three romaria groups. First, he served as an antidote to those moderate leaders who seemed intent on abandoning the millennial dreams that most of the traditionalists continued to embrace. Second, as the purported reincarnation of Pedro Batista, he promised to at least reign in, if not punish, those who had abandoned the antiga lei and those who chose to exploit their poorer and more vulnerable peers. And third, as a male, the Velho appealed to the many who yearned for a patriarch to bolster Dona Dodô's leadership.

The Anthropologist and the Romaria

While in the 1950s and 1960s, Pedro Batista had often admonished his followers to present a secularized discourse and demeanor to outsiders, by the time I arrived in the 1970s there was no such disciplining figure. Moreover, by the mid-1970s the Brazilian military and dominant classes were far more intent on limiting the spread of liberation theology than on eradicating folk Catholicism and popular santos. Consequently, most romeiros felt quite comfortable airing their views about the Velho controversy; indeed, soon after my arrival I was drawn into the maelstrom as each side sought my endorsement of their position. Why and how each faction tried to implicate me revealed as much about their members' preoccupations and interests as it did about their particular understandings regarding the nature of my presence in Santa Brígida.

I believe certain romeiros—especially those belonging to the ranks of the traditionalists—chose to engage me almost immediately because they suspected I was on a divine mission. They sought to impress on me their views on both the Velho and their romeiro rivals. One such zealot was Augustino Veloso, who stopped me on the street with a conspiratorial wink and asked me to follow him to his home for a very important conversation. After we passed through his front door, on which was marked in chalk "Jesus lives here," Augustino bolted the door and the windows securely, explaining that there were troublemakers within ear shot. Refraining from the usual chitchat, Augustino immediately advised me that his Padrinho Pedro had returned in the body of an old, blind penitent. Augustino's voice trembled with anger as he explained that the Velho was being denied his rightful place as head of the romaria by satanic forces within that very body. Augustino suggested that I accompany him and other loyal romeiros when they next visited the Velho, an invitation I later accepted. I suspect that Augustino and other traditionalists believed that I maintained a special spiritual or moral bond with Dona Dodô. After a successful visit with the Velho, they might have thought, I might be inclined to draw her to their side.

Conversely, those romeiros who viewed me as a researcher sought to demonstrate that they were measured individuals who repudiated the ignorance and "fanaticism" of some of their more "backward" and impressionable peers. They asserted that the fanatics were desecrating Pedro Batista's memory and might ignite the kind of violence—and potential state reprisal—associated with the João Gustavo affair. For many romeiros who opposed the Velho, I provided a sympathetic ear and, I suspect, someone who might represent their interests persuasively to Dona Dodô.

My own subject position as an American anthropologist, and as someone who, some suspected, had come on a spiritual mission, likely influenced the type of reception I received, the things I was able to observe, and the discourses I elicited and overheard. As a student of Victor Turner, I was not only committed to studying religious symbols and rituals but also fully prepared to participate in the religious life of the community. Turner was not only an intellectual exponent of "communitas" (1969), he also encouraged his students to seek out instances of such communal practices in their own fieldsites and to personally experience their power to level hierarchy and unleash creativity. In practice, this meant that I endeavored to participate as fully as possible in a broad range of events sponsored and attended by the romaria as a whole, as well as by its diverse segments. My insider/outsider status facilitated boundary crossings that few romeiros could negotiate. My seeming success in ingratiating myself to all sides became apparent when one modernist quipped to a traditionalist, "There's so much bad blood these days that if an election were held for mayor today, the only surefire winner would be Patricia" (Pessar, fieldnotes, 6 August 1974). Furthermore, my own First World sixties sensibility made me "expect" that my informants would share their lives with me. In turn, I would reciprocate by "bearing witness" and "giving voice" to a misunderstood and maligned group of people. Meanwhile, I failed to recognize or interrogate the remarkable openness and generosity with which I was received.

I only came to appreciate my exceptional reception in Santa Brígida after I had the opportunity to compare it with another period of intensive fieldwork.

Participants in the dance of São Jorge and Santa Joana, with author in the middle, 1974. Photo from author's personal archive, photographer unknown.

In the early and mid-1980s I conducted research on international migration in the Dominican Republic and New York. In both sites I found myself confronting suspicions that I was an agent of the Immigration and Naturalization Service and having to convince understandably reluctant people to talk with me. I sorely missed a figure like Dona Dodô who might vouch for me and assure others that it was safe to welcome me into their homes. I will never know the extent to which Dona Dodô's prophecy about the arrival of a messenger of God disposed her to facilitate my exposure to and participation in all facets of the romaria's religious life, which even included permitting me into the male bastion of Os Penitentes. I would like to believe that over the length of my stay, my own very human failings and foibles served to "disenchant" me for her and many others, but I will never know for sure, for despite my attempts to disabuse people of the notion that I had special spiritual powers, they and I knew that such disclaimers were perfectly in keeping with the behavior of a divine emissary.

How did peoples' understandings of who I was affect their encounters with me and the nature of their discourse? Certainly, in interviews and in small gatherings peoples' perceptions of who I was and why I had come to Santa Brígida influenced what they told me or discussed, and how they expressed their views. I have no doubt, for example, that those who believed I had a spiritual mission took special care to impress on me their own faith and abiding devotion to Pedro Batista. Such encounters, however, served as only one venue through which I learned about the romeiros' lives and the ongoing events in Santa Brígida. In the many public airings of contending views about the future of the romaria and the place of the Velho in that future, my presence was largely, if not completely, coincidental to the ensuing discourse. These occasions provided additional and highly valuable information that was not subject to the dialogical constraints of modes of "data" collection in which my presence helped to define the flow and content of the exchange. In the ethnographic materials I present below, I have taken care to present an array of discursive "texts," many of which I first observed while on the margins of discussions and conflicts, and only later recorded in my fieldnotes.

Finally, having been trained to remain "neutral" and "objective," I removed myself from the fray as the controversy over the Velho heated up toward the middle and end of my initial period of fieldwork. Nonetheless, I soon found that while I maintained cordial relations with all sides and took care to participate in, and tape-record when requested, events identified with the traditionalists, moderates, and modernists, the two factions in the Velho controversy sometimes used my presence and my experiences to advance their own positions. To illustrate: when I was hospitalized in Paulo Afonso with a severe case of hepatitis late in my 1973/1974 fieldwork, the pro-Velho forces maintained that I had become ill due to my despair over a divided romaria and my fear that the moderate leaders had sacrificed any chance for mass salvation. The anti-Velho forces countered that I had become the victim of macumba due to my unwillingness to support the pro-Velho faction.[4] I also found that Dona Dodô and others attributed great value to my ability to tape-record events, since these could be listened to and enjoyed by more people at a later date. As becomes clear later in this chapter, while I first approached this taping as a way of reciprocating peoples' generosity in inviting me to their events, I was soon to find that my tapes occasionally further fueled conflicts.

The Velho: God the Holy Ghost

As well as can be reconstructed, the Velho (José Vicente) was born in Pernambuco in the early 1900s but spent many years in Água Branca, Alagoas. Shortly after Pedro Batista's death, he began traveling with key supporters to communities where Batista's pilgrims resided, and he offered his services as a curer and conselheiro. People immediately noted similarities between his demeanor and words and those of Pedro Batista. For his part, the Velho inquired about his visitors and their families in ways that clearly revealed that he was familiar with their pasts. Soon he was sprinkling his conversations with allusions to the many miraculous events with which Pedro Batista was associated, and at some point he elected to change the pronoun from "he" to "I." News of the Velho soon reached Santa Brígida, and early on individuals like Augustino Veloso traveled to the beato's home in Inajá, Pernambuco, to consult with him and urge him to relocate to Santa Brígida.

The Velho's first visit to Santa Brígida in 1971 was strategically planned to coincide with the festival of the community's patron saint, São Pedro. The Velho, a rosy-complected man with a flowing white beard, arrived by truck with a group of romeiros from Pernambuco. His supporters in Santa Brígida led him directly to Pedro Batista's house and seated him in the deceased beato's chair. This act provoked immediate condemnation by moderate leaders who had quickly made their way to the house when they learned of the Velho's arrival. When tempers flared, Dona Dodô placed another chair by the side of Pedro Batista's and suggested that the Velho sit there. Throughout the day the house was filled with romeiros seeking a blessing and beseeching their Padrinho to remain. He said he would like to stay but that it depended on the decision of local officials. For, as his loyal romeiros knew, he never stayed in a place where he was not wanted. As if on cue, moderate leaders proceeded to the offices of the mayor and sheriff, and they demanded that the Velho be expelled. Zezé Ramos's face visibly flushed with anger when he reflected on that day.

> It was horrible. There were two festivals going on, one celebrating São Pedro and the memory of our saintly Padrinho, and the other of ignorant, deluded people, flocking around an impostor. My friends, educated, cultured people from Alagoas and Pernambuco kept coming up to me and asking what was going on. It looked very bad for the romaria, such fanaticism! So finally in the afternoon I went with Comadre Bárbara and Compadre Zé Albino to speak with Joaquim Teixera [the mayor] and other officials. Everyone was disturbed to have important visitors—priests, doctors, and politicians—see such things. So the sheriff approached the Velho and told him that he was creating a disturbance and had better leave before legal proceedings were initiated. . . . You know my Padrinho was a man of courage, and he would face the government and show that he was a person to be reckoned with. But with the suggestion of a problem,

the Velho fled like a scared dog! Such is the so-called mystery of this man whom so many revere even more than Madrinha Dodô! (1974)

In fact the Velho did not fully comply with the orders he was given but instead relocated to the hamlet of Quarenta, fourteen kilometers from the town of Santa Brígida, where he continued to meet with supporters. In Quarenta, he stayed in the home of a woman who had been one of the first romeiro settlers, and her recognition of the Velho as Pedro Batista was an important vote of confidence. At the conclusion of the São Pedro festival, the Velho returned with his companions to Pernambuco.

In this first of several controversial visits, moderate leaders were able to demonstrate that they had the political clout to expel the Velho from the town of Santa Brígida and from the religious festival that they organized and supervised. On the other hand, Velho supporters were buoyed by the tremendous outpouring of interest and support. They vowed it would not be his last visit. Yet, when he returned by bus the following year for the São Pedro festival, authorities had been tipped off and they intercepted him when the bus let off its passengers along the highway outside of town. They informed the Velho that they had been authorized to make out a warrant for his arrest if he entered the town. To avoid trouble, the Velho and his supporters reboarded the bus and did not attend the festivities that year.

There could be no doubt who the victors were in this second round. The Velho supporters had been taken up short. Their Padrinho had been whisked from their midst, and they had not been able to defend him. It was at this point of marked asymmetry in political prowess and power that the Velho supporters tapped into that corpus of highly charged religious symbols applied earlier to the enemies of Pedro Batista. Local authorities like the mayor and sheriff were called Herods and Pontius Pilates, and moderate romeiro leaders were called Judases. Pro-Velho romeiros recalled a verse from one of Pedro Batista's favorite benditos, which advised,

The romeiros will not remember
What their Padrinho told them.
When he reappears
No one will recognize him.

Responding in kind, the anti-Velho forces countered that the Velho and his close supporters were Antichrists. What both sides seemed to agree on was that this conflict symbolized a marked deterioration within the romaria and was an ominous sign that the end was drawing near. The point of contention concerned the actual meaning of "the end." For the Velho supporters it meant the imminent apocalypse and the damnation of their romeiro foes. Conversely, moderate and modernist romeiros who opposed the Velho feared an end in which the "fanatics" temporarily gained control. This, they counseled, would occasion the type of reprisals against the romaria that government authorities had threatened earlier at the time of João Gustavo's death. Both factions were disturbed that Dona Dodô continued to seek unity and refused to join one side or the other.

Pilgrimages to Inajá

As a temporary measure, supporters decided that if the Velho could not come to Santa Brígida, the true romeiros would go to him. Trips to Inajá became frequent, and it was during one of these occasions that the Velho explicitly stated that his real name was Pedro Batista da Silva, curador. He also urged his devotees to collect funds for him to purchase a donkey and saddle so that he might next arrive in Santa Brígida in the same fashion as he had long ago. In 1974, as excitement over the true identity of the Velho grew, I was invited by several traditionalists to accompany them on their next trip to Inajá. While I was eager to travel with the romeiros and observe activities there, I was also mindful that my "pilgrimage" might be used to bolster the pro-Velho cause. Fortunately, Dona Dodô and moderate leaders also encouraged me to make the trip.

Consistent with certain Northeasterners' modes of knowledge and knowing, pro-Velho supporters assured me prior to my departure that it was "through opening my heart" that I would come to appreciate the truth about the Velho. By contrast, their rivals appealed to empiricism and the law. They urged me to observe how his "wily" advisors fed him information, and they alerted me that he was "an impostor who had stolen [Pedro Batista's] identity."

Mindful that I had been drawn into the fray and concerned for my well-being, Dona Dodô arranged for two traditionalist women with whom I was particularly close to accompany me on the day-long trip. They were also eager to go since they had not made up their minds about the authenticity of the Velho. So the three of us carefully observed the Velho and his devotees in Inajá. For me it was a matter of intellectual curiosity: to better understand how a would-be santo operated and to learn how the Velho had managed to garner so much support among Santa Brígida's romeiros. For my two companions the stakes were as high as they could get: recognizing their Padrinho and greatly enhancing their opportunity for salvation, on the one hand, or erroneously casting their lot with a charlatan who might even be the Antichrist, on the other.

The pilgrims who traveled to Inajá expected to view and become involved in "performances" in which claims to charisma are advanced by a would-be santo and his close supporters. These, in turn, are affirmed or rejected by observers. Sitting in front of a simple altar decorated with rustic figures of saints, photographs, ribbons, and streamers, the Velho offered performances that consisted of providing petitioners with homespun advice or a cure. He also delivered long and, in my opinion, rambling speeches and stories, sprinkled with such statements as "I eat nothing; I am all spirit, no flesh or bones" and "How angry I am with those serpents in Santa Brígida who make the poor Virgin suffer so in my absence" (Pessar, fieldnotes, 18 May 1974). One of the most controversial aspects of the Velho's performance was the fact that he was given small amounts of alcohol by his beatos while visitors were present. He and they claimed that this sustained him since he no longer ate regular food. His supporters from Santa Brígida reasoned a bit defensively that their Padrinho had to change his behavior somewhat. This was necessary to test the capacity of his followers to truly recognize him after his "separation."

More dramatic and elaborate performances were offered by several beatas who also cured visitors and seemed to vie with each other for the attention of their guests. On these occasions the women purportedly became possessed by spirits. During my visit these spirits commented on events and individuals in Santa Brígida, thus managing to fuel the flames of controversy. One particularly controversial performance involved a beata who appeared to be possessed by Mãe Quino, Padre Cícero's mother. The stout woman placed the Velho on her knee, whereupon she rocked him and sang him a lullaby. As she sang, she called the Velho both Cícero and Pedro, interchangeably. News of this incident was carried back to Santa Brígida, where it was received with disgust by several moderates and modernists. They argued that no human was pure enough to receive the saintly spirit of Mãe Quino.

My two companions remained skeptical of that performance as well, and they teased me about another beata who broke into loud song when she saw me, praising me as "Her Excellency of Hamérica" at the end of each verse of her song. On a more serious note, each woman separately confided in me that she had seen nothing in Inajá to convince her that the Velho was her Padrinho. Both found his counsel and stories lackluster. Moreover, they suspected that he was nothing more than a poor man being plied with alcohol by others who were enriching themselves on charitable contributions to the Velho. Although I agreed with them, I kept my own counsel, listening closely to the commentaries offered by my many travel companions on our way back to Santa Brígida. When asked about my own views, I replied that I felt it best to reserve judgment until I had had additional opportunities to visit him. This explanation was met with sympathetic comments, the gist of which was that I should continue to open my heart and it would guide me to the correct answer.

I returned from the trip grateful that I had thus far managed to uphold the still-popular tenet of scholarly neutrality and had, until that point, left "the field" "uncontaminated" by my presence. I soon found myself tested when Dona Dodô requested that I visit her home and share my thoughts about the Velho with her.

But first, some background: my trip to Inajá had come on the heels of a letter addressed to Augustino Veloso that the Velho allegedly dictated to one of his literate beatos. It stated, "I will be spending my festival [the upcoming São Pedro festival] with my romeiros. But I will only do this if I know there will be no confusion. I pray the devil has left the hearts of many of my romeiros so they may come back to their Padrinho. . . . I ask you to seek out the officials there and learn if I may spend my festival with my beloved romeiros" (Pessar, fieldnotes, 10 May 1974).

When Augustino showed the letter to the romeiro sheriff, the latter stated that military officials had forbade the Velho to visit Santa Brígida as long as he claimed to be Pedro Batista. The sheriff himself had stated many times that if the Velho presented himself as a poor penitent, there would be no problem, but in stating that he was Pedro Batista, the Velho had become an impostor—a criminal offense. Complicating matters further, after learning about the letter Dona Dodô had approached the sheriff asking him to permit the Velho to attend the festivities. It clearly pained Sheriff João Santos to have to "pull rank" on Dona Dodô. He confided to me, "It was very hard for me to refuse Madrinha Dodô; she wants to please everyone, and she doesn't want to hurt the Velho supporters. But I have my orders. Those of us, a small minority mind you, who have more wisdom and foresight than the weak-minded people here realize that his coming may precipitate another João Gustavo incident" (1974).

A few days later, Dona Dodô found an anonymous letter slipped under her door. It advised that Santa Brígida was no longer the appropriate place for her. One line read, "This is the home of adulterers, macumbeiros, and demons; you must remain in Juazeiro" (ibid.).

Thus when Dona Dodô ushered me alone into a back room of her home and inquired in an uncharacteristically straightforward way whether I had found any special mistério in the old man whom I had visited in Inajá, I knew that she was deeply disturbed by the controversy swirling around her. She sought her own resolution regarding the Velho's claims. One inner voice instructed me about the scholarly "ethics" of neutrality and objectivity. Yet the heart that my romeiro companions had urged me to open recognized Dona Dodô's clear distress and her desire to learn of my views. I should add that at that time I did not know about Dona Dodô's prophecy about the imminent arrival of a divine emissary and the fact that some believed I was that figure. Had I known, I would have felt far more uncomfortable about her question regarding my views on the Velho, but I would not have refused her request to share my views.

I prefaced my remarks by stating that prior to my arrival in Santa Brígida, I had never encountered a person with mistério nor had I been asked to judge the veracity of an individual's spiritual powers. Nonetheless, I told her what had truly been my experience since living there. I encountered some people, like her, who I believed used their spirituality to help others in a wholly altruistic fashion and who seemed humbled rather than self-aggrandized by their "power." Such people also demonstrated their spirituality without benefit of an ensemble of attendant players. This was clearly not the case for the Velho, whose beatos seemed to choreograph his every move and to correct him the many times he faltered. As I voiced these observations, I remember how they seemed at once so strange to me, since matters of saintliness and charisma were foreign to my own life experiences. Nonetheless, I felt certain that if there were such a thing as a living saint, Dona Dodô was decidedly one, and the Velho was not. I also fell back on my own more scientific "canons" to ground me in what I found to be unfamiliar and uncomfortable circumstances. I recalled the work of certain cognitive anthropologists. They taught that a good observer might adequately learn another social group's meaningful categories, whether they be novel terms for color or, in this case, sertanejos' concepts of and norms for mistério.

When I finished speaking, Dona Dodô gently placed my hands in hers and, again uncharacteristically, looked me straight in the eyes. She reassured me that she, too, had reached a similar conclusion: "If he were truly my Padrinho," she stated, "he would have performed a miracle by now; and this old penitent has not" (Pessar, fieldnotes, 19 May 1974). I left her home knowing that I had crossed a line I then believed a researcher should not transgress, but I also knew that I had treated a remarkable woman with the honor and respect she merited—not as a mere key informant. Years later I came to realize that at that moment I had far less freedom of action than the hierarchical researcher-informant diad had led me to believe. Rather, throughout my periods of fieldwork, I, Dona Dodô, and other romeiros dialogically constituted, and continue to reconstitute, the terms by which we permitted ourselves to engage each other.[5]

A Deceased Moderate Leader Turns to São Gonçalo

In a work in which he puzzles over the best way to define the elusive term, *community*, Gavin Smith (1991) recommends the concept of "discursive community." For Smith a discursive community is a group of people who share a corpus of cultural meanings and values even though they debate the appropriateness of variations in core terms and how such variations are best applied in practice. Particularly apposite is Smith's observation that the very desire, if not at times the compulsion, to engage others in debate and contestation over meanings is what socially constitutes a community. Over the course of the 1970s, a highly divided and contentious romaria attempted to remain a community by bringing a common repertoire of meanings about such phenomena as authentic romeiros, mistério, fanaticism, and Antichrists into their public encounters. In these meetings rivals attempted to air their views and convince others about the validity of their particular interpretation.

At that time, of course, the romaria was at a very different phase in its constitution as a community than it had been some twenty years earlier when Pereira de Queiroz praised the Dance of São Gonçalo above all other folkloric practices as "an integrative and cohesive [communal] element" (Queiroz 1958, 73). By the mid-1970s the dance had become a context in which returning spirits stirred the pot of discord through episodes of name-calling and denunciations that the spirits' human hosts would rarely, if ever, have dared to voice publicly.

With the festival of São Pedro nearing and the controversy over the Velho reaching a boiling point, a number of romeiro curers, including Maria Lopes and José Vigário, had purportedly received the tormented spirit of the recently deceased leader of Os Penitentes, João [Oliveira] Manuel Alves. On these occasions João's spirit purportedly lamented that demons were snapping at his heels because he had been unwittingly tempted by Satan into denying José Vigário's mystery and authority and into pronouncing the Velho a fraud. João beseeched the curers to transmit the details of his suffering to his family. He also asked his family to sponsor a Dance of São Gonçalo for the redemption of his soul. It was supposedly his wish to have the traditionalist Lopes family hold the dance at the chapel in Quarenta-e-dois, with José Vigário officiating.

This was a difficult request for the moderate Alves family to honor, especially since they were highly skeptical about the recent proliferation of garrulous spirits. As João's brother and former colônia official Eugenio Alves (1974) commented, "I believe in the cures of my Padrinho, and he exorcised spirits that spoke. But this present situation of everyone receiving spirits, and all the spirits asking for the payment of a promessa to São Gonçalo or accusing people of evil acts, well, I just cannot believe all of this. I fear it is temptation."

On the other hand, as moderate leaders and trusted allies of Dona Dodô, the Alves family had consistently mediated between the demands of the modernists and the traditionalists. By refusing to sponsor a Dance of São Gonçalo, they might seriously jeopardize the respect and credibility they had garnered among the traditionalists. Moreover, the pretext for the performance—that is, the suffering of João in purgatory—was too charged a matter for the Alveses to use as a context to widen the gulf between the traditionalists and moderates, like themselves. Nonetheless, the Alves family were certainly able to communicate their own reticence concerning the performance.

On 9 June 1974, three weeks before the São Pedro festival, a *jornada* was held for João Manuel Alves at the chapel in Quarenta-e-dois. It went on from 8:00 in the morning until 7:00 at night, with Lopes family members participating in the dance and José Vigário in attendance. Strikingly, the Alveses sent the adult members of their family with the least status, two sisters and the youngest brother. The significance of this was not lost on the Lopes family. After she had finished a complete round of the dance, Lenira Lopes took me aside and expressed her annoyance. Her words bespoke her discomfort with the existing stratification within the romaria. More significant, it revealed that poorer romeiros like Lenira had come to harbor *resentment* against certain of their modernist and moderate peers. As Lenira's statement reflects, these traditionalists anticipated that their resentment would be validated and that unity and equality among all true romeiros would reign again once the Velho assumed his rightful place as leader of the romaria: "Do you see, those Alveses act like they're better than us, with their Men's Penitent Society and their involvement in politics. But here it is their brother's spirit being carried off by demons because of his false pride and wrongdoing. And they continue to stay aloof and deceived. When my Padrinho [the Velho] takes his rightful place, it will be too late for those who have forgotten my Padrinho's words: 'He who has made a man rich and given him power can make him small again.' As my Padrinho [José Vigário] says, the day is soon upon us when many romeiros will suffer great agonies due to their evil ways and disbelief" (Pessar, fieldnotes, 9 June 1974).

During the final round of the dance all the participants and bystanders were called to the chapel for the *encerramento* (closing ritual). The closing prayers had just begun when Maria Lopes began to weep and flail her arms. Moving to the front of the chapel, she became rigid and stood perfectly erect. Buzzing began as people came to recognize that she had received the spirit of João Manuel

Alves. To the tune of several benditos, João's spirit began to chant his story of suffering and, now, alleviation. He also used the opportunity to advise his family and friends to remain true to the antiga lei. "God does not like men with long hair, women with short skirts, and disobedience." I was told afterward by several traditionalists that Maria could not possibly have known the melodies the spirit employed while he chanted to the assembled since they were carefully guarded by the men of Os Penitentes. On concluding his remarks the spirit thanked everyone for attending and praying for him. "João" then asked for José Vigário's blessing and pardon, and the latter responded emotionally, "May God bless you."

Talk of the Velho and of João's misguided rejection of him was conspicuously absent from this event. It is likely that "the spirit" did not want to upset the delicate balance—or discursive community—that the dance had momentarily forged. Moreover, curers like Maria, who had previously received João's spirit, had publicly aired the matter of his earlier disbelief and subsequent suffering at the hands of Satan. There would be nothing gained in further subjecting his family to this sordid affair, especially since their general skepticism about returning spirits was well known. Furthermore, too much zeal might result in a backlash on the part of the Alveses and other influential moderates. There was, nonetheless, a clear distinction between the reactions of the Alves and Lopes families to the returning spirit. The former remained solemn and undemonstrative, while the latter wept openly throughout "João's" speech and commented affirmatively and supportively.

Especially dramatic was "João's" request at the end of his remarks for all to approach him and give him their pardon and blessings—a definite reversal of status. During his lifetime João had served as the head of Os Penitentes and was president of the Brotherhood of São Vicente; he was, accordingly, a highly respected and revered leader of the romaria. Under ordinary circumstances, it would have been the Lopeses who would have requested his blessing, rather than the other way around. For the traditionalist Lopes family such a reversal served as a symbolic prologue to that anticipated future when the trend of growing hierarchy and difference within the romaria would end and the authentic romeiros would be rewarded for their unwavering obedience and faith.

The following day brought quite an unexpected escalation in the Velho conflict and heightened animosity between the moderates and traditionalists. It was market day in Santa Brígida, and members of the Lopes family had gone to visit Dona Dodô who was receiving romeiros, as was customary, in Pedro Batista's house. They told her about João's beautiful words and added that fortunately they had requested that I record his statements on my tape recorder.

Dona Dodô immediately called me so that she and the assembled might hear the tapes. Their playing proved to be a highly emotional affair, with Dona Dodô and others weeping throughout and commenting on "how beautiful" and "fine" "João's" oratory was.

Some hours later I was again called to Pedro Batista's home. This time Dona Dodô had gathered some of the most important moderates to listen to João's words. Among those assembled were the sheriff and Zé Albino Sousa. In contrast to the earlier group of listeners, these men sat stony-faced. After hearing "João's" spirit, they politely thanked me and took their leave.

But the incident did not end there. An hour later Zé Albino returned again to Pedro Batista's home where, fortunately, I had decided to remain, chatting in the kitchen with a continuous stream of visitors. Placing himself in front of Pedro Batista's chair in the parlor he shouted, "Oh my Padrinho, I can no longer accept this deception by these demons any longer." He then stated that the Lopeses and "the head demon" José Vigário were all "evil good-for-nothings, macumbeiros, and adulterers, who were dragging Padrinho Pedro's saintly memory through the mud" (Pessar, fieldnotes, 10 June 1974). He went on to contest the very notion that the spirit of João Manuel Alves had entered Maria Lopes. He noted that João was an educated man who spoke "good" Portuguese, while what he heard on the tape was the Portuguese of an illiterate person—Maria Lopes herself. He then began to rail against the Velho and those "ignorant fanatics" like the Lopeses and José Vigário who supported that "drunken dog who dares to say he is my Padrinho." As the coup de grâce, he stated that although Dona Dodô had vowed him to silence, he could no longer remain so. He added that his past respect and devotion to her would fully return only if she openly repudiated the Velho. After revealing the secret of the two disinterments of Pedro Batista's body, he then said in essence: how can a man who passed two months and twenty-four days in the grave without a stain on his saintly body and then disappeared without a trace two years later, come back in the form of a drunk, sorcerer, dancer of candomblé, a bum, reeking of cigarettes and taking part in everything that is worthless! I must speak the truth before the sainted picture of my Padrinho, before we all fall under Satan's power. The romaria is sorely divided and headed toward destruction (ibid.).

In a community where speaking badly of others is considered a serious transgression and might even lead to supernatural punishment ("clicking tongues attract sickness"), such an overt display of verbal aggression, as well as Zé Albino's strongly worded criticism of Dona Dodô, sent shockwaves throughout the community. Contrary to the reaction he had hoped would follow from his disclosure of Pedro Batista's "resurrection," some who had re-

mained undecided about the Velho's true identity took Zé's news as proof that
the Velho really was Batista. As one "convert" told me, "It is suddenly so obvious for those who will see. First my Padrinho Cícero moved on and he was the
Father. Soon my Padrinho Pedro Batista appeared, and he was the Son. Then
because of our sins, my Padrinho moved on in 1967. As God the Son, he, too,
was soon resurrected. Two years later they did not find a single trace of his remains. Well wasn't it exactly in 1969 when the Velho began his wandering and
was recognized as my Padrinho. Those who do not see this either do not have
the merit to know, or have been turned against the Velho by Satan!" (João de
Lima 1974).

The Festival of São Pedro

The festival of São Pedro was traditionally an event that both honored Pedro Batista and contributed to a sense of pride and solidarity within the romaria. Yet as
the 1974 celebration drew near, discord and intrigue greatly dampened the enthusiasm. This was aggravated when, two weeks before the event, the modernist disc jockey announced over his public-address system that the festival dates
had been changed to the last Saturday and Sunday in June. This notice took
most romeiros and baianos by surprise since the actual calendar date for the
saint's day was the final Friday in June. Unbeknownst to most of the town's inhabitants, local politicians and merchants had introduced this change in dates
to permit more visitors from afar to attend the festivities. These modernists
were motivated by economic gain and the desire to demonstrate that Santa Brígida could host a festival that would rival those held in bigger, wealthier towns.
They had, moreover, advised Dona Dodô of this change in scheduling and had
secured her acceptance before going ahead with the change.

When the traditionalists and many of the moderates learned of this change
they were incredulous. They immediately sought out Dona Dodô and asked her
to intercede on their behalf. Under this pressure, and I believe based on her
true inclination, she reversed her decision. She called Mayor Ricardo Barbosa
(a baiano and ally of the modernists) to her house and asked him to change the
dates back to the original Friday and Saturday. He demurred, claiming that all
the publicity had been printed and the band hired for Saturday night. A change
at that late date was impossible.

Disappointed, Dona Dodô and the moderate leaders announced that the
romeiro celebration would be on Friday and Saturday in accordance with tradition and the religious calendar. They also insisted that their celebration was
sacred and directly linked to past São Pedro festivals, while the competing one

reflected values and encouraged practices that Pedro Batista had deplored. The modernists did not entirely challenge this characterization. They countered that only by such innovative actions as moving the festival to the weekend would Santa Brígida *vai pra frente* (move forward). As Mayor Barbosa explained to me, those who complain only want to criticize, but when there is work to be done to improve Santa Brígida, they are nowhere to be found. These are backward, ignorant people. They will only keep us behind. Brazil is progressing, and it is our duty to contribute as much as we can (Pessar, fieldnotes, 18 June 1973).

Thus, with the festival imminent, the romaria found itself deeply divided over two major issues, which served to reveal and accentuate major ideological differences within the romaria. First, the controversy over whether the Velho should be permitted to participate in the festival pitted the modernists and leaders of the moderates against the traditionalists and certain moderates. As the rivals defined and staked out their own positions and proceeded to characterize their nemeses, some drew on tropes of fanaticism and ignorance that had earlier been hurled against *all* of the supporters of Pedro Batista. Moreover, the contenders employed eschatalogical symbols. Thus, depending on one's perspective, the two sides of this highly contentious discursive community were the upholders of rationality and the preservers of Pedro Batista's memory against the fanatics. From another perspective it was the faithful and meritorious struggling against the Judases and Antichrists. As the festival neared, it was generally agreed that the superior political resources the modernists and moderate leaders wielded—that is, the threat of criminal indictment and their closer ties to police and military authorities—had effectively foreclosed the possibility of the Velho participating unimpeded in the saint's day festival.

The other issue that divided the romaria concerned the rescheduling of the dates. Critics viewed this change as a public sanctioning of a move from religion and tradition to profit, entertainment, and innovation. Here the moderates found themselves in agreement with the traditionalists. The moderate leaders had always organized the festival, and they derived prestige from this responsibility. They clearly felt undercut by the unprecedented initiative taken by the modernists and Dona Dodô without having consulted them.

As Dona Dodô had changed her mind concerning the switch in dates of the festival, she advised moderate leaders Zezé and Bárbara to schedule the mass and procession for Friday. For their part, José Vigário and the Lopes family announced that due to the confusion over the timing of the festival, they would sponsor their own festival in the hamlet of Batoque and totally boycott the celebration in Santa Brígida. Traditionalists, like Augustino Veloso (1974), did not miss the opportunity to draw together the two incidents: "So you see how it

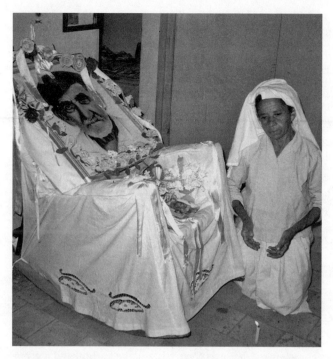

Romeira praying before the "throne" in Pedro Batista's home, 1974.
Photo by the author.

is here. The big families can even tamper with the Bible, changing the date of
São Pedro's birthday! And when my Padrinho [the Velho] wants to celebrate
his birthday and his festival in the city he founded, the Bible changers will not
permit it. It is the work of the Antichrist, pure and simple! And it is a sign of
the times that we must sit back powerless before such evil. But I do not worry,
because I have faith in my Padrinho and in the dawning of a new era."

The Velho's Surprise Visit

To the great astonishment of all of Santa Brígida's romeiros, Friday found the
Velho seated in the front of one of the pickup trucks from Pernambuco. The
truck stopped before Pedro Batista's home, and the seventy year old descended
and was led into the house. Immediately the large photo placed on Pedro Batista's chair was removed and the Velho was invited to be seated. Just as this was
about to happen, Dona Dodô rushed in and suggested that he sit on a nearby
bench in the parlor instead. The sheriff later took me aside and explained that

these had been his instructions to Dona Dodô at an earlier time when he had suspected that the Velho might attempt to attend the festival. "I knew if the Velho sat in my Padrinho's seat, there would be blood spilled. There are people here, including myself, who would not stand for such desecration" (João Santos 1974).

As Pedro Batista's house became inundated with romeiros seeking a blessing and counsel, Dona Dodô again interceded. This time she suggested that the Velho move to her home, which was less centrally located. For a few hours he remained there where he received a large number of visitors. These meetings were disturbed when the sheriff's assistant, Inácio Caetano, also a romeiro and husband of moderate leader Bárbara Santos, entered Dona Dodô's home and approached the Velho. While I did not personally observe this event, I spoke to Inácio about it and interviewed others who were in attendance. The exchange went something like this:

> Inácio: "I have come here as an official of the police to ask you, Sir, what is your name?"
> Velho: "My name is Pedro Batista da Silva, curador."
> Onlookers: "Glory be to God, it is my Padrinho." "Now the truth is finally out." "It is official."
> Inácio: "And when was it that you became Pedro Batista?"
> Velho: "I was resurrected some years ago."
> Inácio: "Well, there seems to be some confusion here over your identity, sir. I have a summons here from the sheriff ordering you and your sponsor in Santa Brígida to present yourselves tomorrow before the judge in Paulo Afonso."
> Velho: "Yes, sir" (Pessar, fieldnotes, 29 June 1974).

At Inácio's departure the Velho made his way to a bed and began to sob. Many romeiros rushed to him and also began to weep. One woman lamented, "They cannot do this to you, my Padrinho. This is your city. Something must be done before those Judases destroy our last chance." The Velho responded, "I am cold. I am dead" (ibid.).

As had occurred several years earlier, the Velho did leave the town but not the municipality. This time he was whisked off to Quarenta-e-dois and the home of Joaquim Lopes. When word reached the Lopes family and José Vigário, they quickly moved their festivities from Batoque to Quarenta-e-dois.

Meanwhile, as a group of romeiros congregated on the veranda of Pedro Batista's house sang a verse of "Happy Birthday" and gazed at a massive birthday cake baked to commemorate Batista's birthday, Zezé Ramos stepped for-

The Velho visits Santa Brígida during the 1974 São Pedro festival. Photo by the author.

ward. Rather than deliver his usual paean to their deceased leader, Zezé's voice crackled with anger and frustration. He stressed the troubling fact that three festivals were operating simultaneously on that day: "Those many so-called ro-meiros who are clustered around that old man, they flock to him, making their own festival and filling my Padrinho's heart with sorrow. There in heaven he looks down to see only a fraction of his flock assembled here at his home to honor him on his birthday. Some are with the Velho and others are in the main square, drinking, smoking, and dancing. We offer our prayers here today for all of those romeiros who are deceived; we pray that they see the error of their ways and return to the only true leader and guide, my Padrinho Pedro Batista da Silva, whom we honor here today" (1974).

For their part, the modernist politicians and merchants who had instigated the change in the dates of the festival were at once disturbed about the Velho's unexpected arrival in Santa Brígida, yet relieved that he had been whisked away from the town before the actual start of their Saturday festival. As one merchant explained a few days later, "Those fanatics who have come with the Velho, they are not the ones who make for a good festival. They never come into the main street to buy things and have fun. If the news had gotten out that the so-called Pedro Batista was here, people from Paulo Afonso and Jeremoabo would have stayed away. They would not have wanted to be associated with such fanaticism. And without the excitement and revenue these visitors bring, we will remain a backward town with no hope of moving forward" (Pedro da Costa 1974).

In discussing what was for most romeiros the very disturbing and controversial step of having a police official issue a warrant in Dona Dodô's house without having advised her beforehand, the mayor stated, "It was official business of the government; it had nothing to do with her. We did not want to implicate her in the matter. She has suffered enough" (Ricardo Barbosa 1974).

Some romeiros again experienced the long hand of the state on the Monday after the close of the festival, when the Velho returned to Inajá. This time Sheriff Santos approached Joaquim Lopes and told him to appear later in the day at the police station. Angry words were exchanged as Santos chided Lopes for harboring the Velho illegally within the municipality. Lopes countered that he had purchased the land with his own money and that it was his home. He added that the São Gonçalo church had been built solely by the Lopes family and was the property of the saint, not the government. Santos insisted that wherever the law was broken, the government had the right and duty to intervene.

In the end, the sheriff's and mayor's threats about bringing Lopes and others before authorities in Paulo Afonso never materialized. I never learned whether the talk of warrants was merely a form of intimidation or whether, as I and others had been assured, legal steps had been taken to charge the Velho as an impostor. Although I might have attempted to clarify this point through interviews in Paulo Afonso, I did not want to draw additional official attention to the matter. When I looked into it much later in 1999 and 2000, no documents were found in police or military archives in Paulo Afonso or Salvador, but these could easily have been discarded or destroyed as were so many documents dating back to the time of the military dictatorship.

Whether or not formal charges were actually being prepared at the time, I am confident that, as in the past, military officials remained in close contact with their informants in Santa Brígida as the Velho's visit unfolded. They may well have calculated that it was wiser for local authorities to use intimidation to persuade the Velho to leave the town peaceably than to actually serve a warrant for his arrest and potentially provoke violence within the romaria.

It was true that the Velho supporters were in the majority and might, under different circumstances, have wielded their electoral power to obtain concessions, as Batista had in the past. During the 1970s and into the early 1980s, however, this was not a viable option. In Santa Brígida, as in all of Brazil, the government's National Renewal Alliance party (ARENA) effectively stifled all opposition; as a result, all segments of the romaria voted for the ARENA candidates.

The Romaria and National Trends

In the 1970s most romeiros drew on biblical themes to account for the conflicts plaguing Santa Brígida. I, by contrast, saw larger structural forces at play. At that time national as well as more local trends in agrarian and industrial capitalism and in state building had significantly improved the lives of only a small segment of Santa Brígida's population. As illustrated by the ghostly detritus of broken-down machines and abandoned warehouses in colônia, neither state propaganda, nationalistic ceremonies, nor impressive public works could resolve a basic contradiction. Powerful capitalists and politicians remained committed only to transforming certain relations of production while keeping control over the nation's productive base and political future in the hands of a small elite. On the one hand, the social stratification, unequal patron-client relations, and mounting class-based antagonism in Santa Brígida were by-products of this larger contradiction. On the other hand, a more localized history of millenarian hopes and the tradition of resentment directed against perceived oppressors informed the particular way the community's poor and disenfranchised struggled against these cruel inequities.

To the outside observer, the controversy also underscored the limitations, incompleteness, and risks of the state's heady pledge to bring unity and progress to all its citizens regardless of class, region, or race. On one side of the divide was that small, upwardly mobile segment of romeiros and baianos who were beneficiaries of the larger national project. They tenaciously defended their gains. And, when feasible, they attempted to mollify their critics by reiterating the government's promises as well as repeating its pleas for order and patience. On the other side were the far more numerous citizens of Santa Brígida who clung to the hope of a better life—whether it be orchestrated by spiritual or secular forces.

Once the fight over the Velho gained in intensity, class divisions—which both romeiro and state ideologies sought to minimize—surfaced with a vengeance. So, too, did another "dirty secret," one regarding race. With Santa Brígida's rivals accusing their foes of resorting to dangerous acts of macumba, and in light of Pedro Batista's and the church's denouncements of such Afro-Brazilian religious practices, the morality of the accused was publicly besmirched. A few incensed moderates went further still, by stressing the dark skin and African ancestry of certain of their traditionalist nemeses. As Zé Albino Sousa charged, "Of course, Maria has used macumba against me. All of her family are macumbeiros; just look at the black color of their skin. They're an evil race of people" (Pessar, fieldnotes, 10 June 1977). It should be noted that Pedro Batista avoided reference to the gradations of pigmentation within his romaria that ranged from extremely fair to dark-skinned. Rather, he most often referred to an individual romeiro or to the collectivity as "caboclo/s." This referred to a mixed-race group composed predominantly of the descendants of Europeans and native Brazilians, capturing the phenotype of the majority of his followers as well as the larger sertanejo population. It also conformed to spiritist beliefs that the indigenous are the most spiritually pure. It is a testament to the heatedness and seriousness of the Velho affair that ordinarily submerged racist sentiments were publicly aired.

At the close of the São Pedro festival and for several years after, the romeiros with whom I spoke and corresponded insisted that the internal rifts created by the Velho controversy had irrevocably destroyed any hope of continued unity and shared mission within the romaria. They pointed as confirming evidence to Dona Dodô's decision to spend ever more protracted periods of time in Juazeiro and to the fact that many refused to participate in nightly romeiro prayer services. The phrase I often heard uttered was, "*a romaria se acabou*" (the romaria is over). Nonetheless, as time went on hard feelings over the handling of the Velho's visit faded. Many apparently found his journey through the sacralizing process ultimately unconvincing. Unlike the leaders considered in chapter 2, the Velho offered lackluster sacralizing performances. Moreover, he could claim no mystery regarding his family; indeed, his critics reviled him for fathering an illegitimate son. Finally, he failed to attract advocates like João Oliveira and Dona Dodô who might have embedded his experiences into a larger folk Catholic, narrative tradition. Nonetheless, some of the still faithful resigned themselves to making periodic trips to visit him in Inajá. And until the Velho's death in the mid-1990s, the most zealous among the traditionalists continued to harbor the hope that he might yet regain his rightful place at the head of the romaria, punish the wayward among them, and set the romaria even more firmly on its millennial mission.

Like the romeiros, over the course of the 1970s and 1980s I worried about the future of the romaria. I suspected that its days as a unified spiritual community were numbered, if not already over. I also believed that its future would be largely determined by how the Velho controversy and related problems of political succession and socioeconomic stratification were managed. Yet, as it has turned out, matters of generational continuity and the growth of modern-ist sensibilities within the romaria have over time proved equally, if not more, determinative and vexing. A generation gap was apparent even during Pedro Batista's declining years, and since then the struggle to convince the young to adhere to the strict romeiro tenets has only intensified. Moderate and tradition-alist parents have found themselves contending with alternative discourses in the schools, in the media (television came to Santa Brígida in 1978), and in the church (the first resident priest arrived in the early 1990s). Moreover, as elderly traditionalists and moderates died, it became increasingly difficult to find ro-meiros with the moral stature and interest to replace the pioneers within the confraternities and, more generally, within the religious life of the romaria.

Some years back, then, it might have seemed perfectly appropriate to con-clude that the romaria would last only as long as those members who had per-sonally known Pedro Batista and had fully embraced the antiga lei were able to assemble to recite their nightly rosaries, sing their own benditos, and honor the memory of Pedro Batista. Their children and grandchildren, it appeared, were fully imbricated in projects of modernity and nationalism within which santos and concerns about the impending apocalypse were alien. The picture is not, however, so simple or modernist in design. Rather, it is certain second-generation romeiro modernists who, with the help of the state, are attempting to revitalize and validate romeiro history and "culture."

CHAPTER SEVEN

CONSTITUTING THE ROMEIROS

INTO "TRADITIONAL" FOLK

In his day Pedro Batista managed to gain state and federal support by both hiding transgressive folk Catholic practices from public view and embracing elements of the dominant discourse of economic development and national progress. By contrast, many of today's younger romeiro leaders proudly display Santa Brígida's folk Catholic traditions and millenarian history. They do so mindful of the current elite projects aimed at preserving "folk" practices lest they be obliterated by "homogenizing" forces of urbanization and globalization. In an ironic recasting of history, state authorities and members of the media contend that valuable, "traditional" cultural practices still exist in Santa Brígida due to the community's long "isolation." This latest representation of Santa Brígida as an isolated backwater effectively erases earlier narratives that portrayed Pedro Batista and Santa Brígida as extremely well connected to and in step with a modernizing Brazilian nation.[1]

Not surprisingly, the romeiros are once again struggling among themselves and with outsiders over matters of representation. Entering into this mix is a new and powerful rhetoric that contains phrases like "cultural rescue," "national patrimony," and "social memory." When state officials personally exhort the romeiros to engage in cultural rescue and to preserve social memory for the general good of the nation, those very demands raise unsettling matters; principal among these is who best and most authoritatively speaks for the romaria. From a more removed, analytical stance, there is also a question of the continuing viability of folk Catholicism as a culture of resistance now that representatives of the state and church have come to celebrate many of its features and practitioners.

In another dramatic twist, as the national and state governments have invested more heavily in recent years in tourism, millenarian communities like Juazeiro, Canudos, and Santa Brígida have suddenly found themselves at a distinct advantage. Consequently, Santa Brígida has been declared a promising site for religious tourism, a development that several young romeiro leaders support enthusiastically, while elderly romeiros have reacted far more cautiously. Once again, Juazeiro and Canudos serve as models against which Santa Brígida's past is reconstituted and its future as a destination of tourism debated and crafted.

A Romeiro Leader for the New Millennium

The romeiro who is most engaged in these new developments and embroiled in the accompanying controversies is Antônio Farias. He is a young man with boundless enthusiasm and a smile to match who until recently served as Santa Brígida's vice mayor. His story is fascinating in several respects. Not since the time of Pedro Batista has there been a romeiro leader more adept than Antônio Farias in developing a discourse about Santa Brígida and proposing local projects to government officials that reflect larger political agendas. Moreover, Farias is another example of a prominent romeiro who, in the pursuit of specific political and social goals, has appropriated and directed to his own ends the presence of researchers and earlier scholarly works on the romaria.[2] Thus, while elsewhere, many subaltern subjects have recently challenged the authority and goals of past and prospective research, in today's Santa Brígida scholars are given honorary citizenship and encouraged to pursue further studies.

ANTÔNIO FARIAS'S YOUTH
Antônio Farias was born on 1 September 1965 in a rural hamlet in Mata Grande, Alagoas. His maternal grandparents were loyal devotees of Padre Cícero, and they were among the first in their community to acknowledge and follow Pedro Batista. They often visited the beato in jail in neighboring Águas Belas, and while Farias's grandparents never settled in Santa Brígida, over the years they made twenty-seven pilgrimages on foot. Many of their relatives did relocate, however, including a sister, children, and grandchildren.

Since Batista was already quite ill at the time of Farias's birth, his parents

The vice mayor and his family, 1998. Photo by Amy Chazkel.

decided to baptize him locally in Mata Grande. Nonetheless, when the toddler was two years old, his mother took him to Santa Brígida to have his name confirmed. "She brought me here, and he was on a hammock. He held me and said Antônio was a good name" (1999).

According to Farias, his mother had long received spirits, and she suffered greatly until she was able to control them, thanks in part to the assistance of curers in Santa Brígida. A highly religious woman, she imparted a love of prayer to her young son. "I used to know a lot," he reported, "I knew the *ofício* (religious service), which is very long. . . . I knew it all. One night I was late and my mother did not wait for me; she prayed alone. She said I was so sad I cried all night long" (1999).

When the boy was seven years old, his aunt Rosa Farias, who had no children of her own, requested that he live with her in Santa Brígida. Farias's parents agreed. Initially the youngster fit right in with the demanding religious life of the romaria. In fact, he was acknowledged to be so gifted that he even prayed over "some more powerful people in Paulo Afonso" (1999) who were friends of his aunt. Yet like so many of his romeiro peers, as he got older, Farias (1999) reports, "I distanced myself from the romaria. I lost interest."

In other significant ways, however, Farias was quite different from the others in his romeiro cohort. Since his aunt also had a home in Paulo Afonso and the schools were better there, he was educated in that city. Later he attended university in Salvador. To his family's great dismay, Farias dropped out of the university shortly before he was to graduate, and he married a young woman from São Paulo. After working in several jobs including as a teacher of English and Portuguese, Farias returned in the early 1990s to Santa Brígida, where he became involved in politics. After serving as a town councilman, in 1994 he assumed the office of vice mayor in 1994 under his aunt, Rosa Farias. She was then serving her second term as mayor.

FARIAS MEETS FOLKLORIST TITUS RIEDL

Referring to his early years as town councilman, Farias (1999) recalls, "I had ideas, but not yet in terms of history and cultural rescue. I did not see it as something that would benefit Santa Brígida or renew it." This changed in the mid-1990s when he first met German folklorist Titus Riedl. The latter had learned of Santa Brígida while conducting research on the cultural practices of the Pankararus, an indigenous group whose members had ties to Pedro Batista, Dona Dodô, and the Velho. This is how Farias (1999) speaks of his early encounter with Riedl.

> This is why I love foreigners. It was because of a foreigner that I became interested in all of this. I always tell Titus, he is the German who came from Ceará. The faith and the cultural practices continued to take place, but I did not notice them or pay attention. Titus was doing this work here. I would chat with him. Many times I would call him to come to Paulo Afonso with me and he would say no. I would say, "You should come. There is going to be a good party and I'll show you around." He would say, "No, I can't go to Paulo Afonso because I have to go to the cemetery late at night to see the Penitents." I would think about the fact that he was young and able to go out . . . but he preferred to go see the Penitents. . . . This was a European from a developed country saying that. . . . I gradually got interested. I went to the cemetery with him a few times. . . . It was after Titus that it all came back to me. The emotion of understanding my history, my roots. . . . Titus was the opening of a new horizon for me.

A REENGAGEMENT WITH MARIA ISAURA PEREIRA
DE QUEIROZ AND THE RESEARCH TEAM FROM
THE UNIVERSITY OF SÃO PAULO

As it turned out, the folklorist was not the only academic to have refocused Antônio's attention on the romaria. Coincidentally, while he was still pondering Riedl's interest in Os Penitentes, a romeiro shared with him a long-guarded copy of Pereira de Queiroz's book on the Dance of São Gonçalo, *Sociologia e Fol-*

clore. According to Farias (1999), "The São Gonçalo book helped me, because I had not seen any importance in those practices."

Riedl also informed Farias that he had heard that a film had been shot in Santa Brígida soon before Batista's death. Farias (1999) claims to have "really become fanatic" on learning about that possibility. He asked Riedl, who was coincidentally traveling to São Paulo for a conference, to try to meet with Pereira de Queiroz to learn more about the film. Reidl had a successful meeting with the sociologist in which he ascertained that the film did indeed exist, and he obtained the name and address of filmmaker, Sérgio Muniz. Farias followed up that eventful meeting with a letter to Queiroz in which he included "a motion from the town council thanking her for everything she had done," and further requesting the names and addresses of the other University of São Paulo (USP) scholars who had conducted research in Santa Brígida.

Having received this information, Farias corresponded with these scholars, as well. He invited them to visit Santa Brígida as honored guests, informed them of his plans to create a museum and documentation center, and he solicited copies of their work. As is evident from the correspondence, most researchers responded warmly to the communication renewed after more than three decades. Those who could also sent copies of their past work on Santa Brígida.

How very different from Pedro Batista was this young leader's disposition to the academy. Consider Batista's 1958 correspondence to a USP scholar who apparently asked for the beato's cooperation in filling out a questionnaire, the findings of which were necessary for a book he was writing. Batista recuses himself by explaining, "I do not have time to take away from my innumerable duties; but more important, I am not enthusiastic about studies on cultural matters" (Pedro Batista da Silva Papers). Two contradictory epistemologies collide here. One suspects that Batista's refusal was strongly influenced by the scholars' use of a survey instrument and his choice of the word *culture*. The researcher required Batista's compliance in converting into scientific "data" phenomena that the beato knew to be nonquantifiable faith and divine calling. By contrast, Farias recognizes that today the romeiros' folk beliefs and practices represent valuable cultural capital (Bourdieu 1986). He seeks the collaboration of scholars to help him reproduce and "advertise" these cultural commodities within Brazil and beyond.

THE RETURN OF THE RESEARCHER FROM O ESTRANGEIRO

As Farias went about his task of reestablishing connections with academics who had conducted research in Santa Brígida, he felt a bit stymied. No one seemed to have an address for Patricia Pessar, the young woman he had recalled seeing in Santa Brígida as a child and whom older romeiros claimed "had become a romeira" (Antônio Farias 1999) after living so long in their midst. While Farias pondered how he might somehow reconnect with me, my own thoughts of Santa Brígida intensified as the new millennium approached and I realized that I had been out of touch for more than ten years. I recalled the refrain I had last heard in Santa Brígida twenty years earlier, "*A mil e tanto chegará, a dois mil não chegará ou passará*" (the year 1,000-and-some will arrive, 2,000 will neither come nor be completed). Unaware of Farias's mission to reconnect with scholars, I myself set out to reestablish contact by writing a letter addressed to the mayor's office. Little did I know that the letter would be read by Mayor Rosa Farias. It was Rosa who years earlier, while visiting from Paulo Afonso in her capacity as a nurse, had been dispatched to my sick bed by Dona Dodô. At that time she immediately diagnosed my hepatitis and arranged for my hospitalization in Paulo Afonso. Declaring that my letter was a "miracle," Rosa immediately shared it with Antônio and instructed him to respond with haste.

He did so, and to my amazement a few weeks later a box postmarked from Brazil was delivered to my office at Yale University. It was brimming with letters, old pictures of me and the home I had lived in, a copy of the Muniz video (which I had never seen), a more recent video produced by a Bahian educational television station, and copies of scholarly works on Santa Brígida written by my predecessors. As Antônio had hoped, this was all the hook I needed to begin to make plans to return to Santa Brígida as soon as possible.

As I proceeded with these plans I was astounded at how time-space compression managed to bring Santa Brígida literally into my home. Not only could I conveniently watch videos of Santa Brígida on my VCR, but I also received numerous phone calls from Antônio filling me in on events in Santa Brígida—this from a locale that in the mid-1970s had had few homes with electricity, no telephones, no televisions, no running water, and that urban Brazilians had referred to jokingly as *o fim do mundo* (the end of the earth). Moreover, Antônio was dialing direct to a place which most of his fellow romeiros had formerly considered so remote and othered that they merely called it, *o estrangeiro* (the "foreign" or "alien" place). Yet now, rather than being bewildered or awed by this faraway place, Antônio responded enthusiastically when I informed him that I had shown the videos he had sent to Portuguese-speaking students at Yale. In a postmodern flourish he responded, "With you and your students, Santa Brígida has crossed the frontiers." While in the 1970s some romeiros constructed me as a figure who had crossed a celestial frontier, in 1999 Antônio and other local politicians praised me in speeches as "a First World scholar" who was willing to leave the comforts of home to live among the romeiros.

This "sacrifice," they informed their audiences, revealed how truly important romeiro culture and history are, even for foreigners like Titus Riedl and me (Pessar, fieldnotes, June–August 1999).

Sérgio Muniz "Brings Back" Padrinho Pedro

If my return proved moving and eventful for many of the romeiros, so too did a brief visit in 1997 by filmmaker Sérgio Muniz. At that time he showed his 1967 film for the first time in Santa Brígida and was accorded the title of honorary citizen of the town. As Antônio's assessment of that event conveys, already by 1997 the vice mayor saw his role in reconstructing and preserving the romaria's past in highly political and contested terms as did his political rivals.

> There was a ceremony, and we were going to explain to the people how he got the title [of honorary citizen]. The way we explained it was by showing the film to the romeiros. You can't imagine the reaction. . . . After thirty-one years the romeiros were seeing their Padrinho again and hearing him speak. They couldn't believe it. Some would come and ask us about it, because our political opponents said it was false, that we had set it up. Many didn't believe it; they thought I had somehow made the whole thing up. But then as they watched, they saw themselves when they were younger, and they saw it was true. . . . To me speaking as a politician, bringing this film back to the community was a great achievement. (1999)[3]

When Farias first contacted Muniz in 1997, he was thrilled to learn that the filmmaker had long harbored the desire to return to Santa Brígida to make a sequel. This matched perfectly with the vice mayor's plan to have the story of the beato and his romeiros disseminated widely throughout Brazil and abroad. Unfortunately Muniz proved unsuccessful in obtaining the considerable funding needed for such a project; yet Farias persevered. Fired up by the idea of a sequel, the vice mayor took advantage of his own political connections, and through the mediation of federal senator Paulo Magalães a meeting was arranged between Farias and the head of Bahia's educational television station, IRDEB.

Pedro Batista: The Counselor Who Succeeded

Although Farias did not know it at the time, the project he was pitching was ideally suited to the philosophy and objectives of the station's new initiative entitled *Bahia singulareplural* (Bahia Singular and Plural). As the name suggests, the statewide and state-funded project aimed, through a series of documentaries and CDs, to produce a *mapeamento cultural* (cultural mapping) of the entire state. The station's director and project manager, Paolo Marconi (1999), indicated that by 1999 they had "recorded 150 cultural productions in approximately 30 towns." And he added, "There is going to be a database of memory that has never existed in any state."

Marconi and his team are proceeding with a sense of urgency, since they believe they are working against powerful forces of globalization and commodification. "My vision is that today popular culture is losing its value due to the homogenization of culture and its products. There is the imposition of a consumer ideology and the market is valued above everything. . . . Our idea is to give a voice to those who don't have one." They reason that by recording and/or filming rural cultural traditions and making these accessible to a broader and more urban audience, they will enhance the esteem of those individuals who are struggling to maintain these traditions and who may, in turn, interest the next generation in sustaining these cultural forms. While Marconi acknowledged that *Bahia singulareplural* might ultimately encourage tourism, he claimed this "may be a consequence [rather than an intention of the project]. . . . I think tourism changes and distorts cultural manifestations," he cautioned.

Paolo Marconi smiled when he recalled the meeting with Antônio that he had reluctantly agreed to a few years back at the behest of the senator. Marconi had never heard of Santa Brígida, and he suspected that the vice mayor was coming in pursuit of a television tower, a request that lay outside his jurisdiction. What Marconi did not know was that the vice mayor was a man on a mission, and he came well armed with research materials, visuals, and his own infectious enthusiasm. According to Marconi, "When he came in he had a bunch of things, a tape, books, I really like those things. I thought, he is bringing something; usually people come here to take something."

Evident in Marconi's decision to make a film about the history and cultural practices of the contemporary romaria is the ongoing impact of the academy on how Santa Brígida is represented and re-represented. Marconi admitted to having been impressed by the former research presence of leading USP scholars, and he was especially heartened by the Muniz film, which would permit visual comparisons. The last key element that entered into his decision was the fact that, on Zezé Ramos's insistence, the romaria was itself attending to matters of social memory. The town was planning a thirty-year commemoration of Pedro Batista's death for November 1997. The procession/pilgrimage from colônia to the center of the town would form the centerpiece of the IRDEB film.

The two films, IRDEB's *Pedro Batista: O conselheiro que deu certo* (Pedro Batista:

The Counselor Who Succeeded) and Muniz's *O povo do velho Pedro*, are intriguing in how they choose to situate their subject matter with respect to earlier millenarian movements. The older film begins with footage of Padre Cícero, explains that the Pedro Batista movement is very much allied to this earlier movement, and mentions the reincarnation motif. Although the second film also treats Padre Cícero, the comparison between Antônio Conselheiro and Pedro Batista is urged from the very moment the subtitle, "The Counselor Who Succeeded," is flashed on the screen. No doubt the decision by the IRDEB crew to reference Canudos and Conselheiro was influenced by the fact that both movements occurred in Bahia state and that their film was financed by Bahian taxpayers and intended primarily for a Bahian audience. Moreover, the filming coincided with the highly publicized and well-commemorated 100th anniversary of Canudos—an event that one opinion maker called "with certainty a major fragment of National Identity and, therefore, one that has to be appropriated by all" (Fialho 1997). It is likely that the subsequent decisions by other television stations in the country (including the major station O Globo) to air IRDEB's film on the beato of Santa Brígida—a messianic leader whose career the filmmakers made sure to juxtapose against Conselheiro's—reflects the centrality of Canudos within the national imaginary.

The film's title was actually suggested by Santa Brígida's mayor and vice mayor. Both are extremely proud of the fact that, unlike the "radical" Conselheiro, their Padrinho had the good sense to forge political alliances with a backlands boss who was able to protect him and his followers. Indeed the mayor told a journalist, "Pedro Batista is the Counselor who actually succeeded. If the one who acted wrongly made history, imagine ours" ("Via Sacra de um beato em terras de Lampião," *Via Bahia*, July 1998, p. 38). The mayor's statement was featured in a magazine published by Bahia state's ministry of culture and tourism. Clearly, in her comparison between the two leaders and their respective histories, Rosa Farias was sending a message to state officials, who had recently poured large sums of money into the restoration and commemoration of Canudos. Santa Brígida's mayor was urging those authorities "to get it right" by turning their attention to a millenarian leader who had *cooperated* with local and state officials.

While the mayor based her pitch on Batista's clear willingness to accommodate to the prevailing power structure, the academy had for some time elected to praise figures like Conselheiro for their daring resistance. The vice mayor found this a bitter pill to swallow, when during a government-funded, regional seminar he had helped organize, the scholars invidiously compared "the heroic" Conselheiro to Pedro Batista, whom they derided as a sellout. A highly disturbed Farias vowed that in the ongoing battle over how history gets constructed, he would not be blindsided again. Rather, he stated that he would bring his own cadre of scholars, including Titus Riedl, to all subsequent seminars. That this criticism was leveled at all and that Farias was unable to deflect it, reflects the fact that many scholars, as well as younger romeiros, have yet to appreciate the religious resistance, defense of folk practices, and alternative modernity that Pedro Batista and Dona Dodô orchestrated so effectively in Santa Brígida.

The current discourse of "cultural rescue" suggests that documentaries are dedicated solely to rescuing the past before it is forgotten. Yet, such symbolic representations also affect how history is remembered and understood, thus influencing how the past will be carried into the future. These points were clearly brought home to me when I returned to Santa Brígida in 1999. I recall having heard only one or two references to Antônio Conselheiro while I resided in Santa Brígida in the 1970s, and these were voiced by baianos. By contrast, Padre Cícero was ever present. He was central to the histories the romeiros told about Pedro Batista and their decision to follow him. He was present in benditos, in ritual practices that included special prayer services held each month on the date of his passing, and in frequent pilgrimages to Juazeiro. And he was prominent in local iconography, which featured his statue outside the romeiro church, at the entrance of the beato's home, and in home altars. There was nary a mention of Antônio Conselheiro in either the 1974 or 1977 São Pedro festivals I attended.

Yet, a quarter of a century later, local and visiting dignitaries repeatedly compared Batista positively to Conselheiro. For example, in a speech, ex-mayor Joaquim Teixeira (1999) stated, "While in Canudos many romeiros died, here we had *ordem e progresso* ["order and progress," the motto on the Brazilian flag]. . . . Today Pedro Batista is known in all Brazil as the 'counselor who succeeded.' " Intriguingly, this point of comparison has also made its way into the lyrics of verses sung by certain local folkloric groups. This change in narration—in concert with the youth's far greater exposure to Canudos than Juazeiro in their school curricula—may mean that in the future Antônio Conselheiro will come to rival Padre Cícero in the retelling of local history.

The making and showing of the IRDEB film, however, had a far more immediate impact on how Pedro Batista is socially constructed and remembered. Shortly after the documentary was aired in Southern Brazil, the mayor's office received a letter from a woman in the state of Paraná. It stated that her elderly mother had viewed the film and that she strongly suspected that Batista was her long-lost uncle. The letter not only cast doubt on accounts of Batista's childhood in the Northeast, but it also implied that the beato had living relatives. While the vice mayor was thrilled by this new, unfolding chapter in the romaria's history and proud of his role in bringing it to light, there were many who did not share his enthusiasm. It will be recalled that the lack of biological kinship is a feature that both characterized the mistério of Padre Cícero and Pedro Batista and served to authenticate their status as santos among their devotees. Elderly romeiros were so deeply disturbed by the news of possible kin that they simply refused to accept its veracity. Moreover, for some this development served as further proof of the generally misguided nature of the vice mayor's cultural politics. Farias (1999) was nonplused as he observed, "Some people who are more ignorant think none of this is worth it, but I was once like that and I understand how they think. The great treasure of Santa Brígida is its history. . . . We can't get attention for Santa Brígida through its many problems: no sewage, no hospital, no doctor, no emergency unit. But when you speak about Pedro Batista and the history, people pay attention."

The municipality's mayor and vice mayor were confident that in the new millennium Santa Brígida's extraordinary cultural capital would distinguish it in the eyes of state and national leaders. And they trusted that the latter would prove more receptive when municipal leaders approached them for much-needed revenues, public works, and services.

Journalists' New Narration of Santa Brígida and Its Romaria

As Farias grew ever more certain that the kind of history and culture captured in the two films represented Santa's Brígida's strategic edge over other poor and remote Bahian municipalities, he added print journalists to his ranks of outside allies and collaborators. Accordingly, Farias made sure to cultivate relationships with those journalists working for major Bahian state newspapers and for local publishers in Paulo Afonso. He invited them to cover religious events, folkloric performances, the inauguration of state-funded public works linked to tourism, and the arrival of researchers, including my research assistants and myself ("Municípios," A Tarde, 27 October 1998, p. 4; "Municípios," A Tarde, 25 June 1999, p. 2).

Farias scored a coup when a highly flattering article entitled "Via Sacra de um beato em terras de Lampião" (A Beato's Via Sacra in the Land of Lampião) appeared in 1998 in the ministry of culture and tourism's magazine Via Bahia. The article includes a sidebar, reminiscent of the New York Times travel section, in which under the headline "Festivals the Entire Year" a calendar of religious and folkloric events is presented for each month of the year (July 1998, pp. 38–39).

So different from the discourse of newspaper articles written in the 1940s, 1950s, or 1960s, a typical headline from the late 1990s reads "Santa Brígida Transforms into a Center of Religiosity" ("A caminhada de Santa Brígida," *A Tarde*, 14 November 1998, p. 11). And an article written about a procession to commemorate the thirty-first anniversary of the death of Pedro Batista includes such passages as: "[It is] a white, clean, and mystical city in the northern corner of Bahia. . . . It represents well that other Bahia, the Bahian sertão, with little African influence. . . . Santa Brígida, like Canudos and Bom Jesus da Lapa, contains the mystical marrow, residue of old medieval sertanejo religious practices linked to Iberian Catholic cults. . . . Through the mystical inheritance of its counselor, the communitarian organization, and religious tourism, Santa Brígida will forge ahead with its integrated and sustainable local development" (*A Tarde*, 19 November 1998, p. 8).

In previous decades the brand of folk Catholicism found in Santa Brígida had been understood by politicians and journalists alike as an obstacle to rural development. Earlier still, the sertanejos' mysticism had been branded fanaticism and attributed to unhealthy racial mixing. By contrast, articles like this one now deemed sertanejo religious practices as attractive to tourists and a means to attain prosperity. Moreover, the rhetoric contributed to that discursive move whereby sertanejos are whitened and socially elevated through their purported ancestral ties to Europe rather than Africa.

Bahia: The Cradle of Brazilian Civilization

Like his Padrinho, Antônio Farias's political career depended on and was greatly spurred by receptive officials in the state and national governments. As exemplified in the assertion by Marinaldo Melo (1999), an official of the Bahian ministry of culture and tourism that Bahia is "the cradle of Brazilian civilization," baianos in general and Bahian state officials in particular have long taken pride in Bahian culture. In searching for the origins of world-renowned traditions in art, music, literature, and dance, Melo suggested that it was "something inherent" in the Bahian people, perhaps fostered by "miscegenation." It was not until 1991, however, that the state government adopted a more pragmatic and interventionist approach to culture, according to Melo. "During other time periods, culture was always revered as something interesting, necessary for social well-being and quality of life. But it was never treated as an economic factor that could bring or add economic benefits, increase income, jobs, and so on, so that with its multiplier effect it could improve everybody's lives, even those who don't work with or get involved with culture" (ibid.).

A crucial step toward increasing such economic benefits occurred in 1995, when the government branch dedicated to cultural matters was moved from the ministry of education and culture to the newly organized ministry of culture and tourism. Explaining the rationale for this move, Melo (1999) continued, "These fundamental changes happened when the government realized that Bahia has strong roots, both with respect to tourism and culture, that both could serve each other reciprocally, so each could develop even more. This is what happened, this model is being implemented. And we feel today that there is an increase in the number of tourists that is a result of induced cultural development. And the reverse is also true; the cultural goods of Bahia are being consumed in greater quantity as the number of tourists increases."[4]

To move forward with its new project, the newly constituted ministry required each municipality in the state to complete a highly detailed cultural census. To ensure that Santa Brígida put its best foot forward, the mayor created the post of secretary of culture with the hope that Titus Riedl would serve as the municipality's first appointee. Although the folklorist declined that position, he did agree to serve briefly as cultural attaché. In this latter capacity, Riedl took the lead in responding to the questionnaire the state distributed for its cultural census. At the same time, he took a proactive stance and sketched out preliminary plans for several cultural/touristic projects.

Antônio Farias, too, seized the moment. He used his connections with officials of the ruling party in Salvador to arrange a meeting with the secretary of the ministry of culture and tourism. At that reunion the vice mayor presented several projects outlined earlier by Riedl, and he was invited to submit a formal proposal to the ministry. Farias leaped at the offer, and in September 1997 he and the mayor proposed that the ministry support and fund a project entitled "Memorial to a Beato."

Remarkably, in the 1950s and again in the 1970s the romaria seemed to receive and to welcome a scholar whose epistemological approach to her subject matter could be well accommodated to—if not, in fact, subtly shaped by—her romeiro "subjects." This clearly happened again in the 1990s. Folklorist Titus Riedl arrived in Santa Brígida at just that moment when local leaders were searching for ways to distinguish their municipality from other equally needy ones, and when officials in Bahia state and the nation were rethinking the value of the "folk" and seeking to better develop the tourist industry. What differentiates the current dialectic between the romaria and the academy from earlier engagements is that younger romeiro leaders like Rosa Farias and Antônio Farias are far more cosmopolitan than their predecessors. Consequently, whenever possible they have attempted to position themselves in an equal or collaborative relationship with interested academics. This was in evidence when they offered Riedl a position in their administration and when Antônio graciously agreed to help me locate a publisher for my book in Brazil.

The proposal the mayor and vice mayor submitted to the ministry of culture and tourism not only faithfully presented the list of new initiatives Riedl had outlined for Santa Brígida during his brief stint as cultural attaché, but it also employed the language of social memory and resistance. Although the stamp of folklorist Riedl was clearly evident, it was the astuteness of the mayor and vice mayor in embracing this language that is most noteworthy, for such terminology was well beyond the bounds of the everyday rhetoric with which they spoke about Pedro Batista, Dona Dodô, and the romaria. For example, the petitioners stated that in the past Santa Brígida had captured the attention of major Brazilian scholars but that after the death of Batista "the phenomena of messianism was almost completely forgotten by the public at large. Nonetheless, without being acknowledged, the principal cultural manifestations and religious 'institutions' endured" thanks in large part to "the spirit of resistance" evinced by "the figure of Madrinha Dodô . . . viewed by many romeiros as a true 'saint.' " In addition to requesting a museum "in honor of Pedro Batista and the romeiros," the mayor and vice mayor proposed the establishment of a documentation center to study Northeastern messianic movements; the construction of an auditorium in which to show videos and perform cultural works; and a commitment to train local artisans in craft production. They concluded their proposal by framing its objectives with an eye both to converting Santa Brígida into a tourist center, since "this municipality is one of the richest places for traditional folklore and popular festivals in Bahia," and to "preserv[ing it] for the public patrimony" (Local Tourism Files, Mayoral Archives, Santa Brígida, Bahia).

References to Batista's political leadership and to the community's impressive economic growth during the 1950s and 1960s were totally absent from the proposal. These accomplishments, so praised in times past, were also largely absent from the actual project the ministry of culture and tourism ultimately implemented. For example, Antônio Farias later suggested that government officials include the renovation of the central plaza of the colônia—the space showcased in the documentary *Um canto de esperança*—in their overall project, "Memorial of a Beato." The officials politely declined. Instead, the way in which state authorities had come to envision Santa Brígida, its beato, and the romaria is nicely captured in a recent document prepared by officials engaged in the museum initiative.

With cultural institutions such as the museum and library, the town of Santa Brígida now offers its inhabitants and tourists its history, which preserves the legacy of the beato Pedro Batista. The town also has the church of São Pedro, monuments honoring the patron of the town, Padre Cícero Romão, and Madrinha Dodô; and it is warmed by the hospitality of its inhabitants. The several cultural practices of the romaria in the Serra do Galeão, which involve romeiros from several places in the Northeast, act as proof of the sertanejo faith. This will certainly promote religious tourism in this town as in Juazeiro do Norte (CE), Bom Jesus da Lapa (BA), Aparecida do Norte (SP), Fatima/Portugal, and Santiago de Compostela/Spain, which would benefit the development of Santa Brígida. (February 2000 Report, Local Tourism Files, Mayoral Archives, Santa Brígida, Bahia)

Clearly the vice mayor's dogged determination and skill in advocating on behalf of his community has been rewarded. Indeed, over the course of the late 1990s the Bahian state government allocated some R$54,000 (U.S.$41,500) for a variety of cultural and touristic ventures in Santa Brígida. At the same time, Farias also participated in federally funded workshops on tourist development, and he even managed to arrange for the members of the Dance of São Gonçalo to accompany him as folkloric performers at a meeting dedicated to tourism in the capital of Brasília. Moreover, Farias succeeded in getting Santa Brígida certified by the federal government as a location worthy of domestic and external investment in tourism.

Celebrating Difference and Appealing to Nostalgia for a Rural Past

In the latest engagement between state agents and the romaria, the latter enjoy far greater freedom to practice cultural forms once branded as dysfunctional and dangerous. How strikingly different is the contemporary moment from the past. Today's Bahian state and federal governments seek to "preserve" culture and social memory in rural communities like Santa Brígida. Regional elites in the late 1930s and early 1940s viewed a wandering beato like Pedro Batista and pilgrims who practiced vigorous, penitential acts in preparation for the apocalypse as artifacts of a sertanejo past that they sought to put well behind them. In doing so, they had multiple aims. These included the desire to change the image of the Northeast as a region that was backward and prone to religious fanaticism into one that was compatible with a nation whose motto was "order and progress." Feelings of embarrassment and defensiveness about sertanejo history and culture likely encouraged a segment of the regional elite to embrace Vargas's strong centralizing imperative. Indeed around the time that Pedro Batista was being denounced as retrograde by regional journalists and jailed as an undesirable character, national unification was being dramatically symbolized in the burning of all state flags in a public ceremony in Rio de Janeiro, then Brazil's capital (Oliven 2000, 131).

The history of the romaria parallels and reflects a larger regional and national history stretching from this earlier period of consolidation to a contemporary Brazil that for several decades has been well integrated from the perspective of national markets, mass communication, telecommunications, and road networks. In the 1960s, during the unifying phase, Pedro Batista showed himself to be an enthusiastic participant in several dimensions of this state initiative, as well as complicit in removing local and regional folk Catholic practices from wider "public" view. With the end of military control in the mid-1980s and the emergence of a unified, modern, and urbanized nation-state, politicians and other segments of the Brazilian elite found themselves prepared to engage and even celebrate difference within Brazil. It is within just such a context that pictorial images of Santa Brígida's romaria have found a place within the national imaginary. For example, photographs of one of the recent celebrations to commemorate Pedro Batista's death (the caminhada) were included among those items featured in São Paulo's *Mostra do Redescobrimento* (A Representation of the Rediscovery), the largest exhibit of Brazilian art ever assembled to commemorate the nation's 500 years since the arrival of the Portuguese. Of course the very act by which the state and its agents affirm difference and afford it a place within the nation can be viewed as a form of cooptation which effectively narrows those social and cultural spaces available for the creation and maintenance of counterhegemonic subjectivities, beliefs, and practices.

In addition to this celebration of difference within the national imaginary, other factors associated with urbanization and nostalgia further contribute to newfound interest in locales like Santa Brígida. Although TV Bahia's Paolo Marconi may speak about using the media to encourage pride in local Bahian cultural practices and to promote their preservation, the actual producers of these traditions are not lacking in strong local and regional identities. What they do lack is the money and technology (e.g., CD players and VCRs) to consume the documentary CDs and videocassettes that IRDB has created. Whether one speaks of regional Brazilian identities constituted around the sertanejo's Northeast, the state of Bahia's multiple cultures (i.e., *Bahia singulareplural*) or the Gaúcho's Rio Grande do Sul—these largely appeal to and are marketed to those urban Brazilians who maintain a nostalgia for a form of rural life that has become a thing of the past for them (Oliven 2000). These individuals also fear that the penetration of mass culture into rural areas will soon eradicate their objects of nostalgic desire.

Santa Brígida's 2000 São Pedro celebration exemplified a successful partnership: it was forged between state representatives who endeavored to capture and retain regional/rural difference and local leaders who embraced this elite project as their own.

The 2000 São Pedro Festival and Its Inaugurations

Three short years after the mayor and vice mayor first penned their proposal for tourist development in Santa Brígida, they and Bahian state dignitaries assembled to preside over the inauguration of three new buildings: the Pedro Batista Museum, an auditorium/theater, and a library/documentation center. In keeping with the state project of religious tourism, the ceremonies coincided with the town's São Pedro festival. In the mid-1970s it was the Velho who generated great excitement during several São Pedro festivals; a quarter of a century later, the Velho was all but forgotten. It was visiting government officials who were now being feted.

The speeches delivered at the inaugurations for the new structures that emerged from the project "Memorial to a Beato" provide a flavor for the ways in which the 2000 São Pedro festival had become an affair of state and a platform for electoral politics. In the rhetoric of his speeches, the vice mayor attempted to implicate visiting officials from the ministry of culture and tourism in future plans for cultural rescue and touristic development. Indeed, he went so far as to suggest that the state government stand in for Pedro Batista as the community's godfather. Undersecretary of the ministry Sônia Bastos praised Santa Brígida for fulfilling the state's goals for its citizens: to retain their history and culture and to champion tourism. Moreover, in her speeches was further evidence that, unlike their predecessors, state authorities now valued Pedro Batista and his romeiros for their faith and for their "premodern" traditions.

On a crisp June night Antônio Farias stood proudly before the new auditorium named after his party's state leader and federal senator, Paulo Magalhães. The vice mayor was flanked by local and state officials, visiting scholars, journalists, and members of groups like São Gonçalo, São Jorge, and the Bacamateiros who had just performed in honor of the invited guests. Farias chose his words carefully, not only because influential guests were present but also because this was an election year and a few of the new installations, like the museum, had proven highly controversial. After acknowledging his esteemed visitors, Antônio proclaimed,

> The fight for the defense and the rescuing of our culture is embodied in this building. Dr. Sônia [Bastos], we want to move beyond an economy of subsistence agriculture that is strongly tied to the phenomenon of the drought. . . . The town barely has any commerce and definitely no industry. The only institution that employs people is the mayor's office. The mayor's office is not able to employ all due to the lack of funds and the few available resources. This is why the partnership with the state government is so important. . . .
>
> I want to thank Dr. Sônia for her presence. . . . Santa Brígida is in need of padrinhos. We miss our Padrinho Pedro Batista and our Madrinha Dodô. Today the greatest honor in Santa Brígida is to be a godfather or a godmother. . . . [Nonetheless,] you can't become a godfather from one minute to the next. You have to be a friend, show the work you are doing, and help this needy community in the sertão. This community needs the recognition of the state government so that it can bring tourists here, so that they will visit the museum, see films [about Santa Brígida] in this auditorium, stay in a small hotel, buy handicrafts, and eat at a restaurant. In this way we can create another alternative for development, and an alternative to the harsh reality of subsistence agriculture. (Antônio Farias 2000)

Two elements in the vice mayor's speech are particularly noteworthy. First, he positioned Santa Brígida's challenges within a larger set of state and national concerns. He therefore echoed official discourse when he cautioned that subsistence agriculture could not sustain rural households, that government jobs were insufficient, and that new industries like tourism were therefore required. Second, the institution of patronage reappeared, with Farias arguing that state and federal authorities had to make strong commitments to and serve as patrons for those rural communities that were attempting to launch tourism. Accordingly, he informed his guests that, while the romeiros could in the past have depended on specific individuals like Pedro Batista to sustain them economically, they now had to turn to the state for such protection and support.

Farias then handed the microphone to Sônia Bastos, who began by praising and endorsing the current leadership of Santa Brígida—an unusual endorsement since bureaucrats are expected to remain removed from everyday politics. For those local critics of the mayor and vice mayor and their tourism venture, the undersecretary's remarks only underscored how politicized and partisan romeiro history and culture seemed to have become.

> My dear friends of Santa Brígida, I could not miss this opportunity to congratulate you on behalf of the governor, his administrators, and the secretary of culture and tourism, whom I am representing for having selected this team of administrators for your town. The buildings we have inaugurated today are proof of the hard work and love of Antônio and Rosa for their hometown. I would like to ask you not to let the important cultural practices I just witnessed die or fade away. This is your culture. This is what makes Santa Brígida different from the other towns in the state of Bahia. Those of you who performed here have a great responsibility to transmit this culture to the next generations. You must teach them these dances and these folkloric practices. . . . This is the trait unique to your town. Don't let this culture disappear. Another important aspect is the romaria. Romaria represents faith, faith in the supernatural. The purity of your hearts is perceived by God. I believe in the people of Santa Brígida. You are honest, you work hard, you are sincere, and you have elected sincere, hardworking, and honest people such as those who stand here with me today. (Sônia Bastos 2000)

A short while later the undersecretary was again representing the secretary of culture and tourism as she stood before the new municipal library named in her honor. This time she took the opportunity to link the government's project of cultural preservation with the romeiros' faith and their wisdom in revering "traditional" sertanejo practices: "This municipality, which is located in the heart of the sertão, had the perceptiveness to continue to value its roots and the history of its people. You have discovered that culture is the reality of memory. Culture is inspiration for its people. Culture is to provide the opportunity for every citizen to learn. . . . The home of the beato is a testimony of the people who lived here, of the habits of the sertanejo *before the television arrived and taught them about modernity*. The history of the people is the story of a man who drew multitudes of people, of a man who hoped to build a better world *through his faith*" (ibid.; emphasis added).

The undersecretary's revision of history aside, one of the striking features of Santa Brígida in the 1950s and 1960s was Pedro Batista's ability to maintain and mutually reinforce folk Catholicism and economic modernization. This synergy was certainly unusual at the time, and it complicates familiar binary notions of "tradition" and "modernity." At a critical moment in the codification of the community's history, official discourses such as that offered by the undersecretary may lead people to conclude erroneously that the longevity of Santa Brígida's folk practices results from its isolation, as measured, for example, by the late arrival of television and "modernity." More important, it may promote undue pessimism and feelings of resignation about the future vitality and continued "authenticity" of "traditional" cultural practices now that "modernity" has arrived in Santa Brígida.

How was the undersecretary's speech received by her audience? Certainly, the mayor and vice mayor beamed as they received her endorsement for the upcoming elections. Antônio Farias, in particular, had to be well satisfied that Bastos had made reference to matters of Santa Brígida's unique history and culture. These were points he had been emphasizing with authorities for years, and she had taken the further step of linking initiatives in Santa Brígida to the state's larger politics of social memory and tourism. Nonetheless, I suspect that a goodly number of older romeiros found her remarks devoid of any appreciation of the romaria's true identity and mission. This had been brought home to me a year earlier at the São Pedro festivities, when after similar speech-making a disgruntled Fernando Reis (1999) motioned me aside and said, "All the others do is talk, talk, talk. You say few things and what you say comes from the heart. Only you know the mystery of my Padrinho; none of the others do."

Look What They Have Done to My Padrinho's Home — It's a Mess!

Although the festival's orators championed tourism based on the community's faith, folk culture, and millenarian history, the larger romaria had to be convinced. One might well suspect that the notion of enhancing religious tourism would, on the face of it, have proven congenial to Dona Dodô and to other older romeiros. After all, she had encouraged religious pilgrimages to São Francisco de Canínde, and one of her achievements after Batista's death had been to organize and head an annual pilgrimage on foot to Juazeiro. Indeed, when traditional romeiros imagined proper and respectful touristic development in Santa Brígida, they conjured up visions of Juazeiro. In the view of many, what distinguished the places Dona Dodô frequented and took them to visit in Juazeiro was the care guardians had taken to preserve the priest's belongings "as Padre Cícero had left them, to leave them *untouched* " (Samuel Rodrigues 1999). Many pointed approvingly, for example, to Padre Cícero's home, and they clearly also saw it as a model for how they had long endeavored to preserve Pedro Batista's home.

Yet, when Antônio first began approaching well-respected romeiros to request their tacit approval for the renovation of the beato's belongings and to donate their own artifacts for the proposed museum, he was roundly rebuffed. As he explained, "The first thing we had to do was organize Pedro Batista's belongings, those things that were in his wardrobe thirty-three years after his death. The documents were falling apart. The romeiros did not want these objects to be touched and wanted to leave them where they were until the world came to an end. This was always the answer I was given when I asked. . . . It was a very slow process" (Antônio Farias 1999).

The decision to add a museum to the rear of Pedro Batista's home greatly exacerbated this initial resistance. Titus Riedl, who first proposed the museum venture, was sensitive to romeiros' sentiments regarding religious sanctity and preservation. He had proposed that the museum be situated in a wholly separate building. The state's curators, on the other hand, argued that it ought to be attached to the beato's home. This would facilitate the flow of visitors and showcase the two complementary touristic venues. What this latter plan failed to appreciate was that, unlike a museum or even Padre Cícero's home in Juazeiro, Batista's home was a living and highly communitarian space. Its sanctity fostered individual and collective acts of prayer and devotion, while its sociability facilitated informal gatherings and more formal collective celebrations and feasting. The rear space of the home, which the museum effectively appropriated, had been the site where invited guests who did not have kin in Santa Brígida might hitch up a hammock and reside without charge. It concerned romeiros that the mayor's office and the state of Bahia had usurped this collective space and were now making it available to unknown tourists.[5]

Another even graver problem with the architectural design was that it necessitated the tearing down of a back wall of the beato's home to add on rooms for the museum. Although the vice mayor had consulted with Dona Dodô before going ahead with this step, by most accounts she was deeply upset when the actual demolition and construction began. As the resident priest, Padre Gilberto de Lima (1999) observed, "If you change things in Pedro Batista's home, you will anger people. That has to remain the same. People do not accept change in the sacred things of Pedro Batista." Many told me that Dona Dodô wept openly every time she passed the house. And she would comment to people who visited her there, "Look what they are doing to my Padrinho's house—it's a mess (bagaceira)!" (Elsa Conceição 1999). Critics of the mayor and vice mayor even claimed that it was Dona Dodô's despair over, in their words, the "desecration" of their Padrinho's home that led her to depart for Juazeiro not long after the construction commenced. Her actions definitively sealed the fate of the museum project for some.

Pedro Batista's personal effects displayed prior to processing by museum curators, 1999. Photo by the author.

Despite an extremely rocky start, Farias did succeed in convincing the caretakers of both Pedro Batista's home and Dona Dodô's effects to allow him to borrow and restore many prized objects and place them in the museum. When the museum was eventually opened to the public, it was greeted with general enthusiasm and approval by those romeiros who chose to visit. As its designers had hoped, social memory was resuscitated. It was evoked by exhibits featuring examples of religious devotion, such as ex-votos and a collection of hundreds of pebbles romeiros had deposited in Batista's home to mark each time they had offered a rosary for his improved health; photos of romeiro folkloric practices; traditional material culture belonging to Pedro Batista (e.g., his clothing, razor, and medications); and correspondences between the leader and prominent politicians. Older romeiros could be seen gesturing to specific items on display, such as an old sewing machine used to make the beato's clothing, and relating anecdotes associated with them. One middle-aged woman proclaimed that she felt as if her Padrinho was there in the museum with her.

Many seemed eager to purchase souvenirs on sale in the tiny gift shop. These included plaster statues of Dona Dodô and rustic shell figurines with photographs of Pedro Batista and Padre Cícero prominently featured. Nowhere in view were the more elaborate woven straw bags and leatherwork that had been featured years back in the government documentary on colônia to demonstrate the locals' industriousness and marketable skills. Apparently, their producers had either died or migrated, and no local market existed to encourage others to continue the craft. Instead, it was the entrepreneurial Antônio Farias who gathered shells from coastal beaches and showed a local woman with an artistic bent how to fashion figurines into "authentic" souvenirs.

The museum's tasteful displays and glassed-in sacred items seemed to assuage many older romeiros who had feared that, in the hands of outsiders, their Padrinho's personal effects might not receive the respect they and he merited. To the contrary, the very attention the displays and brief accompanying texts drew to these artifacts and to the romeiros' history and cultural practices seemed to underscore the importance that state officials and professionals, like the undersecretary and curators, accorded Pedro Batista and his romaria.

Dona Dodô and Religious Tourism

On 4 September 1998 Dona Dodô passed away in her sleep at the advanced age of ninety-five. She was then residing in her second home in Juazeiro during what some claim was a self-imposed exile, occasioned by her despair over the construction of the museum. How her funeral was orchestrated is the last example of controversy over politics, culture, and tourism considered herein.

Two priests, Padre de Lima of Santa Brígida and Monsenhor Murilo de Sá Barreto of Juazeiro, insist that Dona Dodô explicitly told them of her wish to be buried in whichever city she happened to die in. Consequently, when she died in Juazeiro, Monsenhor Murilo and her small group of followers there attended to the burial plans. Some even hinted that she might be buried within Padre Cícero's original church and Juazeiro's main cathedral, Nossa Senhora das Dores.

The mourners immediately telephoned Santa Brígida, assuming that the sad news would occasion the swift departure of a large entourage of romeiros to Juazeiro. Instead, they were advised to cease their arrangements pending a visit by the mayor and Dona Dodô's nephews. When the contingent arrived in Juazeiro, they immediately demanded to take the body back to Santa Brígida for burial. Monsenhor Murilo initially refused, but he was forced to recant after a lawyer advised him that a verbal understanding with the deceased was not legally binding. Under such circumstances, Dona Dodô's next of kin had the right to determine where she would be buried, and they opted for Santa Brígida. Several of Dona Dodô's closest supporters from Juazeiro and Santa Brígida recoiled at the news. They openly accused the mayor and vice mayor of unduly influencing Dona Dodô's kin and, more seriously, of playing politics

Maria das Dores in the São Pedro church shortly before her death in 1998.
Photo from author's personal archive, photographer unknown.

at a time when the romaria ought to unite and honor their deceased leader's wishes. Some even suggested ominously that Dona Dodô's burial site had fallen hostage to the politics of religious tourism.

This accusation gained greater currency when the funeral procession, numbering in the thousands, reached the plaza in front of São Pedro church in Santa Brígida. There the mourners were confronted with the sight of several men digging a grave beside the mayor's office. The romeiros were informed that this would be the site of their Madrinha's burial. Shortly thereafter, a small church, Nossa Senhora das Dores, would be erected over the makeshift plot. This church would draw even more romeiros in religious tourism to Santa Brígida, the mayor and vice mayor explained.

This development clearly horrified most onlookers, first and foremost because the setting had been used until then as a refuse dump; second, because most romeiros had assumed that Dona Dodô would be buried in the cemetery alongside their Padrinho; and third, because this decision had been made almost unilaterally without consultation with several of the most respected romeiro leaders. The situation quickly deteriorated as several well-regarded romeiro men shouted: "We will all jump into the grave alongside our Madrinha, and you will have to bury us all if you dare place her in that garbage pit!" (Samuel Rodrigues 1999). In response to this dramatic provocation and the priests' similar opposition to the burial plans, the vice mayor grabbed a microphone and denounced those "half romeiros" who were too ignorant to know how to truly honor their deceased leader (ibid.). As tempers flared, visiting dignitaries and clergy feared that violence might soon ensue. Indeed, veiled references to Canudos and to João Gustavo could be heard as the assembled multitude waited for some resolution to this unhappy affair. Fortunately, Padre Mario (now a bishop) finally got the feuding sides to agree to a vote, and amid a din of keening and denunciations, a clear majority raised their hands in favor of a cemetery burial.

The controversy over Dona Dodô's burial and its resolution brought to the fore the pressing matter of succession. It also set the stage for renegotiations over the evolving relationship between the romaria and the state and church. Long before Dona Dodô's death, romeiros and others had pondered her replacement. Zezé's name had been raised often as a likely successor. Nonetheless, many expressed reservations about his obvious lack of mistério. As Miguel Duarte (1977) explained, "Zezé, well he's just the same as me. All a person needs to do is learn to read, pick up the Bible, and they are equal to Zezé. Only my Padrinho and Madrinha Dodô have this dom de Deus [gift from God]." Others lamented Zezé's inability to be impartial and to forge consensus. His critics observed that his past attempts to assert leadership, as during the Velho incident, merely heightened tensions. This uncertainty over succession, combined with the state's demonstrated capacity to consolidate its power and increase its legibility throughout Brazil, made it far easier for romeiro politicians like Rosa Farias and Antônio Farias to claim that they were speaking for the romaria.

Reminiscent of Pedro Batista's funeral, the controversy over Dona Dodô's burial revealed tensions between the romaria and the state. When a sea of hands went up in repudiation of the mayor's and vice mayor's plan, the majority of romeiros proclaimed the following: at least at that moment and in that instance, they were obligated to reject that local and state project intent on converting both Santa Brígida's history and its contemporary life into commodities for the tourist market. A few weeks after the funeral, elderly romeiros spread the rumor that in his capacity as municipal notary, Zezé had drawn up legal documents declaring the mayor solely responsible for the romaria. Although the rumor proved false, it did crystallize fears that the state, acting through its local intermediaries, had successfully forced its way into the very heart of the romaria.[6] This was surely a disturbing thought. Even the highly accommodating and nationalistic Pedro Batista had zealously shielded the true essence and well-being of the romaria from state scrutiny and control.

Dissent over who best represented Dona Dodô's interests and the manner in which she should be remembered lingered well beyond the disturbing events of her funeral. Stymied in their plans to construct a church in her honor, the mayor and vice mayor resorted to using municipal funds for the creation of both a mural depicting a pastoral scene of the morning of her death and a large statue of Dona Dodô. If the intent of these commemorative public works was to reclaim Dona Dodô and charge her with advancing the political goals of "faith and tourism" (Rosa Farias 1999), the romeiros who visit these images have cooperated, in part, by "enchanting" them. For example, romeiros are fond of recounting that Dona Dodô has already repaid the sculptor of her piece with a miracle. Apparently, shortly after having completed this commission, he received word that he had won a major artistic competition for another of his works. For their part, many devout romeiros approach the statue as they would the image of any powerful saint. Consequently, they place ribbons on it to thank Dona Dodô for having interceded with God on their behalf after they made a vow, and they drink the rain water that gathers at the statue's base, convinced that it has curative powers.

Several romeiros recently took a bolder step toward appropriating the statue for the romaria rather than for outside tourists. They insisted that the statue be renovated to resemble their Madrinha more respectfully and faithfully. This

Bronze statue of Maria das Dores with ribbons offered as promessas, 1999.
Photo by the author.

initially meant altering the bronze statue so that the dress Dona Dodô is wearing might be lengthened to the ankles; then, against the sculptor's wishes, they
invited a more willing and "rustic" artist from Juazeiro to paint her face tan and
her dress white. Critics complained that the statue's bronze color was inappro-
priate and disrespectful to their Madrinha who had always rejected grandeur.
The move to lengthen her dress and paint it white better captured her humility
and purity, as well as her customary dress. The application of tan paint to her
face reclaimed her as a cabocla—a true daughter of the sertão. It should be
added that despite these concessions, a few remained so aggrieved by the way
Dona Dodô's funeral had been handled that they averted their eyes whenever
they passed the statue.

During the funeral and in its aftermath, important matters also emerged
regarding the church's relationship and commitment to the romaria. Paradoxi-
cally, in this most recent phase of the romaria's history, the resident priest
Padre de Lima has fashioned himself into the defender of the more traditional
segment of the romaria. Moreover, he has staked claims to perpetuating Dona
Dodô's memory. For example, de Lima stood in for the deceased leader when
he organized a pilgrimage of thirteen cars and trucks bound for Juazeiro in
February 2000, where more than 300 persons attended a mass he and a local
priest celebrated in Dona Dodô's memory. He also conducts a special mass for
the deceased leader monthly in Santa Brígida on the date of her death. At these
times he often refers to her as a "santa." Finally, in an obvious concession to
popular faith, the priest has allowed a large portrait of Dona Dodô to be placed
in the church on the seat she occupied in later years. Like the new statue in the
plaza, this portrait, too, has been converted into an object of veneration.

To account for Padre de Lima's striking concessions to popular religious belief and practice, one must look to broader developments within the Brazilian
Catholic church. Since the 1960s, more progressive elements within the church
have agreed to tolerate a certain degree of unorthodoxy while endeavoring to
shape this faith along more acceptable channels of religiosity. Clergy who have
ministered to romeiros in pilgrimage centers like Juazeiro and Bom Jesus da
Lapa describe the process as a negotiation (Barreto 1998; Steil 1996), one in
which pilgrims infuse religious sites with their own popular beliefs and unorthodox practices and church leaders attempt to incorporate some of these
into institutional orthodoxy and reject others as unacceptable superstition.[7]
With respect to this more inclusive stance, Padre de Lima (1999) stated, "One
has to adapt to the history and conditions of the place where one lives. It's no
use hitting your head against a brick wall. You have to work to take down the
walls. You have to bring the people, especially the older people with you. We

must also adapt to their ways. They are not the only ones who should adapt to us."

As de Lima's statement attests, to keep backlanders' faith alive, the church has adapted by celebrating the contributions made by popular religious figures like Antônio Conselheiro and Pedro Batista. Moreover, in the wake of liberation theology Antônio Conselheiro has been recast as a humble defender of economic and social justice. Indeed, every year since 1983 an official mass entitled "Popular Celebration for the Martyrs of Canudos" has been celebrated on the grounds of the bloody battle (Pinho 1997, 181). The Catholic Church has also compromised by adopting a popular vernacular, as when a figure like Dona Dodô is referred to as a saint. According to Padre de Lima (1999),

> Popular religiosity occurred because there were no priests in certain regions. . . . People wanted to pray. . . . In Paraíba there was Padre Ibiapina and others. Padre Cícero, Antônio Conselheiro in Canudos, Pedro Batista here. . . . We should thank God for the existence of such people who were devoted to religion. [Religion] was very serious and strong. Today this has been lost because of technology and other things. . . .
>
> Madrinha Dodô was a saint. Why do I consider her a saint? Because she did not keep anything for herself. She did not worry about herself. She worried about others. She worried about the priest, the poor, the rich, everyone. She was a saint. I am thankful for having met her. She was a person sent by God.

As the Catholic Church in Brazil has found itself losing ground to Protestantism, a strong charismatic movement has emerged. Charismatic priests like Padre de Lima are far more comfortable with expressions of emotion and enchantment, such as those present in the romeiros' brand of folk Catholicism, than their more orthodox counterparts.

Where Padre de Lima firmly draws the line in Santa Brígida, however, is over matters of spirit possession, which he asserts "the Church does not permit." This posture has affected the ways in which conflict is expressed and managed today in Santa Brígida. In the mid-1970s episodes of spirit possession often occurred during highly public religious services in the romeiro church. During the Velho controversy, spirits would enter the bodies of those who were "receptacles" and denounce fellow romeiros for improper understandings and wrongdoing. Yet in 1998, following the upheaval over Dona Dodô's burial, Padre de Lima squelched a potential episode of spirit possession that threatened to disturb his mass. As he recounted, "A person started speaking, but I knew. She had said to me some days earlier at my home, 'The church needs a priest, and the mayor's office needs a mayor.'" [So when I saw her entering a trance during the mass] I said, 'No, you can't do this. Be quiet. Stay in your normal state.' She went for two months without speaking to me. . . . It is not that the people are wrong. It is their culture. . . . Some things I tolerate, but other things I cannot permit" (1999).

Although many welcomed the priest's overall receptivity to romeiro beliefs and practices, others harbored grievances and suspicions. For example, with priests and nuns stationed permanently in Santa Brígida as of 1990, moderate leaders like Zezé and Barbara experienced a gradual but definite reduction in their authority as religious leaders. Although moderate leaders had been instrumental in the construction of the São Pedro church and had led countless prayer services at its altar, they eventually found themselves outranked and sidelined by the resident priests. The latter asserted ever-increasing control over the church's physical and spiritual space (forbidding the placement of a portrait of Pedro Batista in the church, for example) and orchestrated the community's ritual cycle. These church authorities also introduced new entities such as the youth chorus, which came to be featured in formal church services, rather than the female prayer leaders recruited and trained by Dona Dodô. The chorus replaced the *rezadeiras*' dirge-like hymns decrying sin and recommending penitence with upbeat hymns praising Jesus' love. While trying hard not to appear critical of the church, rezadeira Dina de Lima (1999) could not resist commenting that "these new prayers are so catchy and happy. God forgive me, but I cannot believe they are as powerful and effective as the old benditos."

More damning, critics believed that the priest was using the pulpit to garner support among the electorate and to advance his own political agenda. Like so many other points of contention, this controversy erupted during Dona Dodô's funeral. As tempers flared over the appropriate burial site, the mayor said rhetorically, "I need to know whether I am dealing with a priest or a rival politician" (Rosa Farias 1999). Here she alluded to suspicions that Padre de Lima would run as her adversary in the 2000 mayoral elections. Many of the older and most devout romeiros felt conflicted about such an eventuality. On the one hand, they had come to view the priest as an articulate spokesperson for their interests and as a trusted guardian of Dona Dodô's memory and legacy. On the other hand, if he so chose to declare himself a mayoral candidate, he would seriously blur the lines between religion and politics, a boundary crossing they believed to be ill-advised, at the very least, if not extremely dangerous.

Ultimately, Padre de Lima chose not to run for office, but he did campaign vigorously for Rosa's and Antônio's rivals. As the campaign heated up, Antônio denounced the priest in ever more vitriolic terms. Some contend that his disrespectful rhetoric ultimately cost the vice mayor's party the elections. In this re-gard, it is noteworthy that the Lopes family cast their numerous votes for Padre de Lima's candidate, despite the fact that they benefited greatly from Rosa's ad-ministration. For example, they received running water and electricity in their homes in the hamlet of Quarenta-e-dois and were featured in many folkloric presentations arranged by the vice mayor. In the end, the Lopeses demonstrated their traditionalist sensibilities. At a time in the romaria's history when many considered the church to be the most responsible guardian of social memory, vituperative attacks on its leader could not, and would not, be tolerated. Indeed an astute Padre de Lima (1999) had observed a year earlier, "Whether one likes it or not, the people [here] admire the church and the priest."

Millenarianism and Tourism

As controversy over the future direction of Santa Brígida grips the commu-nity, two pressing questions remain. How are the initiatives intended to convert Santa Brígida and its romaria into a tourist destination and to repackage its religious practices into generic folklore likely to affect the romeiros? And how successful is Santa Brígida likely to be as a magnet for religious tourism?

My initial perusal of the materials Antônio Farias had mailed to me in New Haven in 1998 and my subsequent telephone conversations with him made clear that he and the mayor were enthusiastic collaborators in the state project of tourism and cultural rescue. As I prepared to return to Santa Brígida, I won-dered how other romeiros greeted the prospect of a museum and the arrival of tourists. I recalled a conversation I had had decades earlier with a crusty Scottish Highlander. The old man lamented that "Highland Gaelic culture had died" the moment certain Scots agreed to build museums to display Gaelic cul-tural artifacts and to perform folkloric events for tourists. I wondered if some of Santa Brígida's romeiros had reached a similar conclusion with respect to recent developments there. As I mused, I recalled the refrain from years past, which ominously intoned "a romaria se acabou."

Of course, such concerns strike at the very heart of the matter concerning the effects of the current state projects on the romaria. Consequently, I should be clear that I do not subscribe to the view that cultures somehow die when their products are converted into artifacts placed in museum cases or when these are commodified for touristic consumption. Similarly, I do not share cer-tain assumptions behind projects of cultural rescue, such as the commonly held belief that mass culture represents a global menace to local cultures. Both views reflect and help to perpetuate the romantic notion of a once-timeless traditional people and their authentic folkloric traditions. Such arguments hold that certain people have somehow managed, over prolonged periods of time, to remain sheltered from potentially altering historical processes. This narrative of traditional cultures and traditional peoples forecloses historical agency. Its proponents obscure the fact that in the past, as well as in the present, members of such "remote" and "timeless" societies have sought to engage with historical processes and to be recognized as prime negotiators in how such process would be received and instantiated locally (see Handler 1988; Gewertz and Errington 1991). Without an appreciation for the historical interplay among global, national, and local forces and social actors, then, one misses the play of accommodation and resistance, which over time has been so central to the practitioners of Brazilian folk Catholicism in general and to Santa Brígida's romeiros in particular.

The genius of Pedro Batista was his ability to at once accommodate sufficiently to the state and keep the church at arms distance so as to negotiate a safe haven for his romeiros to practice the antiga lei and prepare for the apocalypse. What for Batista and his romeiros were beliefs and practices rich in mistério and danger that had to be hidden or obscured from state and church authorities have today been appropriated and labeled by the latter as "national patrimony" and "authentic faith." Within this new historical panorama of detente and cultural inclusion there is reason to question whether, and for how long, Santa Brígida's romeiros will be able to sustain vestiges of folk Catholicism's culture of resistance. As in the past, the romeiros are facing the current conjuncture with a measure of accommodation and resistance. However, during the years that stretch from Batista's thaumaturgical days to the present, the number of romeiros who manage to engage in explicitly transgressive organizations and acts that resist the meanings and disciplining pressures of the church and state has greatly diminished. This underscores the relative success of both institutions in their dialectical struggles with the subaltern classes and their popular cultures.

However, it is also true that when romeiros assemble to publicly commemorate such events as the inauguration of a public building or the arrival of a dignitary, they continue to mark these occasions with religious performances. While in other towns the national anthem or stirring speeches about national and regional heroes predominate, in Santa Brígida dances and brincadeiras (more ludic performances) that refer to God, the saints, and popular santos figure centrally. References to past and contemporary politicians are usually secondary. In this way the romeiros continue to modulate those secularizing and nationalist trends long evident elsewhere in Brazil. Moreover, in retaining

these performances and, in many cases, managing to recruit younger participants, the romeiros are holding the line against the alleged homogenization
of popular culture.

The group that has remained most resistant to accommodation and cooptation is Os Penitentes. They reject efforts by representatives of the media and
the state to appropriate folkloric practices as elements of the national patrimony to be marketed as items for broader consumption. Consequently, unlike
his peers, the head of Os Penitentes has firmly refused to allow his brotherhood's rituals to be filmed by outsiders. He and his fellow penitents have made
it clear that their prayers are intended only for a sacred audience. A very telling
incident occurred recently when Antônio Farias reproduced an old photo he
had been lent of Pedro Batista and the leaders of Os Penitentes in which their
faces are clearly visible. The vice mayor reproduced this striking photo without permission and proceeded to place it alongside several other photos of the
romaria; all of which were superimposed on a publicity poster advertising an
upcoming event of religious tourism in Santa Brígida. Over the next couple of
nights members of Os Penitentes systematically scouted out the posters tacked
up around the town and tore off the offending photo. This represented a clear
repudiation of efforts to use their image—and, by extension, their endorsement—to market religious tourism.

But have their more cooperative peers been coopted in some way by their decisions to perform before cameras and to participate in wholly secular, folkloric
events? Is there something unprecedented and ultimately threatening to the in-
tegrity of romeiro cultural practices in these new performances? While cultural
purists would reply in the affirmative, the fact that compromises are currently
being made with respect to external demands and opportunities is hardly new.
Even in the 1960s, Dona Dodô had begun to do away with certain penitential
practices and to reform others when she realized that many romeiros could no
longer sustain the rigors they demanded. Even then, Os Penitentes was prized
for its members' exceptional ability to adhere to the dictates of the *antiga lei*.
But how do public folkloric performances accord with the original romeiro
mission to direct all acts of penitence to the collective goals of securing mass
salvation and ushering in Heaven on Earth? Even here compromises have long
been under way. With the death of Pedro Batista and the refusal to permit the
Velho to replace him, the grand salvationist and millennial goals were replaced
by more modest ones. These focused on *individual* responsibility for spiritual
well-being and personal salvation. Dona Dodô both acknowledged this change
and abetted it. She did so most dramatically during the 1980s when she not
only granted approval to a few middle-aged beatas who sought her permis-

sion to marry but also encouraged others to follow suit. This action ultimately led to the abandonment of the lay sisterhood of beatas—the very organization charged, since the days of Padre Ibiapina's charity houses, with resisting church reform and ministering to the povo's pursuit of salvation before the imminent apocalypse.

Another element that has helped ease the transition from yesterday's penitence to today's entertainment is found in the very constitution of the romeiros' dances and brincadeiras. Apparently Dona Dodô recognized from the beginning that most romeiros could not maintain lives based solely on demanding penitence, and she feared that without some license for play people would turn to such "immoral" acts as gambling and drinking. Consequently, she permitted the ludic to enter into such religious devotions as the Dances of Santa Joana, and São Jorge. The existence of this marriage between prayer and play came through clearly in the commentaries delivered by leaders of various romeiro dances and brincadeiras when they were interviewed by IRDEB filmmakers. These romeiros were the subjects of *O pequeno grande mundo de Santa Brígida*, a documentary on what the narrator calls Santa Brígida's "cultural manifestations" and "folkloric practices" (IRDEB 2000). Such secularized and scientific terms hardly conform to the discourse of the romeiro commentators, who never use the term *folklore*. Rather, they make clear to their audience that their practices are, foremost, inspired by and directed toward God and the saints. As the leader of the group, Mineiro Pau, expressed it, they are "part prayer and penitence" and "part play" (ibid.). What the viewers of the documentary were privy to, then, was "play." That dimension of their devotion reserved for penitence remained a community trust—still safe from mass consumption.

Nonetheless, over the years leaders of these groups have had to moderate their demands and expectations. This has occurred both with respect to the moral prerequisites for new recruits and to the overall decorum of the audience. The only group today that does not pair devotion with play is Os Penitentes. For this reason, it is considered the most efficacious and fina of all. It is also why its members refuse to appear before an audience, and why it has had difficulties for many years in recruiting youthful members.

I do not want to leave the impression that tourism poses no problem or contradictions for the romaria. Clearly, proponents of tourism pursue contradictory aims depending on whether they reside within or outside of Santa Brígida. Segments of the outside elite have come to value the romaria for its purported isolation from modernity, its lack of development, and its capacity to maintain wholesome social norms and traditional religious practices long abandoned throughout most of Brazil. For a jaded audience, the romaria provides a wellspring of nostalgic memories about a bygone world. This is hardly the vision or aim held by the mayor, vice mayor, and their local supporters, however. They view tourism as a vehicle for more rapid development in Santa Brígida and as a way to close the cultural and economic gaps between the rural municipality and a more urbanized Brazil. This is also the aspiration of one of the youthful dancers of São Jorge who hopes to be discovered by a theatrical agent while he is performing with the group! In a sense, contemporary romeiro politicians like Antônio and Rosa share Pedro Batista's vision that religion and economic modernity can be mutually reinforcing.

Juazeiro, a highly successful destination of religious tourism that receives some two million tourists annually, has managed this balancing act expertly. On the one hand, it appears to have successfully retained traditional religious and cultural practices; on the other, it is prospering economically. It is instructive to explore how this feat has been accomplished in Juazeiro before considering whether it might be replicated in Santa Brígida. In Juazeiro local politicians and church leaders have crafted a pilgrimage center that attracts the faithful, ministers to their spiritual needs, and fulfills their desire to consume religious iconography. Juazeiro simultaneously offers visitors a window onto Brazil's millenarian history and provides nonbelievers the spectacle of "authentic" folk Catholicism and rustic folk art. Recently, through the creation of a living museum (museu-vivo) local officials, in collaboration with the state and federal governments, have taken a further step in marketing Juazeiro's "faith" and "history" more broadly. Mayor Mauro Sampaio (2000) commented, "It is a museum that is known nationally. When [the federal minister of culture] was there he said that it is no less impressive than any European museum. We felt honored by this. The images of Padre Cícero were made in Paris, by internationally renowned artists. Each part of the museum features images of Padre Cícero showing one aspect of his life. We also kept the ex-votos there, which are part of popular religion."

Already in the works is a Padre Cícero theme park, which will boast a tower soaring 111 meters high. According to Juazeiro's mayor, "It will be the largest religious tower in the world. On top there will be a cross, and on the bottom a basilica . . . very open, as Christ always advised us to be with the people" (ibid.) The mayor anticipates receiving upward of four million visitors annually once this project is completed.

Mayor Sampaio freely admitted that the ambitious project of religious tourism could never have been undertaken without a strong partnership between the government and the Catholic Church: "Our priest, Padre Murilo de Sá Barreto speaks the language of the romeiro. Earlier clerics . . . did not defend

Padre Cícero. Today Padre Murilo defends the virtues of Padre Cícero, and he discusses the injustices he suffered. . . . His preaching focuses on popular religion. . . . Padre Cícero has now been integrated into the Catholic Church [which attracts increasingly large numbers of pilgrims to Juazeiro]."

Critics of Santa Brígida's current plans for tourism, like Padre de Lima, worry that, unlike in Juazeiro, politicians are proceeding without input from church officials.[8] Critics also worry that the religious fervor that continues to draw outsiders to Juazeiro cannot be equally sustained in Santa Brígida. They point to the lack of a charismatic leader, to the unlikelihood that Santa Brígida's millenarian history alone will draw tourists, and to a younger generation who are attracted to the dances and brincadeiras solely for their entertainment value and financial rewards. Padre de Lima (1999) touches on all these points.

> Today Madrinha Dodô is gone and many people no longer come here. You need someone like her to draw people here. . . . The mayor's office can bring multitudes of people in trucks from the outside, but that is not worth anything. People have to come with their hearts. . . . .
>
> You can have tourism and folklore, but if you don't have religiosity it is nothing more than folklore. Juazeiro does not exist because of folklore; it exists because of its powerful religiosity. . . . The vice-mayor is trying to rescue Santa Brígida's culture, but he is forgetting about the religious aspect. . . .
>
> In Canudos there was that effort to create a romaria of sorts. But people went there and they didn't see anything. They went there, but there was nothing really to attract them. . . . People go to Juazeiro to ask for blessings and to take part in religious ceremonies. [If Santa Brígida doesn't follow that model] it will become like Canudos, where people go to look at the place, but there is nothing religious there. Many people don't go to Canudos anymore. I hope this doesn't happen with Santa Brígida.

Where the priest, mayor, and vice mayor do agree is in their convictions that Juazeiro is the more appropriate model for Santa Brígida to emulate. The mayor proposes that Santa Brígida "get into the [entrepreneurial] spirit of Juazeiro" and begin to build small lodgings, rent rooms, and open modest restaurants rather than offering such services at little or no cost to most visitors (Rosa Farias 1999). For his part, the vice mayor envisions a twelve-meter-high sculpture of Pedro Batista mounted in the hillside in imitation of a similar monument in honor of Padre Cícero in Juazeiro. He states, "The idea of placing this statue in the hillside would draw tourists. It would spark the curiosity of people in the region if they heard there was something similar to Juazeiro here. After all, everyone always says Padre Cícero and Pedro Batista are one" (Antônio Farias 1999).

In addition to concern about Santa Brígida's continuing viability as an attractive site for religious tourism, there is also a general preoccupation with the fact that the plans for tourist development are very much tied to a specific group of local politicians with ties to the ruling party in Bahia state. For example IRDEB's Paolo Marconi (1999) observed, "I don't know how the state can help keep these very spontaneous traditions alive without interfering and drawing politics into it and controlling it. There are folkloric [groups and] practices in the interior that exist today only through the support of the municipal government. . . . If the municipal government is an adversary of such a group, then they won't receive uniforms and the group will not perform for four years."

As luck would have it, Santa Brígida may be faced with just such a problem if the newly elected mayor and his staff decide to place little, if any, priority on developing the previous administration's cultural and touristic initiatives. Having been forewarned by bureaucrats of just such an eventuality, Antônio Farias and his close associates have once again demonstrated that they are very much in step with current historical and political trends. With easy and direct access to municipal and state funds gone, Farias and the ex-mayor have created a nongovernmental body, Centro Comunitário Pedro Batista (Pedro Batista Community Center). Farias has already contacted me to help him establish ties with potential North American funders to support the center's activities. In this spirit, he has managed to have the films about Santa Brígida translated into English and Spanish. In the future, Santa Brígida's highly "traditional" and localized practices and memories may be sustained, in part, by foreign funding and the concerted efforts of locals and internationals who share a transnational imaginary and a transnational field of social action.

The Official Embrace of "the Folk" and Their "Folklore"

The contemporary elite project aimed at recapturing "the folk" and their traditions for the benefit of local communities and the nation is a measure far less radical, inclusive, and respectful than it might initially appear. For example, in the Bahian state project to record still-popular cultural traditions found in the countryside, urban filmmakers uncritically attach the term *folklore* to these expressions rather than presenting and analyzing the terms the performers themselves employ. Apposite is Candido da Costa e Silva's (1982) criticism that in dominant scholarship the folk have yet to be given an adequate opportunity to express their own beliefs and views. In the case of the romeiros who are fea-

Romeiro children
participating in an
Easter procession, 1974.
Photo by the author.

tured prominently in several of the documentaries, the unproblematic use of
the term *folklore* avoids an important matter. I refer to those social processes
involved in the decentering of religious faith and intention from collective performances such that they increasingly assume features of secular, folkloric performances. Moreover, in largely displacing religion from their overall treatment
of these performances, the filmmakers erase the long history in which many
of these "folkloric" performances were maintained despite repression by the
church and state. Indeed, when matters of resistance are broached at all in
the films, it is done so in the context of a contemporary struggle: one pitting
a previous, largely isolated, and "unified" folk against homogenizing forces
within larger national and global economies. Such a presentist posture deflects
attention from important points of current debate and disagreement among
the folk, in part because locals have long differed in how they should personally confront, respond to, and internalize outside forces. In the present, as in
the past, romeiro penitential performances and brincadeiras become strategic
sites within which romeiros contest the proper reception and incorporation of
outside cultural, social, political, and economic developments.

If Santa Brígida does find its way into the tourist circuit—a big if—it is likely
that, as with other instances of commodified culture, one will find one or a
combination of the following responses. Some will come to resent and perhaps

Romeiro children twenty-five years later participating in a far more secular and folkloric dance commemorating São João, 1999. Photo by the author.

parody the tourist gaze (Olwig 1999). Some will find a way of fashioning and performing folklore while shielding intimate faith and sacred communal secrets from public view (Gewertz and Errington 1991). Hybrid forms combining selective elements of romeiro culture and other genres may well emerge. Individuals and the community will most likely struggle over the most appropriate ways to maintain the correct balance between spiritual penitence and brincadeiras in religious performances, and between honoring God and the saints and performing for remuneration (Castile 1996).

The romeiros will also join the ranks of other subaltern producers of such manifestations of popular culture as carnival, samba, and umbanda. All have faced the dilemma of appreciating inclusion and the ability to profit monetarily from the elite embrace, yet struggling to hold onto certain features of those alternative subjectivities, cultural forms, and social spaces that foster challenges to elite domination (Brown 1994; Miceli 1984). It remains unclear who, if anyone, among Santa Brígida's youthful generation will take up this latter call once their more passionate and contentious elders pass away.

What is clear, however, is that despite official moves to celebrate and domesticate millenarian symbols and specific historical episodes of popular mobilization, millenarianism continues to inspire resistance and political protest. This is evidenced in the sermons and special masses delivered by progressive priests who recall the names and struggles of past millenarian leaders. Such resistance also resonates in those claims of a shared lineage among the fallen at Canudos and Contestado and some of todays activists; these activists include contemporary agrarian rebels of the *movimento sem terra* who have invaded and who farm the underutilized properties of large landowners in many parts of Brazil (Moura 2000).

MILLENARIANISM, STATE FORMATION, AND RESISTANCE

More than once while writing this book and struggling to tame its many elements and fulfill its larger ambitions, I asked myself, "Why not write a case study of the Pedro Batista movement and be done with it?" Although certainly expedient, to have done so would have been to enclose my subject in far too restrictive a format. My engagement over three decades with the topic of Brazilian millenarianism and my years spent with Brazilian millenarianists convinced me that a more sweeping narrative and hybridized genre were required to tell the story I needed to tell. Others may find that more conventional formats or another experimental form work best for them. I would hope, however, that in the future scholars will take up my challenge to recognize Brazilian millenarianism as a traveling cultural formation. It is in historical motion, reflects ongoing social production among a wide range of actors and institutions, involves intertexual comparisons and borrowing among movements, deals with matters and emotions of spirituality and faith, and is subject to political contestation and accommodation.

This study has touched on several dimensions of Brazilian millenarianism that have received inadequate attention. By examining millenarianism as a cultural formation over the longue durée, I have mapped its multiple roles and changing course over several centuries of Brazilian history. In doing so, one comes to appreciate that in Brazil millenarianism is a symbolic resource that people have long struggled over and deployed in the pursuit of power, wealth, salvation, distinctiveness, and unity (Bourdieu 1986). From the very start, millennial symbols featured prominently in geopolitical assertions about Portugal's imperial destiny in Brazil and beyond. Such meanings were employed in attempts to legitimate conquest and to avoid the use of force by persuading the "pagan" and "uncivilized races" to bend to their conquerors' will. Since those early days, millenarian and apocalyptic symbols have resurfaced repeatedly. They have been found in national leaders' more secularized (though no less magical) discourses about Brazil's coming of age: initially as a fully modern country and, later, as a superpower. Images of the apocalypse, Judgment Day, and the divine kingdom have also helped to fuel and channel poor backlanders' resentment, which has been directed against the rich and powerful who have failed to represent and incorporate the subaltern justly and adequately in their grand plans. Finally, like the tale of the sorcerer and his apprentice, many now fear that processes of modernization, standardization, and globalization have stripped the nation of much of its distinctive character. Consequently, after centuries of repression and denigration, certain popular millenarian beliefs, practices, and practitioners have found a valued place within the state's and the Catholic Church's agendas, and those previously branded fanatics have been celebrated as authentic and valuable Brazilian folk.

Precisely because millenarian meanings amount to symbolic capital in Brazil, they have been the source of contestation and struggle among and between members of the dominant and subaltern classes. Repeatedly, popular millenarianists' beliefs and motives have been distorted and othered by elite members of the church, state, and intelligentsia. This has been done in the name of ultramontane reform, republicanism, Positivism, nationalism, modernization, and cultural rescue. Such hegemonic projects have explicitly or implicitly intruded into millenarian scholarship. The result is works that often fail to adequately portray and analyze those folk religious epistemologies and spiritual subjectivities Brazilian backlanders have brought to bear as they interpreted and participated in profound local, regional, and national transformations. In the late 1800s and early 1900s millenarianism provided the meanings, motives, and inspiration with which many thousands of dispossessed backlanders not only challenged the elite and fashioned more acceptable leaders but also charted a more ethical and desirable route into modernity.

Symbols that Are Good to Think On

Claude Levi-Strauss (1967) tells us that myths are good to think on. Certainly in Brazil the narrative of the messiah and the millennium have long inspired thinking about such heady matters as destiny/history, power, social justice, national belonging, and supernatural versus human agency. The apocalypse, the millennium, the messiah, and the Antichrist have provided a rich vocabulary for both the powerful and the subaltern to ponder their times, to reflect on their place, and to imagine their future. Precisely because millenarianism affords such a powerful and widely shared language, I have sought to widen the circle of actors and institutions conventionally included in studies of millenarianism. In addition to featuring millenarianists, politicians, and clergy, I have figured into this study other significant players in the social production of millenarianism, such as scholars, journalists, filmmakers, and curators. Moreover, I have gone against the grain of most scholarship on nineteenth- and twentieth-century Brazilian millenarianism by refusing to reserve for the subaltern alone the meanings and emotions tied to millenarian discourses.

It is my contention that many members of the intelligentsia have been drawn to episodes of millenarianism due to more than the simple desire to document them faithfully. Some of the best have used the context of millenarianism and its rich vocabulary to advance claims about and to help forge the Brazilian people and nation. A fine example is Euclides da Cunha whose work has been cited throughout this study. At the turn of the twentieth-century his *Os Sertões* told a story of national destiny. It was an epic about the fashioning of a people—a "triumph" of eugenics in which the weaker races would either be subsumed by their lighter-skinned compatriots or totally disappear. It was also a tale about place, one in which a modern Brazil would cast off the shackles of the backward Northeast and rise up along the nation's urban coastal rim and in the commercial, central South. Da Cunha also celebrated a society in which reason would triumph over religion. It did not take long for *Os Sertões* to be recognized as a national treasure, "the Bible of Brazilian nationality" (Levine 1992, 18).

Due to the significance millenarianism has long enjoyed within the national imaginary, scholars have been able to use it as a springboard into larger national debates. For example, professor of legal and forensic medicine, Raimundo Nina Rodrigues (1897) appropriated the case of Antônio Conselheiro and Canudos to forward several claims about the nation and its citizenry. Pointing to the "fanatics" of Canudos, he decried the degenerative effects for the nation of miscegenation and insisted that the sertanejos' underdeveloped minds rendered them incapable of understanding republicanism—a more abstract form of governance than the previous monarchy (Levine 1992; Villa 1997). Studies of millenarianism have also contributed to a larger national dialogue over the ability of the tropics to support a modern people and nation, and the role of certain regions and their populations in building, claiming, and governing such a nation (Queiroz 1965b). For Brazilians who confronted years of censorship and authoritarian rule and who ultimately emerged from its grip, millenarian movements provided a context to probe the contours and the promise of popular political struggle for a more democratic nation (Amado 1978; Arruda 1993: Moura 2000). This book shares this concern. It also seeks to enter into dialogue with discussions over the impacts of cultural globalization on Brazil.

Popular Culture and Resistance

Matters of resistance and popular culture have featured prominently in this study. The relational dimension on which the notion of millenarianism as popular culture depends proves wholly incompatible with older scholarship predicated on the notion of two purportedly autonomous Brazils (one modern and the other premodern). Equally faulty are those related claims about religion having served as a social glue that returned momentarily disorganized rural people to a more pristine (and ahistorical) steady state. Later studies have advanced scholars' understanding by situating local episodes of millenarianism within their broader national and international contexts (e.g., della Cava 1970). Where these latter studies falter, however, is in their failure to recognize that conflicts over power emerged along multiple scales and in multiple locations, not merely along the fault lines of class and public politics. Consequently, these works have remained largely silent on matters of hegemony and popular culture. On a related point, they have failed to explore the many sites, myriad actors, and intertextuality among movements that are part of the ongoing struggles over the representations of millenarianists, the nature of their agency, their goals, and legacy.

That body of scholarship suffering most from a unitary notion of power and a disregard for religion as popular culture is the one produced by certain Marxists, like Rui Facó (1963) and Edmundo Moniz (1978). In these writings the millenarianists' religious discourse serves no other purpose than to mask class struggle. By privileging acts of class struggle and finding them even where the empirical evidence indicates otherwise, these researchers miss the type of accommodation a millenarian figure like Pedro Batista brokered with powerholders in order to negotiate a safe haven for the practice of charismatic authority, communal social relations, and a millenarian brand of folk Catholicism.[1] This study contributes to that newer body of scholarship that not only examines the sacralization of rule throughout Brazilian political history but also probes how popular classes have both collaborated in and contested their subordination

(Azevedo 1981; Schultz 2001; Oliveira 1997). Popular millenarian mobilization may be a symptom and expression of a breakdown in the state's hegemonic mission, as occurred at the turn of the twentieth century (see also Oliveira 1985). It may also reemerge *within* a routinizing movement, as has been the case in the Pedro Batista movement. There, millenarian symbols and desire continued to attract those who neither saw their millennial dreams realized nor benefited greatly from the elite projects that have rewarded a small segment of their community.

Studies of Brazilian millenarianism hold the promise of refining scholarly understandings of resistance. Consider, for example, James Holston's almost apologetic admission about the followers of the Valley of Dawn, a millenarian religion practiced by thousands of residents of Brasília: "The estrangement of the state does not generate alienated rebels or engaged reformists. In fact, it does not lead directly to political mobilization at all. Thus, I cannot easily call the Valley's religious practice a form of resistance to the kinds of oppression the poor suffer in the secular world" (1999, 607).

Scholars have become habituated of late to authors' claims to have found instances of resistance in even the most seemingly trivial and mundane actions of subaltern actors. In reaching these conclusions authors have been guided by many of the same works central to this study. That is, they have combined Marxist understandings of political economy, poststructuralist notions of power as decentered, and an appreciation of culture as a strategic site for contestation between dominant and popular classes (Foucault 1990; Bourdieu 1977; Williams 1977). While praising the move to decenter power, critics have recently raised concern over the imprecise use and abuse of the term *resistance*, some suggesting the need for a larger and more flexible set of terms and operations regarding matters of domination and subordination (e.g., Abu Lughod 1990; Gutmann 1993; Rubin 1996; Brown 1996). In this work I, too, have worried about my use of the terms *resistance* and *protest*, especially with regard to the important matter of how Brazilian millenarian subjects actually viewed their own agency. The history of Brazilian millenarianism affords a revealing case with which to contemplate such issues and to consider the merits of an expanded grammar of motivations, agencies, and contingencies.

If nothing more, our engagement with Brazilian millenarianism over the centuries cautions against any sweeping and totalizing narrative of millenarianism as "protest," "compensation," "accommodation," and so forth. Surely for the Portuguese colonizers and missionaries there was nary a trace of resistance and protest in the millenarian symbols so central to their statecraft. In their writings on the hegemonic process, Philip Corrigan, Harvie Ramsey, and

Derek Sayer assert that rituals of rule, along with their constituent "categories of moral absolutism," make possible a way of discussing political priorities that render unsayable much of what is lived as political problems (1980, 17–19). For Brazil's subaltern peoples millenarian discourse became what Ranajit Guha calls a "borrowed language," which induces the subordinated to "speak in the language of [their] enemy" (1983, 75). It is equally true, however, that millenarianism and Catholicism, more generally, harbored potentially subversive elements, which included the former's invitation to symbolic inversion and the latter's notion of resentment.

I would therefore amend the claims of Corrigan, Ramsey, and Sayer and propose that elite rituals and other such hegemonic ventures intended to impose domination and forge popular consent frequently displace the "publicly unsayable" into forms of popular culture, including Scott's hidden transcripts. These popular forms await historical conjunctures, like the turn of the twentieth century in Brazil, when the unsayable can, and must, be openly voiced and put into practice. In the cases of Canudos and Contestado, millenarianists appropriated the language of their oppressors and fashioned it quite explicitly into an ideology of struggle, social justice, and societal redemption through divine intervention. Moreover, the social memory and spirit of earlier millenarian leaders and their devotees have continued to resonate in the words and actions of adherents of Brazil's liberation theology and its *"igreja dos pobres"* (church of the poor) (Barreto 1998) and in the contemporary struggles of rural activists (Moura 2000).

Authors like Jeffrey Rubin (1996) have, in my view, correctly proposed that the term *resistance* be preserved for acts that entail aspects of consciousness, collective action, and direct challenge to structures of power. Canudos and Contestado certainly meet this criteria. On the other hand, as consummate backland bosses, Padre Cícero and Pedro Batista did not represent overt threats to the state nor did they encourage their followers in such a direction. Rather they targeted other arenas of power: the church and those dispersed sites for the propagation of a modernist agenda based on individualism, secularism, alienated labor, accumulation, and conspicuous consumption. Theirs, too, deserves the label of resistance, but it is of a type left unacknowledged if the meaning of resistance is *exclusively* understood to be overt challenges to *state* authority.

By neither explicitly challenging the state nor being perceived by key power-holders as doing so, Padre Cícero and Pedro Batista managed simultaneously to accommodate and resist larger structures of power. In seeking to capture this dialectic within the larger rubric of resistance, I favor the concept of "negotiation," which refers to "the quotidian struggle for value and power, for freedom and autonomy" (Alonzo 1992, 183). This is a concept I believe Pedro Batista and his romeiros would recognize as an apt description of their leader's genius: o conselheiro quem deu certo.

Negotiations over such matters as representation, value, and the freedom and autonomy to pursue spiritual and social lives at odds with the mainstream continue today both within the romaria and between it and outside institutions. On the one hand, one may interpret as new and positive the mayor's and vice mayor's access and facility in transacting with state officials, journalists, filmmakers, and scholars over the modes of appropriation and representation of romeiro history and culture. On the other hand, one may rightly conclude that these romeiro leaders are so completely in step with and implicated in the larger state agenda of tourism, cultural rescue, and the commodification of popular culture that they pose no real threat to the larger hegemonic project.

Does this mean that we have come full circle? Has that brand of popular millenarianism long practiced by Brazilian backlanders been leached of its potential as a discourse and practice of alterity and protest? Does it now simply conform to the interests of the dominant classes? On the one hand, certainly none of the messianic figures featured in this study could have ever imagined that their lives and popular mobilizations would have become cultural fodder for urban Brazilians' nostalgia about an authentic rural past; neither could they have foreseen that their struggles and religious convictions and practices would be commemorated in state-supported folkloric events, museums, and theme parks. Similarly, it would have been outside the ken of those romeiros persecuted by church and state officials for their devotion to Padre Cícero to imagine that during the 1998 presidential election both Fernando Henríque Cardoso and Luís Inácio da Silva (Lula) would launch their political campaigns in the Northeast at the Horto beneath the massive statue of Padre Cícero. On the other hand, whether millenarianists are remembered nostalgically by members of the dominant classes as the "martyrs of Canudos" or celebrated like Santa Brígida's romeiros as authentic folk valuable to the national patrimony, millenarian ideology, subjectivities, and practices help to nourish the critical imaginations and cultural creativity of many Brazilians.[2]

Having said this, there is reason to question whether and how precisely that brand of folk Catholicism featured in this study will remain a source and inspiration for popular struggle among Brazil's youth. Youthful Brazilians in their roles as students, viewers of television and film, and parishioners have been exposed to the revisionist narratives of the late-nineteenth- and early-twentieth-century millenarian leaders and their followers. It is perhaps inevitable that in the testimonies, songs, poems, and commemorative dramas composed by

young people in towns like Canudos and Santa Brígida the supernatural qualities that so captivate the imaginations of their elders are either minimized or
wholly absent. Instead, heroes are praised for their organizational genius, their
commitment to social justice, and, in the case of Conselheiro, his fight for liberation. Through the workings of social memory, yesterday's charismatic santos have been transformed into highly secular master planners and champions
of social justice. They are viewed as exemplars who emerged from the ranks of
the common people and continue to exhort them to higher principles. Thus a
popular young poet resident in Canudos writes of Conselheiro,

> What longing (*saudade*) for Antônio . . .
> Antônio persecuted
> Antônio defender of the oppressed people.
> What longing for Antônio
> Antônio of truth
> Antônio of equality. (Pinho 1997, 193)

For her part, a fifteen-year-old romeira in Santa Brígida lamented never
having met Pedro Batista, adding, "I know he was a very great man who fought
for the poor people and gave them land. My teacher said that we should be
proud to live in Santa Brígida and should always remember that Pedro Batista
was a poor backlander who was not afraid to defend his people. . . . The older
people talk about his miracles, but I don't know about that stuff" (Lourdes
Reis 1999).

AN AMERICAN ANTHROPOLOGIST AND

A PERUVIAN NOVELIST MEET OVER LUNCH

I also don't know much about miracles or prophecy, but I choose to add a post-script to his narrative that relates an episode that continues to send shivers down my spine more than a decade since it occurred. It was 1985 and I was attending a conference at Georgetown University in which Mario Vargas Llosa was the keynote speaker. The author's wife, Patricia, accompanied him to the event, and the organizers quickly became concerned that no one had been tapped to keep her company. As a Georgetown faculty member and one of the few female conference participants, I was requested to provide this service. I gladly accepted, and Patricia and I were soon engaged in animated discussion. Part of our interchange involved my telling her that one of the characters in her husband's novel about Canudos (*The War of the End of the World*) bore an uncanny resemblance to Dona Dodô. I wondered out loud whether he had actually inter-viewed her while conducting research for his book. As our conversation moved into the dining room where a formal lunch had been prepared, Mrs. Vargas Llosa insisted that I sit with her and her husband and pose my question directly to him.

The impromptu change in seating arrangements seemed to rest poorly with some at the main table. Consequently, I bowed to hierarchy and protocol and kept an exceedingly low profile throughout most of the meal. During a lapse in the conversation, Patricia urged me to speak of Santa Brígida and Dona Dodô with Vargas Llosa. As much of the previous conversation had been conducted in Spanish, I proceeded with some trepidation to frame my observations and queries in Spanish as well. Almost immediately my words were met with a booming shout from the novelist, "Patricia, Patricia, tú eres Patricia!" (Patricia, Patricia, you are Patricia). Before my rattled senses were able to fully assimilate his words, I was quite certain that, in my inelegant Spanish, I had managed to deeply offend him. Sensing my discomfort and having gained the attention of all at our table and well beyond, Vargas Llosa switched to English and explained that he had indeed visited and interviewed Dona Dodô and that she had made a lasting impression on him. At the end of their conversation she had requested, "When you see Patricia, please tell her how much we miss her and how we look forward to her return." Perplexed but dutiful, the novelist returned to his wife Patricia and told her of the mystical beata's request. He continued with a smile, "My Patricia told me, 'Look Mario, there is more to this story,' and she was right. Finally, many years later, here at Georgetown University I can give the message I promised to deliver to the right Patricia!"

I am well aware that one reading of this vignette, with which I am wholly comfortable, holds that within Dona Dodô's social geography Mario Vargas Llosa and I both belonged to that far distant place she and others called o estrangeiro. Just as her social universe was a highly intimate place, so from her perspective might be o estrangeiro. Nonetheless, in spatial geography Peru and the United States are very far apart and have large populations; moreover as an anthropologist my path rarely crosses with those of Latin American novelists. Hence the suspicion of mistério and the shivers down my spine when I recall that Vargas Llosa, the author of a renowned novel about Canudos, had ultimately found the right Patricia for Dona Dodô's message of saudade and her appeal for reconnection. My letters and small gifts to her over the years have responded in small measure to this appeal, as did my last visit to Santa Brígida, which unfortunately occurred after her death. This book is yet another expression of reconnection and commemoration.

NOTES

Introduction

1 Scholars differ with respect to their dating of these movements. Many assign the beginning date to the year when the religious figure first settled in a "holy city" and attracted followers to his side, and they set the ending date to coincide with the death of the leader and/or the violent destruction of his community. For reasons that will become clear shortly, I prefer the move by Gunter Paolo Süss to employ a starting date that reflects the early careers of the messianic figures prior to their creation of holy cities. Süss does, however, use the conventional approach to fixing an end date. Accordingly, he presents the following chronologies: Contestado, 1844–1912 [sic, 1914]; Canudos, 1867–1897; and Juazeiro (1870–1934) (1979, 68). By contrast, I argue that one must be more flexible in establishing end dates as well, in order to capture the important fact that these movements continue to live on into the present in popular and elite memory and practice.

There is also disagreement among scholars with respect to the number of followers belonging to each movement. For example, Todd Diacon (1991, 3) cites a figure of some 20,000 Contestado followers, while Süss (1979, 68) claims only 15,000. The highest estimate of millenarians at Canudos is set at 25,000, a figure that Hoornaert (1997, 24) reports but disputes. Süss, on the other hand, places the figure at a far more modest 6,000 (1979, 68). Joaseiro attracted approximately 30,000 followers according to Süss (ibid).

2 The Brazilian Northeast, which is the setting for most of this study, consists of two distinct zones. The first is the humid coastal region of cacao and sugar production. It is where Brazil's colonization began and home of the important colonial city of Salvador. To the west of the lush and wealthy coast lies the broad *sertão*, or backlands, a semi-arid region covered with scrub brush (*caatinga*) and cactus. The sertão is subject to periodic droughts which result in famine and mass migration.

At the time of Pedro Batista's journey across the sertão, the majority of the residents (*sertanejos*) were small farmers and sharecroppers. For the most part, their livelihoods depended on animal husbandry (e.g., cattle and pigs) and subsistence agriculture (beans, maize, manioc, and cotton). Many also participated in seasonal migrations to the coastal sugar and cacao estates (Johnson 1971; Anthony Hall 1978).

3 There is no single explanation for the emergence of all millenarian movements. Nonetheless, certain circumstances appear to favor their development. Catastrophe or the fear of imminent catastrophe (e.g., famines or plagues) is one such condition. The alleged inability or failure of figures of authority to regulate relations between the social and supernatural spheres is another. A third factor is the disruption of economic and status relations often caused by colonization, capitalism, or both, and the subsequent inability of the aggrieved to organize for the purpose of defending and furthering their interests by secular means. Finally, ideology and ritual practices contribute to the phenomenon, as the emergence of such movements cannot be reduced to social circumstances alone.

4 Although he does not develop his observation as fully as I do in this book, Robert Levine is correct, in my estimation, when he concludes, "The reforms sought by the ultramontane clerics for backland Catholic practice were likely as troubling to sertanejos as the fall of the monarchy, the advent of the railroad, and the penetration of the republican government" (1992, 226). For an excellent development of this theme see Oliveira 1985.

5 Notable exceptions to this practice within the scholarship on Brazilian millenarianism include Monteiro 1974, Oliveira 1985, Hoornaert 1997, and Villa 1997.

6 In the narrative of this book I will refer to Brazilian scholars by their full last names, as is standard practice in Brazil. These scholars' works, however, will for the most part be referenced using the Library of Congress system employing the final family name.

7 See Diacon 1991 for a discussion of the problems of bringing contemporary ethnographic research on religion and mentalité to historical studies of Brazilian millenarianism.

8 In light of this study's hybrid nature, I have combined different styles in citing primary materials. Archival papers are referenced in both individual chapters and the bibliography, in accordance with the dictates of historical research. Following the conventional practice in anthropology to protect anonymity—particularly in small communities like Santa Brígida—pseudonyms are given to all persons interviewed in that town, with the exception of Dona Dodô. Not only is her identity crucial to the narrative, but she also granted me permission to use her name in my writings. Similarly, individuals who reside outside Santa Brígida (in Salvador, Água Branca, and Jeremoabo) and understood that quotes would be attributed to them personally have been cited by name in the book.

   In researching and writing *From Fanatics to Folk* I have drawn on many primary sources. These include my own fieldnotes, taped interviews, and taped speeches, as well as newspaper articles and other archival materials. Fieldnotes and taped interviews and speeches are referenced only in the body of the text.

9 The brand of Ibero-American folk Catholicism featured in this study has its foundation in religious teachings introduced during the colonial period by such Catholic missionary orders as the Jesuits, Benedictines, Franciscans, Carmelites, Capuchins, and Oratorians. These discourses and religious practices were commonly placed in the service of the state and dominant classes. Nonetheless, they sometimes competed with and became hybridized through an encounter with more popular religious beliefs and customs (e.g., witchcraft and lay religious healers) introduced by more humble Portuguese colonists (Souza 1986). Added to the mix were spiritual elements embraced by indigenous and African slaves who were resettled by missionaries and the colonists in centralized villages and large estates (Oliveira 1997). Despite such cross-fertilization Brazilian folk Catholicism retains its Ibero-Catholic core. This distinguishes it from other traditions also found in Brazil, such as Afro-Brazilian *candomblé* and *umbanda*, European-derived spiritism / Kardecism (introduced into Brazil in the mid-1800s), Protestantism, and indigenous religions. For studies of these other religious forms, see Landes 1947, Carneiro 1961, Camargo 1961, Bastide 1978, Brown 1994, Ireland 1992, Freston 1994, Clastres 1978, and Castro 1986.

10 This is a conclusion I reached early in my writing on millenarianism (e.g., Pessar 1980) and thus independent of Eduardo Hoornaert (1998). Nonetheless, I am pleased to see his endorsement of such a position as well.

1. The World Turned Upside Down

1 Medieval catechists maintained that the earthly realm was inherently evil and was becoming increasingly so, as witnessed by ominous natural disasters and social upheavals. They also preached about the imminent Second Coming. In the late Middle Ages, as the monarchical realms coalesced in western Europe and rulers came to battle each other and Muslim "infidels," the role of savior shifted from Jesus to such "miraculous" kings as Charlemagne, King Arthur, and Portugal's "founding father" Prince Afonso Henriques. Portugal's origin myth contends that Christ appeared to the prince immediately before the decisive battle of Ourique in 1199, not only promising victory against the Moorish kings but also vowing to create a universal Christian empire under the tutelage of the prince's descendants (Carvalho 2000).

In the sermon cited above, Vieira invoked Portugal's messianic tradition and revealed that its monarchy, then under the direction of Dom João IV (1640–1656), was the universal fifth empire prophesied in the Book of Daniel. Indicative of the general instability of millenarian discourse (whether in the service of elite or subaltern classes), following the king's untimely death, both Vieira and his late patron were investigated by the Inquisition (the king posthumously) (Schultz 2001). This was followed years later by a censuring of the Jesuit by both the Pope and the Holy Office of Coimbra (Cohen 1998).

Millenarianism was not the only, or even the most prominent, set of symbols authenticating monarchical rule in Portugal and Brazil during the long colonial period. Nonetheless, this discourse was highly salient in certain periods, including the early years of conquest, the reigns of João IV and João V (1706–1750) (Cohen 1998; Schultz 2001), and again in the early 1800s following the Napoleonic conflict (which were narrated throughout the Portuguese world in eschatological terms) and the relocation of the royal court to Brazil. In Portugal this unfortunate exile was believed to be necessary "to usher in a new and glorious reign with Europe at the center of imperial transcendence" (Schultz 2001, 86). By contrast, in Brazil clergy proclaimed that Rio de Janeiro was not only " 'a new Court, a new Athens, a new Lisbon,' but also 'a new Jerusalem, comparable to the one that John saw in his Apocalypse' " (ibid.).

2   Vieira's messianic prophecies about the imminent resurrection of Portuguese king João IV ultimately led to censure by the Inquisition and his confinement to his quarters. Although the authorities sought to silence him, religious historians conclude that his prolific writings and the numerous sermons he delivered in Salvador, Bahia, on messianic themes gave the decisive impetus to the continuation of these beliefs and expectations in Brazil for centuries to come (Myscofski 1991; Cohen 1998).

3   For insightful discussions of how Catholicism abetted the hegemonic project in early colonial Brazil, see Hoornaert 1974 and Oliveira 1985. Both authors discuss the practice of elevating in stature such so-called warrior-saints as Saint George and Saint Sebastian. Warrior-saints' banners were carried into battle against indigenous groups who actively resisted colonization, and churches honoring the saints were built on the sites of victorious battles. The colonists' victories over both native peoples and European rivals (e.g., the Dutch) reinforced beliefs about Portugal's sanctified mission and millennial destiny.

4   Priests who were commonly relatives of the plantation owners delivered sermons that sanctified hierarchy, patriarchy, and submission to authority, often asking the plantation's slaves to appreciate the similarities between their material and spiritual conditions and Christ's Passion. An early sermon exhorted: "There is not a type of work nor way of life more similar to the Cross and Passion than yours on these plantations. Fortunate are you who recognize the gift of your divine state, how conformity to and imitation of such a high and divine resemblance enhances and sanctifies the work. . . . The shackles, the prisons, the whips, the wounds, the curses, of all this is your imitation composed, and if it is accompanied with patience so it too will possess the merit of martyrdom" (Hoornaert 1974, 86).

5   For a discussion of these mutually beneficial displays of hegemonic authority see de Groot 1996.

6   Brazilians gained independence from Portugal in 1822, but this hardly represented a clean break from the monarchical system (see Costa 1985). Rather, at the time,

the Portuguese king returned to Europe leaving behind his Braganca heirs, Pedro I and later Pedro II, to rule over the fledgling Brazilian empire (1822–1889).

See Schultz 2001 (chap. 7) for a discussion of how the transition from monarchy to republic occasioned new discourses on power and rights. For example, one constitutionalist writer stated that the king had not "descended from the Heavens" but rather, as "the wisest, and most distinguished of Citizens," had been "elected" to serve as "trustee and administrator of the Laws" (255).

7 Due to its exemplary role in the reconquest and in the spread of Christianity, several popes granted to the Portuguese crown and its colonial administrators what amounted to virtual control over the new church in Brazil. Many scholars have remarked that despite the clear ideological and social benefits the church afforded the colonial administration, from the very beginning the state sought to curtail ecclesiastical power (Haring 1958; Bruneau 1974; de Groot 1996).

8 Dom Vital clearly received encouragement from the Vatican. In 1874, for example, Pius IX wrote to the young bishop, "You have acted wisely, continue. We cannot refrain from commending the zeal with which you have striven and are striving to resist so great an evil. We commit full power to you" (quoted in Thornton 1948, 162).

9 In separate processes, the two bishops were condemned to four years of forced labor. These sentences were soon commuted to four years of normal imprisonment, and shortly after the bishops were granted amnesty.

10 Irmandades ranked among the most important institutions in colonial Brazil. Much of the work that was done by the government or by the church in Spanish America was done in Brazil by these religious brotherhoods. It was just such responsibility and power in the hands of the laity that ultramontane clergy sought to transfer to church authorities in nineteenth-century Brazil (Azzi 1977, de Groot 1996).

11 When the Jesuits were expelled in 1759, Brazil lost its most dedicated and independent-minded clergy. By the end of the colonial period, Brazil counted seven dioceses with an average of 514,000 parishioners. By contrast, in 1800 Spanish America had forty-five dioceses, with an average of one diocese for every 300,000 persons (de Groot 1996, 14). Later, under the empire state, authorities suppressed all religious orders, and the number of priests and nuns in Brazil declined precipitously (Bruneau 1982).

12 In 1880 bishop Dom Macedo Costa wrote, "Festivals of Our Lady only for gambling . . . commerce . . . dancing . . . and drinking? This cannot be! This is a dishonor to religion and to the civilization of our country!" (cited in Azzi 1977, 68).

13 The bishops also hoped that by controlling major sites of popular devotion they might better channel devotees' offerings and charity toward the church now that the republican state had ceased its contributions to the seminaries and for the maintenance of churches (Azzi 1977).

14 Ibiapina's charity houses belong to a line of analogous institutions for women dating back to the early colonial period. Initially, "official" convents for women

were prohibited due to the scarcity of Portugese women and to the crown's explicit policy of encouraging them to marry in order to populate Brazil with Portuguese colonizers. Nonetheless, over time lay religious orders for women were founded to meet the demand of women who strongly resisted marriage and sought to dedicate themselves fully to religion, to discipline and reform women who had broken the norms of proper feminine comportment, and to provide educational institutions for young women in preparation for marriage and domestic life. It is noteworthy that during the colonial period the few canonically approved convents only accepted elite white women, while unofficial orders accepted less privileged members (Paz 1998). See Mott 1992 for a study of Nossa Senhora do Bom Parto (Our Lady of the Good Childbirth), a lay order founded by Rosa Egipcíca, a black ex-prostitute.

15 I regret that I never asked Maria das Dores about this connection. Nonetheless, given her direct links to Padre Ibiapina (through Padre Cícero and other priests who kept his teachings and practices alive) and her keen sense of responsibility for sustaining those penitential and charitable practices necessary for individual and collective salvation, I strongly suspect that her decision to establish the lay order of beatas was inspired by Ibiapina's prophecy.

16 For an excellent study on Padre Ibiapina and his casas de caridade see Hoornaert 1981.

17 This is a precursor of a contemporary problem that Nancy Scheper-Hughes points out in her ethnographic study *Death Without Weeping* (1992). She observes that in the Northeast proponents of liberation theology discouraged those religious rituals that traditionally accompanied the death of babies and supported the belief that such infant deaths were blessings. Church officials advised mothers that God wanted their babies to live but failed to offer any concrete way (or ethical justification) to assist poor women in birth control.

18 On 4 September 1878 the *Jornal do Comércio* reported that a jury in Souza, Paraíba, had absolved a mother for the murder and cannibalizing of her two children due to "the irresistible fear of dying from hunger" (Villa 2000, 69).

19 Military titles were awarded either as a result of service as the head of a national guard brigade in a given municipality or through the purchase of this honorific. There is a large literature on the institution of coronelismo; see for example Leal 1949; Lewin 1987; Chilcote 1990.

20 The selective and instrumental use of violence was the crux of the bands' political strategy. This included assaults on farms, villages, and occasionally on cities of many thousands of inhabitants. Bands also engaged in extortion, ransom, "taxation" of commerce, sale of "protection," and mercenary activities for the highest-paying coronel. Works on Brazilian banditry include Facó 1963, Queiroz 1992, Souza 1972, and Chandler 1978.

21 I reached this conclusion before having read Ribeiro de Oliveira's *Religião e Dominação de Classe* in which he also advances this argument. See in particular chapters 5 and 6 of that excellent study.

22 The early days of republicanism marked the most "radical" movement away from identifying the leaders and the nation with God and Catholicism. It was a time when influential politicians and opinion makers broke with the Catholic Church and joined a Positivist sect based on humanism. For these individuals ineluctable principles of positivism, evolutionism, and social Darwinism were guiding Brazil's future and inspiring its leaders. Accordingly, they militated for the removal of "superstitious" references to God in official state documents such as the federal and state constitutions. The Vargas Revolution of 1930 securely repositioned God and Catholicism within the symbols and rituals of the dominant hegemonic order where they have remained ever since. For an excellent study of what he calls "Brazilian civil religion," see Azevedo 1981.

23 Ralph Della Cava (1970) notes that printed texts of Friar Vitale da Frascarolo's apocalyptic prophecy, first delivered in the early nineteenth century, continued to circulate throughout the Northeast for almost a century after his death. Della Cava also observes that its message was firmly believed by rich and poor alike (15). In fact, I saw a copy of the friar's text in a poor romeiro's home in Juazeiro in 1999.

24 The friar is better known in the Northeast under the Brazilianized name of Frei Vidal. His photo can still be found decorating the walls of Northerners' homes, and chapbooks containing his prophecies are available for purchase.

25 The Contestado millenarianists similarly expelled Friar Rogério Neuhaus from their compound. This was after João Maria refused to accept communion and informed the friar that his own prayers were worth far more than a Mass (Monteiro 1974). By contrast, Padre Cícero, who continued after his censuring to pursue both reinstatement by the church and official recognition of the miracle at Juazeiro, attempted to control highly unorthodox religious claims and practices among his followers. On this latter initiative see Pessar 1991.

26 For a collection of Conselheiro's writings see Nogueira 1978.

27 See Levine 1992, Otten 1994, Diacon 1991, and Queiroz 1965b for reference to the promonarchical leanings of the millenarianists of the three movements.

28 See Della Cava 1970, Monteiro 1977, Oliveira 1985, and Pessar 1991 for discussions of how Padre Cícero maintained control over politics and popular Catholicism in Juazeiro.

29 Euclides da Cunha's Os sertões (Rebellion in the backlands, 1944), published originally in 1902, is an example. See Levine 1992 and Villa 1997 for discussions of elite rhetoric about Canudos.

2. The Povo Make a Saint

1 A newspaper article published in 1942 claims that Pedro Batista was fifty-six years old at that time. If correct, his year of birth would have been 1885 or 1886 ("Encontra-se, atualmente na Baia, o beato Pedro Batista," Jornal de Alagoas, 25 February 1942, p. 6).

2   It was not possible to determine exactly when this incident occurred since the informant was uncertain of (and I believe uninterested in) the actual timing. What is clear from the account, however, is that if it did occur, it took place prior to Batista's years as a thaumaturge.

3   None of the people I interviewed provided me with these precise dates; and in fact there are discrepancies in the dates various authors use. For example Pereira de Queiroz (1965a and b) begins her account of the beato's penitential journey in 1942, while a short history of the municipality of Jeremoabo has Pedro Batista settling with his romeiros in 1937 (Almeida 1998); a brief historical account of Pedro Batista once again places the date at 1942 (Gonzalez 1996).

   The chronology I present here is based in part on a 1942 newspaper article that reports that in 1942 Pedro Batista told the police who had imprisoned him in Água Branca, Alagoas, that he was in the fourth year of a seven-year mission. Such a statement would mean that Pedro Batista began his penitential journey in 1938. The majority of accounts assert that Pedro Batista settled in Santa Brígida in June of 1945, a date that is consistent with a seven-year mission beginning in 1938.

4   See Candace Slater's cogent critique (1982) of those authors who fail to appreciate the complexity of the cordel by emphasizing solely its more reactionary aspects or its unique crystallization of the conerns of the Northeastern masses. She correctly argues that even within the most conservative and pious stories, "One glimpses obscene gestures, the sudden clenching of a fist" (217).

5   According to his followers, Pedro Batista strongly dissuaded them from publicly using the honorific "saint" when they referred to him. He did, however, inform them that twelve apostles wandered the world, and he led them to suspect that he was one of these saintly men. Much evidence indicates Pedro Batista's status as a popular santo in the romeiros' discourse and actions. Moreover, in 1958 the romeiros built a church in Santa Brígida that they named São Pedro. Romeiros have told me that while Batista continued to deny a direct association between him and the saint, many romeiros insisted that the church belonged equally to the two "saints."

6   A breakaway faction of the Roman Catholic Church, Igreja Católica Apostólica Brasileira (Brazilian Apostolic Catholic Church), actually declared Padre Cícero a saint in 1973. According to Candace Slater, most devotees are aware of the priest's lack of official standing (1986, 39). Another popular figure considered to be a santo by many Northeasterners is Italian-born Frei Damião (Moura 1978; Souto 1998). For thirty-six years the itinerant Capuchin friar preached throughout the sertão, where he was revered as a curer and miracle worker. Upon the nonagenarian's death in 1997, President Fernando Henrique Cardoso declared three days of national mourning. The bishop of Patrolina, Pernambuco, also asked the Vatican to beatify Frei Damião.

   In May 2003 Pope John Paul II canonized Brazil's first officially recognized saint, Madre Paulina de Coração de Jesús (Puma 2003). For social scientific studies of the canonization of saints by the Catholic Church, see Delooz 1983; Margolies 1988; Woodward 1996; and Puma 2003.

7 I use the masculine pronoun because all of the figures I consider here are men.

8 I continue to use the term *millenarian leader* to describe those popular figures whose teachings are directly informed by millenarian and apocalyptic meanings and who head movements that engage in practices long associated with a collective pursuit of salvation and the Kingdom of God on earth.

9 This binary does not include the politics of redistribution in its understanding of politics. Moreover, in such a system of classification, the church belongs to política, although specific priests such as Padre Cícero may break ranks and enter into the domain of religião. This is a move which, not surprisingly, is denounced by the church and leads in turn to further praise on the part of the povo.

10 Several nonromeiro residents of Santa Brígida (*baianos*) recounted that Pedro Batista had allegedly contracted the services of a local bandit, Pedro Grande, to intercept and kill men who had been dispatched to assassinate him at the behest of a rival political chief in Água Branca. Fortunately, the assassination attempt was called off. Nonetheless, baianos used this incident to invidiously compare Pedro Batista with "Padre Cícero who never had to resort to bandits and assassins to get his way. He was truly different, a man of God. Pedro Batista was just like you or me" (José Marques 1973). Needless to say, romeiros deemed this story slanderous, and they insisted that Batista would never have needed, nor resorted, to such violence.

11 Slater (1986) notes that this story of Padre Cícero's exchange at birth recalls a whole class of tales involving wondrous births. Indeed, several romeiros who related this story to me indicated in further conversation that the circumstances of Padre Cícero's birth were a sign that he and Jesus Christ, in their words, "were one."

12 The honorific godfather is an assertion of spiritual kinship rather than a biological one.

13 Levine writes of Antônio Conselheiro, "He often chided penitents who genuflected before him, remarking, 'I am Maciel by name and a Conselheiro only in my heart' " (1992, 133).

14 This is codified in the statement, "May God pay you," which the recipient of charity commonly says to the bestower of the gift.

15 The beato's retaliation is in keeping with backland notions about the right and need of the powerful to forcefully redress challenges to their authority by those less powerful (Slater 1986, 114). In this way, those who tell this story are making a statement about the relative power of João Maria and the wealthy farmer.

16 This letter and others composed by Conselheiro's nemesis, the Baron of Geremoabo (Bastos 1995), express concern both that the religious leader had siphoned off badly needed labor and that he encouraged practices that ran counter to regional and national trends leading to the proletarianization of sharecroppers, tenant farmers, and small farmers.

17 There are also similarities in terminology and beliefs. For example, both romeiros and practitioners of Afro-Brazilian religions speak of spirit mediums as *guias*, and in the two symbolic systems the spirits of *caboclos* ("uncivilized" Indians) are believed to be the purest and most intelligent (see Burdick 1993). It should be noted that romeiros have never discussed such parallels with me. In fact they view all Afro-Brazilian religions (i.e., Umbanda, Macumba, and Candomblé) to be satanical. Occasionally romeiras who don long, white dresses are confused by outsiders with practitioners of Brazilian Candomblé who also wear such clothing. Such mistaken identity troubles and offends romeiros.

18 René Ribeiro (1970) notes that scholars have underestimated the aesthetic appeal millenarian movements hold for their followers. It is certainly the case that in their reminiscences about Pedro Batista, romeiros often spoke in great detail and quite animatedly about highly dramatic cures in which the beato successfully battled the forces of evil.

19 This statement contains that inversionary brand of repudiation of the rich and powerful and ethical affirmation of the poor and weak that James Scott (1990) locates in the popular classes' hidden transcripts.

20 Obviously many poor backlanders were skeptical about or totally rejected Batista's status as a curer and/or a santo. Marco Ribeiro (2000), who took his ill mother to a curing ritual, had this to say about his encounter with Batista in early 1940s: "At that time there was so much ignorance. . . . I did not see anything, but she had faith. Any smart person can do that. You arrive at someone's home and say, 'I have a toothache. I would like you to pray over it.' Sometimes all you have to do is put your finger on it and the pain goes away; just from the person having the impression that you know how to pray. That's how it was."

21 The terms the romeiros used most often for these narratives are um *exemplo* (an example or exemplum) or um *caso* (a case). When I explicitly requested that they tell me stories about Pedro Batista or Padre Cícero, I used the term *história* (a purportedly true story).

22 This legend also touches on the mistério associated with a santo's name.

23 Often the setting for this tale is Águas Belas rather than Água Branca.

3. The Coronel and the Beato

1 Lampião's consort, Maria Bonita, was born and resided in Santa Brígida. Her home is still standing there, and her youngest brother is still alive. He assured me in a recent interview that she earned her name "Beautiful Mary" for good reason (Pessar, fieldnotes, 20 July 1999).

2 Glória is now part of the municipality of Paulo Afonso.

3 Batista evidently told Pereira de Queiroz that he was attracted to Santa Brígida because it was "an abandoned place, far away from everything, that no one liked" (Queiroz 1965b, 273).

4 It is generally agreed among romeiros and baianos that Batista arrived on 13 June 1945, although various scholarly works and newspaper articles cite alternative dates such as 1942 (Gonzalez 1996) and 1944 (Queiroz 1965b).

5 The fact that Batista appears not to have sought permission earlier from any other political boss to settle elsewhere is probably tied to the fact that his seven-year mission came to a close in the summer of 1945. I do wonder, however, whether his detractors in places like Águas Belas and Água Branca might have reversed their positions and supported Batista had he sought to settle there. I suspect not, however, since I do not believe the political benefits the beato and his romeiros might have brought to these politicians matched those they held for Coronel Sá, the Bahian chefe político.

6 The UDN opposed Vargas and the two parties he created, the Social Democratic Party (PSD) and the Brazilian Labor Party (PTB).

7 Beginning in 1937 Vargas canceled elections on the grounds of communist threat and national security risks.

8 Vargas committed suicide in August 1954 following a public ultimatum delivered by thirty generals that he step down from the presidency. For a study of Vargas and his era, see Levine 1998.

9 Their ties to Juazeiro remain firm today despite the fact that it is now more than a century since the miracle was proclaimed. For example, priests from Juazeiro annually celebrate a special mass for the romeiros in Água Branca and Águas Belas, as well as in their surrounding hamlets. Furthermore, massive pilgrimages are routinely organized from these locales to Juazeiro during saint's day festivals.

10 See Paz 1998 for a feminist analysis of Padre Cícero's beatas.

11 Having said this, I recognize that more detailed archival research than I have been able to conduct thus far in the backland towns and hamlets from which Batista drew his followers would be necessary to make this claim with full certainty.

12 In the mid-1970s a few, very poor romeiros who had settled in the town subsequent to Batista's death admitted to having been drawn to Santa Brígida both for its spirituality and for its possession of more economic opportunities and social services than their former hamlets afforded.

13 Apparently, many of the abandoned female heads of family had been left behind by migrant husbands. The 1930s and 1940s witnessed great increases in the incidence of migration both within the Northeast and to the South (see Villa 2000).

14 By contrast, Dona Dodô favored celibacy and a life dedicated to spiritual and communal service for women and men who proved reluctant to marry. I can only surmise that the leaders discussed their differences in those cases when romeiros expressed especially strong reservations about matrimony. I suspect that had Renata Torres been successful in gaining her parent's support, she might have been saved from such an early marriage. Certainly, there were, and continue to be, a number of highly respected, unmarried individuals in Santa Brígida. Until recently, several of these women belonged to Dona Dodô's sisterhood of romeira beatas.

With regard to sexual preference, Pedro Batista strongly denounced open displays of homosexuality, and he ostracized or banished the few who were "credibly" suspected of performing homosexual acts. On the other hand, there are individuals whom community members and/or outsiders believe to be homosexual but who refrain from acting on this sexual preference openly within Santa Brígida.

15 During my interviews and casual conversations about romeiros' lives prior to resettlement, I have only heard of one case in which a man claimed that his father was deeply concerned about potential persecution at the hands of a local political boss opposed to Batista. This fear led the man initially to move to another community during Batista's traveling days and later to relocate permanently to Santa Brígida. What proved far more common were statements such as that contained in the third testimony; that is, romeiros complained of taunting, belittling, and ostracism by certain neighbors and social superiors due to their beliefs in Batista and to their commitment to follow his teachings.

16 This does raise the intriguing question of why it was that in the late 1960s (only months before his death), Pedro Batista elected to publicly proclaim in Muniz's film his status as a judge of all souls. I am able to offer two possible explanations. First, as chapter 6 documents, Batista's charismatic authority suffered in his last years, and he may have viewed the film as a mechanism to reassert his spiritual power. Second, outsiders, including Muniz, note that toward the end of his life Batista appeared to be suffering from senility. It might also have been the case that with his mental capacities diminished, Batista dropped the pose that politicians demanded and revealed for posterity that identity that he and his followers knew to be true.

17 Unlike my Brazilian predecessors, I was privileged with sufficient funding to permit a far longer period of fieldwork in Santa Brígida than these other researchers could manage. My initial eighteen months of research and residence in Santa Brígida impressed many romeiros, who were used to outsiders who remained for far shorter periods.

18 An additional motive for my avoiding politics had to do with the times. While in the democratic 1990s I felt comfortable in probing past and present relations between the romaria and larger political and military institutions, I did not feel so in the mid-1970s at the height of a violent and repressive dictatorship. In such an environment, I tread lightly so as not to draw undue attention to the romaria and to my role as a researcher in their midst. I should add that in 1974 the mayor of Santa Brígida was asked to appear before the military commander in the strategically important, neighboring city of Paulo Afonso (site of a major hydroelectric dam) to explain my presence in the town. I, too, was asked for an explanation by the clearly sheepish mayor. Many romeiros apologized for this official inquiry and expressed their support for me. Indeed, several men even stated with bravado that they would take up arms to protect me should I be further harassed by military officials.

4. Pray Like You're Going to Die Today

1   This is also a homily Padre Cícero championed.

2   See Montenegro 1973 (58) for a discussion of romeiro concern with the exploitation by local merchants of pilgrims who visited Juazeiro during and after Padre Cícero's lifetime.

3   See Della Cava 1970 (84) for a description of Padre Cícero's prophecies about the imminent arrival of the Day of Judgment that would occur in Juazeiro.

4   Batista informed his followers that he had already died after the long illness that had left him bedridden. At the time he received his penitential mission from God, he was provided with another spirit.

5   The baianos refused to permit the romeiros to conduct their services in the baiano church.

6   A rosary was dedicated each day of the week to the following: Nossa Senhora do Carmo (Monday), São Francisco (Tuesday), Nossa Senhora de Solidade (Wednesday), Bom Jesus (Thursday), A Cruz (Friday), Nossa Senhora da Boa Morte (Saturday), Espírito Santo (Sunday). Other saints or holy persons with special rosaries included Padre Cícero and Santa Helena.

7   For a study on the origins and survival of such penitential societies see Silva 1962.

8   An exception was made in the case of Dona Dodô who often accompanied the men but remained in the back of the procession of penitents. Toward the end of my first year-and-a-half of fieldwork, the head of the penitents and Dona Dodô invited me to attend an evening prayer. This was a very moving experience for me, and it was capped by each man's removing his hood so that I might see his face. Each then proceeded to shake my hand.

9   One hears again strains of da Cunha's (1944) social Darwinism and racism in the monsignor's discourse. The former used such words as "extravagant superstition" (111), "barbarous fetishism" (118), and "collective psychosis" (148) when describing the religious beliefs of sertanejos.

10 Della Cava quotes a Cariry Valley historian and contemporary of Padre Cícero as having written, "Padre Cícero was . . . one of the greatest forces for progress in the economic life of Southern Ceará" (1970, 90). Among the advances della Cava notes are tremendous increases in agricultural production due to the massive influx of labor, the creation of many new sugar mills, and the establishment of flourishing artisan industries.

11 One tarefa measures approximately 4,356 square meters of land.

12 For a brief discussion of the early colonization regime and its problems see Galjart 1968; for a treatment of land reform and colonization programs in Brazil during the 1960s and 1970s see Cehelsky 1979.

13 In 1965 twenty hectares (slightly less than fifty acres) was considered the minimum amount of land needed to support a farming family in Brazil. At that time half of all farm land was owned by 1.5 percent of all property owners. The great majority

of all land owners (some 63 percent) owned only 6.3 percent of all farm land, and 45 percent of all individually held properties were 10 hectares (24.7 acres) or less (IBRA 1967).

14 It has been suggested that Castelo Branco's sensitivity to agrarian problems and to the potential for rural social unrest was reinforced by his earlier participation in a seminar on agrarian issues held at the Jaoquim Nambuco Institute of Social Sciences. There he exchanged ideas with sociologist Gilberto Freyre, leader of the peasant leagues Francisco Julião, and Fathers Melo and Crespo who sought to counter the radicalizing influence of the peasant leagues by establishing church sponsored unions in Pernambuco (Cehelsky 1979).

15 The name of the colonization program had been changed from INCA to INDA.

5. Pedro Batista "Moves On"

1 I heard this claim advanced in 1973/1974 and again in 1999 by both romeiros and baianos. Nonetheless, we were unable to uncover in Paulo Afonso or Salvador any official military correspondences regarding its role in the burial controversy. Moreover, although he was out of town immediately prior to the burial, then mayor and military intermediary Luís da Silva disputes this claim.

2 This is the same man who wrote the chapbook about Pedro Batista's life. Oliveira Brito was one of the officials who defended Pedro Batista when he was summoned to appear in Jeremoabo by Major Felipe Borges de Castro.

3 The actual letter is dated 1968, but this appears to be a typo since the contents refer to events that had occurred only days before the letter was written.

6. The Romaria Is Over

1 José Vigario first visited Santa Brígida in the late 1940s, and Pedro Batista allegedly insisted that he settle to help lead the romaria. The former had lived as a beato in Juazeiro for many years until he left in disgust, concluding that the politicians and merchants had defamed Padre Cícero's memory. While residing in Santa Brígida and serving as a curer and advisor to Batista, José Vigario was accused of practicing homosexual acts with young boys. José insisted on his innocence and took the case before a judge in Jeremoabo who claimed there was insufficient evidence. After the incident, Pedro Batista persuaded the beato to settle in Batoque so that he might oversee the many romeiros who worked and lived on Batista's farm there.

2 According to tradition, the Dance of São Gonçalo was created in Portugal by the saint after whom it is named. São Gonçalo allegedly encountered twelve prostitutes, and in order to save them he taught them the dance and its verses while he played the adufo (a percussion instrument). The women danced so vigorously during the day that when nightfall arrived they were too tired to practice their trade.

God miraculously furnished the saint with money, which he distributed among the repentant women.

3 In 1974, 317 elderly residents of Santa Brígida were receiving government pensions. Two-thirds of these were romeiros. Initially, most romeiros were suspicious of the program, but with the encouragement of Dona Dodô, local clergy, and romeiro municipal officials, people slowly applied for social-security benefits.

4 During my hospitalization Dona Dodô once again demonstrated her great kindness and generosity. At a time when it was unclear whether the hospital would process the paperwork I needed to get reimbursed from my health plan in the United States, Dona Dodô insisted on assuming all costs for my treatment despite my strong protests. She argued that while I lived in Santa Brígida I was a guest of the romaria, and since I had no family there they were responsible for me. Fortunately, the hospital administrators did submit the appropriate forms, and my expenses were fully covered.

5 I should add that I was concerned at that time that our frank discussion might be aired more publicly by her and that it might add further fuel to the controversy over the Velho. From what I could determine, though, she kept our discussion in confidence as I did at that time. Before our meeting she had publicly voiced her concern about the Velho having not performed a miracle as yet, and after our reunion she continued to stress this point publicly.

7. Romeiros into "Traditional" Folk

1 According to the 1990 census, 17,037 persons resided in the municipality of Santa Brígida.

2 In his study of local intellectuals and the Gaúcho Traditionalist Movement in Rio Grande do Sul, Ruben George Oliven points to a somewhat analogous process wherein the creators of this movement drew on academic knowledge (in this case produced by North American and European social scientists) to legitimate their popular culture movement. Oliven calls this "the circulation of ideas between academic and nonacademic circles" (2000, 134); such circulation also typifies Antônio Faria's efforts both to bring scholarship on romeiro history and cultural practices to the attention of state officials, journalists, and potential funders in the private sphere and to legitimate the importance of his initiative.

3 The act of showing the film in Santa Brígida for the first time some thirty years after it had been shot is, in itself, a striking example of time-space compression. On the one hand, most of the romeiros I spoke to were pleased that Farias had subsequently arranged for it to be aired on major television stations in Brazil, as this enabled their small community to come to the attention of the rest of the nation. On the other hand, the film's telescoping of time served as a sobering reminder of just how far the romaria had moved from its earlier days of far greater commitment to the antiga

lei. As I discuss later with reference to more contemporary films about the romaria, this and other cinematographic representations affect the ways in which today's inhabitants of Santa Brígida remember and codify their past.

4 In 1997 Bahia state earned a very healthy U.S.$1,620,700 in profits from tourism, some 4.3 percent of total state revenues (Antônio 1998, 14).

5 Ultimately, a building close to Batista's home was purchased by the municipal government. It was converted into a space where visitors could hitch their hammocks and stay for the night.

6 They were buttressed in this claim by the fact that Zezé supported the Farias administration.

7 See Carlos Alberto Steil (1996) for a discussion of the negotiations between pilgrims and the priests assigned to the Bahian pilgrimage site of Bom Jesus da Lapa. According to Steil, the pilgrims forced the clergy to widen the boundaries of official Catholicism while the priests seek interpretations that integrate popular beliefs into the institutional orthodoxy. For example, at Bom Jesus da Lapa in 1983 and at other sanctuaries, ex-votos (associated with the miraculous powers of saints) were removed from the main sanctuary and relegated to less visible spaces. This step, reminiscent of earlier ultramontane reforms, aimed to shift the focus from the healing powers of the saints to those possessed by Jesus and also to discipline parishioners to concentrate on the power of the sacraments as administered by ordained ministers.

8 Brazilian pilgrimage centers are sites that commonly provoke competition and tensions between officials of the church and state; see for example Steil 1996.

Conclusion

1 To feature Conselheiro and his followers as revolutionaries, Facó recasts them as the initial instigators of the armed combat, thereby contradicting plentiful military and journalist documentation to the contrary.

2 For discussions of the notion of Brazilian national patrimony see Miceli 1984 and Chuva 1995. See Holston 1999 for a discussion of how the Valley of Dawn mirrors modernity back to modernist Brasília; as such, it demands "a bureaucracy that is indeed rational, a meritocracy that delivers as promised, a legal system that not only achieves justice but also works for the common citizen, an intellectual center where national problems are actually solved and where all members have access to resources that lead to mastery, self-discipline, and pride" (624).

BIBLIOGRAPHY

Newspapers and Magazines

Correio da Bahia (Salvador)
Diário da Bahia (Salvador)
Diário de Notícias (Salvador)
Diário Oficial Estado (Salvador)
Diário Oficial União (Brasília)
Estado da Bahia (Salvador)
Gazeta de Alagoas (Maceo)

Imparcial (Salvador)
Jornal de Alagoas (Maceo)
Povo (Fortaleza)
Paulo Afonso Magazine (Paulo Afonso)
A Tarde (Salvador)
Veja (São Paulo)
Via Bahia (Salvador)

Films

Marconi, Paolo, project coordinator. 1998. Pedro Batista: O conselheiro que deu certo. 1998. Instituto de Radiofusão Educativa da Bahia (IRDEB). Videocasette.
Marconi, Paolo, project coordinator. 2000. O pequeno grande mundo de Santa Brígida. 2000. Instituto de Radiofusão Educativa da Bahia (IRDEB). Videocasette.
Muniz, Sérgio, producer and director. 1967. O povo do velho Pedro. Videocasette.
Santana, Oscar, producer and director. 1965. Um canto de esperança. Videocasette.

Archives and Personal Papers

Arquivo Nacional, Rio de Janeiro. Published guides, unpublished finding aids, document collections.
Bahiatursa, Salvador. Folder on Santa Brígida.
Batista da Silva, Pedro. Papers. Pedro Batista Museum, Santa Brígida, Bahia.
Centro de Estudos Euclides da Cunha, Salvador.
Estado de Bahia, Arquivo Publico, Salvador.
Fundação Gétulio Vargas, Rio de Janeiro, Inventório, vol. 2, 1941–45.

Gabinete Arquiespiscopal, Salvador.

Instituto Brasileiro de Geografia e Estatística, Salvador. Folder on Santa Brígida.

Instituto de Patrimônio Histórico e Artístico Nacional (IPHAN), Rio de Janeiro.

Jeremoabo Town Records, Land Estate Section, Jeremoabo, Bahia.

Mayoral Archives, Santa Brígida, Bahia. Documents on cultural rescue and religious tourism.

Oliviera, Lindoaldo Alves de. Papers. Santa Brígida, Bahia.

Tribunal Superior Eleitoral, Salvador. Electoral Results and Data for Santa Brígida and Jeremoabo, 1946–1996.

Primary Resources

Abu-Lughod, Lila. 1990. "The Romance of Resistance: Tracing Transformations of Power through Bedouin Women." *American Ethnologist* 17, no. 1: 41–55.

Albuquerque, Durval Muniz de, Jr. 1999. *A invenção do nordeste e outras artes*. São Paulo: Cortez.

Alden, Dauril. 1969. "Black Robes versus White Settlers: The Struggle for 'Freedom of the Indians' in Colonial Brazil." In *Attitudes of Colonial Power toward the American Indian*, edited by Howard Peckham and Charles Gibson, 19–46. Salt Lake City: University of Utah Press.

Almeida, Marco Antônio Dantas de. 1998. *Jeremoabo: Breve resumo da história de uma terra e do seu povo*. Jeremoabo, Bahia.

Amado, Janaína. 1978. *Conflito social no Brasil: A revolta dos "Mucker."* São Paulo: Duas Cidades.

Andrade, Manoel Correia de. 1980. *The Land and People of Northeast Brazil*. Albuquerque: University of New Mexico Press.

Antônio, Jorge. 1998. "Uma economia de resultados." *Via Bahia* 11, no. 5: 14.

Appadurai, Arjun. 1990. "Disjuncture and Difference in the Global Economy." *Public Culture* 2, no. 2:1–24.

———. 1995. *Modernity at Large*. Minneapolis: University of Minnesota Press.

Arruda, João. 1993. *Canudos: Messianismo e conflito social*. Forteleza: Editições UFC/ SECULT.

Azevedo, Thales de. 1981. *A religião civil Brasileira: Um instrumento político*. Petrópolis, Brazil: Editora Vozes.

Azzi, Riolando. 1976a. "Elementos para a história do catolicismo popular." *Revista Eclestiástica Brasileira* 36, no. 141: 95–130.

———. 1976b. "Ermitães e irmãos uma forma de vida religiosa no Brasil antigo." *Convergência* 9, no. 94: 370–83.

———. 1977. *O episcopado do Brasil frente ao catolicismo popular*. Petrópolis, Brazil: Editora Vozes.

———. 1978. *O católicismo popular no Brazil: Aspectos históricos*. Petrópolis, Brazil: Editora Vozes.

Baretto, Margarita. 2000. *Turismo e legado cultural*. Campinas, Brazil: Papirus.

Barman, Roderick. 1977. "The Brazilian Peasantry Reexamined: The Implications of the Quebra-Quilo Revolt, 1874–1875." *Hispanic American Historical Review* 57, no. 3: 401–24.

Barreto, Padre Murilo de Sá. 1998. *Testemunho, serviço e fidelidade*. Juazeiro do Norte: Paróquia de Nossa Senhora das Dores.

Barros, Luitgarde Oliveira Cavalcanti. 1997. "Do Ceará, três santos do nordeste." *Revista Canudos* 1, no. 1: 37–53.

Bastide, Roger. 1978. *The African Religions in Brazil*. Baltimore, Md.: Johns Hopkins University Press.

Bastos, José Augusto Cabral Barreto. 1995. *Incompreensível e bárbaro inimigo: A guerra simbólica contra Canudos*. Salvador: EDUFBA.

Berger, Peter. 1967. *The Sacred Canopy*. New York: Doubleday.

Birman, Patrícia, and Márcia Pereira Leite. 2000. "Whatever Happened to What Used to Be the Largest Catholic Church in the World?" *Daedulus* 129, no. 2: 271–90.

Blake, Stanley. 2001. "The Invention of the Nordestino: Race, Region and Identity in Northeastern Brazil, 1889–1945." Ph.D. diss., State University of New York, Stony Brook.

Boaventura, Edivaldo. 1997. *O parque estadual de Canudos*. Salvador: Secretária de Cultura e Turismo.

Borges, Dane. 1999. "A Mirror of Progress." In *The Brazil Reader: History, Culture, Politics*, edited by Robert Levine, 93–99. Durham, N.C.: Duke University Press.

———. 2001. "Healing and Mischief: Witchcraft in Brazilian Law and Literature, 1890–1920." In *Crime and Punishment in Latin America*, edited by Ricardo Salvatore, Carlos Aguirre, and Gilbert Joseph, 180–210. Durham, N.C.: Duke University Press.

Bourdieu, Pierre. 1977. *Outline of a Theory of Practice*. Cambridge: Cambridge University Press.

———. 1986. "The Forms of Capital." In *Handbook of Theory and Research for the Sociology of Education*, edited by John G. Richardson, 241–58. New York: Greenwood.

Brown, Diana DeG. 1994. *Umbanda: Religion and Politics in Urban Brazil*. New York: Columbia University Press.

Brown, Michael. 1996. "On Resisting Resistance." *American Anthropologist* 98, no. 4: 729–35.

Bruneau, Thomas C. 1974. *The Political Transformation of the Brazilian Church*. New York: Cambridge University Press.

———. 1982. *The Church in Brazil: The Politics of Religion*. Austin: University of Texas Press.

Burdick, John. 1993. *Looking for God in Brazil*. Berkeley: University of California Press.

Camargo, Candido Procopio Ferreira de. 1961. *Kardecismo e Umbanda*. São Paulo: Livraria Pioneira Editora.

Carneiro, Edison. 1961. *Candomblés da Bahia*. Rio de Janeiro: Editora Conquista.

Carvalho, José Murilo de. 2000. "Dreams Do Come Untrue." *Daedulus* 129, no. 2: 82.

Castile, George Pierre. 1996. "The Commodification of Indian Identity." *American Eth-nologist* 98, no. 4: 743–49.

Castro, Eduardo B. Viveiros de. 1986. "Escatologia pessoal e poder entre os Arawete." *Religião e sociedade* 13, no. 3: 2–26.

Cehelsky, Marta. 1979. *Land Reform in Brazil: The Management of Change.* Boulder, Colo.: Westview Press.

Chandler, Billy Jaynes. 1972. *The Feitosas and the Sertão dos Inhamuns.* Gainesville: University of Florida Press.

———. 1978. *The Bandit King: Lampião of Brazil.* College Station: Texas A&M University Press.

Chilcote, Ronald. 1990. *Power and the Ruling Classes in Northeast Brazil: Juazeiro and Petrolina in Transition.* Cambridge: Cambridge University Press.

———, ed. 1972. *Protest and Resistance in Angola and Brazil.* Berkeley: University of California Press.

Chuva, Márcia. 1995. *A invenção patrímonio.* Rio de Janeiro: IPHAN.

Clastres, Helene. 1978. *Terra sem mal: O profestismo Tupi-guarani.* São Paulo: Editora Brasiliense.

Cohen, Thomas M. 1991. "Millenarian Themes in the Writing of Antônio Vieira." *Luso-Brazilian Review* 28, no. 1: 23–46.

———. 1998. *Fire of Tongues: Antônio Vieira and the Missionary Church in Brazil and Portugal.* Stanford: Stanford University Press.

Cohn, Norman. 1961. *The Pursuit of the Millennium.* New York: Oxford University Press.

Corrigan, Philip, Harvie Ramsay, and Derek Sayer. 1980. "The State as a Relation of Production." In *Capitalism, State Formation, and Marxist Theory,* edited by Philip Corrigan, 1–26. London: Quartet Books.

Costa, Emilia Viotti da. 1985. *The Brazilian Empire: Myths and Histories.* Chicago: Dorsey Press.

———. 1994. *Cross of Glory, Tears of Blood: The Demerara Slave Rebellion of 1822.* New York: Oxford University Press.

Couto, Manoel José Gonçalves. 1873. *Missão abreviada para despertar os descuidados, converter os peccadores e sustentar o fructo das missões.* Porto, Portugal: Sebastião José Pereira.

da Cunha, Euclides. 1944. *Rebellion in the Backlands.* Chicago: University of Chicago Press.

de Certeau, Michel. 1988. *The Writing of History.* New York: Columbia University Press.

———. 2000. *The Certeau Reader.* Edited by Graham Ward. Oxford: Blackwell Publishers.

De Groot, C. G. 1996. *Brazilian Catholicism and the Ultramontane Reform, 1850–1930.* Amsterdam: Centre for Latin American Research and Documentation.

Della Cava, Ralph. 1968. "Brazilian Millenarianism and National Institutions: A Reappraisal of Canudos and Juazeiro." *Hispanic American Historical Review* 48, no. 3: 402–20.

———. 1970. *Miracle at Juazeiro.* New York: Columbia University Press.

Delooz, Pierre. 1983. "Toward a Sociological Study of Canonized Sainthood in the

Catholic Church." In *Saints and Their Cults: Studies in Religious Sociology, Folklore, and History*, edited by Stephen Wilson, 189–216. Cambridge: Cambridge University Press.

Diacon, Todd A. 1991. *Millenarian Vision, Capitalist Reality: Brazil's Contestado Rebellion, 1912–1916*. Durham, N.C.: Duke University Press.

Diaz, Clímaco. 1997. "Canudos: poesia e mistério de Machado de Assis." *Revista Canudos* 1, no. 1: 91–103.

Duarte, Raymundo. 1963. "Um movimento messianico no interior da Bahia." *Revista de Antropologia* 1, no 1: 45–51.

Dumont, Luis. 1970. *Homo Hierarchicus*. Chicago: University of Chicago Press.

Estrela, Raimundo. 1997. *Pau-de-Colher: Um pequeno Canudos*. Salvador, Bahia: Assembleia Legislativa do Estado da Bahia.

Facó, Rui. 1963. *Cangaceiros e fanáticos*. Rio de Janeiro: Civilização Brasileira.

Fausto, Boris, ed. 1977. *História geral da civilização brasileira*. Volume 3. São Paulo: DIFEL.

Fernandes, Aníbal. 1938. *O Folclore Mágico do Nordeste*. Rio de Janeiro: Civilização Brasileira Editora.

Fialho, Nadia Hage. 1997. "Prefácio." *Revista Canudos* 1, no. 1: 2.

Fogelson, Raymond, and Richard Adams, eds. 1977. *The Anthropology of Power*. New York: Academic Press.

Forman, Shepard. 1975. *The Brazilian Peasantry*. New York: Columbia University Press.

Foucault, Michel. 1990. *The History of Sexuality*. Volume 1. New York: Vintage Books.

Freston, Paul. 1994. *Nem anjos nem demônios: Interpretações sociológicas do pentecostalismo*. Petrópolis, Brazil: Editora Vozes.

Freyre, Gilberto. 1946. *The Masters and Slaves*. New York: Knopf.

Fukui, Lia Freitas Garcia. 1979. *Sertão e bairro rural: Parentesco e família entre sitantes tradicionais*. São Paulo: Editora Ática.

Galjart, Benno. 1968. *Itaguái: Old Habits and New Techniques in a Brazilian Land Settlement*. Wageningen, Netherlands: Center for Agricultural Publishing and Documentation.

Galvão, Eduardo. 1957. *Santos e Visagens*. Rio de Janeiro: Companhia Editora Nacional Rio de Janeiro.

Geertz, Clifford. 1957. "Ritual and Social Change: A Javanese Example." *American Anthropologist* 59: 32–54.

———. 1963. *Agricultural Involution*. Berkeley: University of California Press.

Gewertz, Deborah, and Frederick Errington. 1991. *Twisted Histories, Altered Contexts: Representing the Chambri in a World System*. New York: Cambridge University Press.

Gonzalez, Olegário Miguez. 1996. *Pedro Batista: Lider messianico de Santa Brígida*. Salvador, Bahia: Empresa Gráfica Bahia.

Gramsci, Antonio. 1971. *Selections from the Prison Notebooks of Antonio Gramsci*. Edited by Quintin Hoare and Geoffrey Nowell Smith. New York: International Publishers.

Greenfield, Gerald M. 1999. "Drought and the Image of the Northeast." In *The Brazil Reader: History, Culture, Politics*, edited by Robert Levine, 100–103. Durham, N.C.: Duke University Press.

Guha, Ranajit. 1983. *Elementary Aspects of Peasant Insurgency in Colonial India*. Delhi: Oxford University Press.

Gutmann, Matthew. 1993. "Rituals of Resistance: A Critique of the Theory of Everyday Forms of Resistance." *Latin American Perspectives* 2, no. 2: 74–92.

Hall, Anthony. 1978. *Drought and Irrigation in Northeast Brazil*. New York: Cambridge University Press.

Hall, Stuart. 1981. "Notes on Deconstructing the 'Popular.' " In *People's History and Socialist Theory*, edited by Raphael Samuel, 227–40. London: Routledge and Kegan Paul.

Handler, Richard. 1988. *Nationalism and the Politics of Culture in Quebec*. Madison: University of Wisconsin Press.

Haring, Charles. 1958. *Empire in Brazil*. Cambridge, Mass.: Harvard University Press.

Harris, Marvin. 1966. *Town and Country in Brazil*. New York: Norton Press.

Hirshman, Albert O. 1965. *Journeys Toward Progress*. New York: Doubleday.

Hobsbawm, Eric. 1959. *Primitive Rebels*. Manchester: University of Manchester Press.

Holmes, Derek. 1978. *The Triumph of the Holy See*. London: Burns and Oates.

Holston, James. 1989. *Modernist City: An Anthropological Critique of Brasilia*. Chicago: University of Chicago Press.

———. 1999. "Alternative Modernities: Statecraft and Religious Imagination in the Valley of the Dawn." *American Ethnologist* 26, no. 3: 605–31.

Hoornaert, Eduardo. 1973. *Verdadeira e falsa religião no nordeste*. Salvador: Editora Beneditina.

———. 1974. *Formação do catolicismo Brasiliero, 1550–1800*. Petrópolis, Brazil: Editora Vozes.

———. 1977. *História da igreja no Brasil*. Petrópolis, Brazil: Editora Vozes.

———. 1981. *Crônica das casas de caridade: Fundadas pelo Padre Ibiapina*. São Paulo: Edições Loyola.

———. 1997. *Os anjos de Canudos: Uma revisão histórica*. Petrópolis, Brazil: Editora Vozes.

Ianni, Octávio. 1992. *A idéia Brasil moderno*. São Paulo: Editora Brasilense.

IBRA. 1967. *Estrutura agrária brasileira*. Rio de Janeiro: Instituto Brasileiro de Reforma Agrária.

Ireland, Rowan. 1992. *Kingdoms Come: Religion and Politics in Brazil*. Pittsburgh, Penn.: Pittsburgh University Press.

Johnson, Allen. 1971. *Sharecroppers of the Sertão*. Stanford, Calif.: Stanford University Press.

Joseph, Gilbert M., and Daniel Nugent. 1994. "Popular Culture and State Formation in Revolutionary Mexico." In *Everyday Forms of State Formation: Revolution and the Negotiation of Rule in Modern Mexico*, edited by Gilbert M. Joseph and Daniel Nugent, 3–23. Durham, N.C.: Duke University Press.

Landes, Ruth. 1947. *City of Women*. New York: MacMillan.

Lanternari, Vittorio. 1963. *The Religions of the Oppressed: A Study of Modern Messianic Cults*. New York: Alfred A. Knopf.

Leal, Victor Nunes. 1949. *Coronelismo, enxada, e voto: O município e regime representativo no Brasil*. Rio de Janeiro: Livraria Forense.

Leers, Bernardino. 1977. *Catolicismo popular e mundo rural: Um ensaio pastoral.* Petrópolis, Brazil: Editora Vozes.

Levine, Robert. 1992. *Vale of Tears: Revisiting the Canudos Massacre in Northeastern Brazil, 1893– 1897.* Berkeley: University of California Press.

———, ed. 1999. *The Brazil Reader: History, Culture, Politics.* Durham, N.C.: Duke University Press.

Lévi-Strauss, Claude. 1967. *Structural Anthropology.* New York: Doubleday.

Lewin, Linda. 1987. *Politics and Parentela in Paraíba.* Princeton, N.J.: Princeton University Press.

Lima, Amazonas Alves. 1968. "Características psicológicas de uma comunidade rural baiana." Projecto Santa Brígida, University of São Paulo.

Lima, João. 1953. *Vida de uma dama brasileira.* Rio de Janeiro: Companhia Brasileira de Artes Gráficas.

Mainwaring, Scott. 1986. *The Catholic Church and Politics in Brazil, 1916–1985.* Stanford, Calif.: Stanford University Press.

Margolies, Louise. 1988. "The Canonization of a Venezuelan Folk Saint: The Case of José Gregorio Hernández." *Journal of Latin American Lore* 14, no. 1: 93–110.

Marques, Daniel Walker Almeida, and J. C. Bruno. 1988. *O pensamento vivo de Padre Cícero.* São Paulo: Martin Claret Editores.

Marx, Karl. 1973. *Grundrisse.* New York: Random House/Vintage.

Matta, Roberto da. 1991. *Carnivals, Rogues, and Heroes: An Interpretation of the Brazilian Dilemma.* Notre Dame, Ind.: University of Notre Dame Press.

Meznar, Joan Elen. 1986. "Deference and Dependence: The World of Small Farmers in a Northeastern Brazilian Community, 1850–1900." Ph.D. diss., University of Texas, Austin.

Miceli, Sérgio. 1984. *Estado e cultura no Brasil.* São Paulo: DIFEL.

Moniz, Edmundo. 1978. *A guerra social de Canudos.* Rio de Janeiro: Civilização Brasileira.

Monteiro, Duglas Teixeira. 1974. *Os errantes do novo século: Um estudo sobre o surto milenarista do Contestado.* São Paulo: Livraria Duas Cidades.

———. 1977. "Um confronto entre Juazeiro, Canudos, e Contestado," In *História geral da civilização brasileira,* volume 3, edited by Boris Fausto, 38–92. São Paulo: DIFEL.

Monteiro, Hamilton de Mattos. 1980. *Crise agrária e luta de classes: O Nordeste brasileiro entre 1850 e 1889.* Brasília: Editora Horizonte.

Montenegro, Abelardo. 1954. *Antônio Conselheiro.* Fortaleza, Brazil: A. Batista Fontenele.

———. 1973. *Fanáticos e cangaçeiros.* Fortaleza, Brazil: Editôra Henriqueta Galeano.

Mott, Luís. 1992. *Rosa Egipcíaca: Uma santa africana no Brasil.* Rio de Janeiro: Bertrand.

Moura, Abdalaziz de. 1978. *Frei Damião e os impasses da religião popular.* Petrópolis, Brazil: Editora Vozes.

Moura, Clóvis. 2000. *Sociologia política da guerra camponesa de Canudos.* São Paulo: Editora Expressão Popular.

Myscofski, Carole A. 1988. *When Men Walk Dry: Portuguese Messianism in Brazil.* Atlanta, Ga.: Scholars Press.

———. 1991. "Messianic Themes in Portuguese and Brazilian Literature in the Sixteenth and Seventh Centuries." *Luso-Brazilian Review* 28, no. 1: 77–94.

Neto, José Oliveira. N.d. *O fim do mundo em 1999*. Fortaleza, Brazil: Universidade Federal de Pernambuco.

Nogueira, Ataliba. 1978. *Antônio Conselheiro e Canudos*. São Paulo: Editora Nacional.

Nugent, Daniel, and Ana María Alonso. 1994. "Multiple Selective Traditions in Agrarian Reform and Agrarian Struggle." In *Everyday Forms of State Formation*, edited by Gilbert M. Joseph and Daniel Nugent, 209–46. Durham, N.C.: Duke University Press.

O'Brien, Jay, and William Roseberry, eds. 1991. *Golden Ages, Dark Ages*. Berkeley: University of California Press.

Oliveira, João. N.d. "Vida e morte do meu padrinho." Santa Brígida, Bahia: Mayor's Office.

Oliveira, Pedro A. Ribeiro de. 1985. *Religião e dominação de classe: gênese, estrutura e funcão do catolicismo romanizado no Brasil*. Petrópolis, Brazil: Editora Vozes.

———. 1997. "Adeus á sociologia da religião popular." *Religião e Sociedade* 18, no. 2: 43–61.

Oliven, Ruben George. 2000. " 'The Largest Popular Culture Movement in the Western World': Intellectuals and Gaúcho Traditionalism in Brazil." *American Ethnologist* 27, no. 2: 128–46.

Olwig, Karen Fog. 1999. "The Burden of Heritage: Claiming a Place for a West Indian Culture." *American Ethnologist* 26, no. 2: 370–88.

Otten, Alexandre. 1990. *Só Deus é grande*. São Paulo: Loyola.

———. 1994. "Apocalíptica popular: Uma dimensão da visão escatológica de Antônio Conselheiro." *Religião e Sociedade* 16, no. 3: 64–79.

Palacin, Padre Luíz Gomes, S. J. 1987. *História da diocese de Paulo Afonso*. Diocese de Paulo Afonso, Paulo Afonso, Bahia.

Pang, Eul-Soo. 1981–1982. "Banditry and Messianism in Brazil, 1870–1940." *Proceedings of the Pacific Coast Council on Latin American Studies* 8: 1–23.

Paz, Renata Marinho. 1998. *As beatas do Padre Cícero: Participação feminina leiga no movimento sócio-religioso de Juazeiro do Norte*. Juazeiro do Norte: Edições IPESC-URCA.

Peckham, Howard, and Charles Gibson, eds. 1969. *Attitudes of Colonial Power Toward the American Indian*. Salt Lake City: University of Utah Press.

Pessar, Patricia R. 1976. "When Prophecy Prevails: The Pedro Batista Movement." Ph.D. diss., University of Chicago.

———. 1981. "Unmasking the Politics of Religion: The Case of Brazilian Millenarianism." *Journal of Latin American Lore* 7, no. 2: 255–78.

———. 1982. "Millenarian Movements in Rural Brazil: Prophecy and Protest." *Religion* 12: 187–213.

———. 1991. "Three Moments in Brazilian Millenarianism: The Interrelationship Between Politics and Religion." *Luso-Brazilian Review* 28, no. 1: 95–116.

Pinho, Patricia de Santana. 1997. "Revisando Canudos hoje no imaginário popular." *Revista Canudos* 1, no. 1: 173–203.

Puma, Joseph. 2003. "The Making of Madre Paulina: Discursive and Visual Representations of Brazil's First Roman Catholic Saint." Unpublished manuscript.

Putnam, Samuel 1944. Translator's Introduction to Euclides da Cunha, *Rebellion in the
Backlands*, iii–xviii. Chicago: University of Chicago Press.

Queiroz, Maria Isaura Pereira de. 1958. *Sociologia e folclore: A danca de São Gonçalo num po-
voado baiano*. Salvador, Bahia: Livraria Progresso Editora.

———. 1965a. "Messiahs in Brazil." *Past and Present* 31: 62–86.

———. 1965b. *O messianismo no Brasil e no mundo*. São Paulo: Dominus.

———. 1973. *O campesinato brasileiro*. Petrópolis, Brazil: Editora Vozes.

———. 1992. *Os cangaceiros: La epopeya bandolera del nordeste de brasil*. Bogotá, Colombia:
El Áncora Editores.

Queiroz, Maurício Vinhas de. 1966. *Messianismo e conflito social*. Rio de Janeiro: Editora
Civilização Brasileira.

Ribeiro, René. 1970. "Brazilian Messianic Movements." In *Millennial Dreams in Action*,
edited by Sylvia Thrupp, 55–69. The Hague: Mouton.

Richardson, John G., ed. 1986. *Handbook of Theory and Research for the Sociology of Education*.
New York: Greenwood.

Riedl, Titus. N.d. "Viva a Boa Morte: a precária sobrevivência de uma comunidade religiosa no sertão nordestino." Unpublished manuscript.

Rodrigues, Raimundo Nina. 1897. "A loucura epidemica de Canudos:" *Revista Brasileira*
2: 129–218.

Roseberry, William. 1989. *Anthropologies and Histories: Essays in Culture, History, and Political
Economy*. New Brunswick: Rutgers University Press.

———. 1994. "Hegemony and the Language of Contention." In *Everyday Forms of State
Formation: Revolution and the Negotiation of Rule in Modern Mexico*, edited by Gilbert M.
Joseph and Daniel Nugent, 355–66. Durham, N.C.: Duke University Press.

Roseberry, William, and Jay O'Brien. 1991. Introduction to *Golden Ages, Dark Ages: Imagining the Past in Anthropology and History*, edited by Jay O' Brien and William Roseberry,
1–18. Berkeley: University of California Press.

Rowe, William, and Vivian Schelling. 1991. *Memory and Modernity: Popular Culture in Latin
America*. New York: Verso.

Rubin, Jeffrey. 1996. "The Ambiguity of Resistance." *Studies in Law, Politics, and Society* 5:
237–60.

Salvatore, Ricardo, Carlos Aguirre, and Gilbert Joseph, eds. 2001. *Crime and Punishment
in Latin America*. Durham, N.C.: Duke University Press.

Samuel, Raphael, ed. 1981. *People's History and Socialist Theory*. London: Routledge and
Kegan Paul.

Sayer, Derek. 1994. "Everyday Forms of State Formation: Some Dissident Remarks on
'Hegemony.' " In *Everyday Forms of State Formation: Revolution and the Negotiation of Rule
in Modern Mexico*, edited by Gilbert M. Joseph and Daniel Nugent, 367–77. Durham,
N.C.: Duke University Press.

Scheper-Hughes, Nancy. 1992. *Death without Weeping: The Violence of Everyday Life in Brazil.* Berkeley: University of California Press.

Schultz, Kristin. 2001. *Tropical Versailles.* New York: Routledge.

Scott, James C. 1976. *The Moral Economy of the Peasant: Rebellion and Subsistence in Southeast Asia.* New Haven, Conn.: Yale University Press.

———. 1990. *Domination and the Arts of Resistance: Hidden Transcripts.* New Haven, Conn.: Yale University Press.

Siegel, Bernard. 1977. "The Contestado Rebellion, 1912–1916." In *The Anthropology of Power,* edited by Raymond Fogelson and Richard Adams, 325–36. New York: Academic Press.

Silva, A. 1982. *Cartas de Padre Cícero.* Salvador, Bahia: Escola Profissionais Salesianas.

Silva, Candido da Costa e. 1982. *Roteiro de vida e de morte: Um estudo do catolicismo no sertão da Bahia.* São Paulo: Editora Atica.

Silva, Fernando Altenfelder. 1962. "As lamentacações e os grupos de flagelados de São Francisco." *Sociologia* 24, no. 1:15–28.

Slater, Candace. 1982. *Stories on a String.* Berkeley: University of California Press.

———. 1986. *Trails of Miracles: Stories from a Pilgrimage in Northeast Brazil.* Berkeley: University of California Press.

Smith, Gavin. 1991. "The Production of Culture in Local Rebellion." In *Golden Ages, Dark Ages,* edited by Jay O'Brien and William Roseberry, 180–207. Berkeley: University of California Press.

Souto Maior, Mário. 1998. *Frei Damião: Um santo?* Recife, Brazil: Editora Massangana.

Souza, Amaury de. 1972. "The Cangaço and the Politics of Violence in Northeast Brazil." In *Protest and Resistance in Angola and Brazil,* edited by Richard Chilcote, 109–32. Berkeley: University of California Press.

Souza, Laura de Mello e. 1986. *O diabo e a terra de santa cruz: Feiticeria e religiosidade popular no Brasil colonial.* São Paulo: Companhia das Letras.

Steil, Carlos Alberto. 1996. *O sertão das romarias: Um estudo antropológico sobre o santúario de Bom Jesus da Lapa, Bahia.* Petrópolis, Brazil: Editora Vozes.

Süss, Gunter Paulo. 1979. *Catolicismo popular no brasil.* Rio de Janeiro: Zahar.

Taussig, Michael. 1987. *Shamanism, Colonialism, and the Wild Man: A Study in Terror and Healing.* Chicago: University of Chicago Press.

Thompson, E. P. 1971. "The Moral Economy of the English Crowd in the Eighteenth Century." *Past and Present* 50: 76–136.

Thornton, Mary Crescentia. 1948. *The Church and Freemasonry in Brazil, 1872–1875.* Washington: Catholic University of America Press.

Thrupp, Sylvia, ed. 1970. *Millennial Dreams in Action.* The Hague: Mouton.

Torres, Quiteria. 1990. "Religiosas de Água Branca." Unpublished manuscript.

Trouillot, Michel-Rolph. 1995. *Silencing the Past: The Production of History.* Boston: Beacon Press.

Turner, Victor W. 1957. *Schism and Continuity in an African Society.* Manchester, England: Manchester University Press.

———.1968. *The Drums of Affliction*. Oxford: Clarendon Press.

———. 1969. *The Ritual Process*. Chicago: Aldine Publisher.

Vanderwood, Paul. 1998. *The Power of God against the Guns of Government: Religious Upheaval in Mexico in the Turn of the 19th Century*. Stanford, Calif.: Stanford University Press.

Van Young, Eric. 1999. "The New Cultural History Comes to Old Mexico." *Hispanic American Historical Review* 79, no. 2: 211–47.

Vargas Llosa, Mario. 1984. *The War of the End of the World*. New York: Farrar Straus Giroux.

Venceu, Marcos Guedes. 1986. "A cruz e o barrette: Tempo e história no conflito de Canudos." *Religião e Sociedade* 13, no. 2: 38–56.

Villa, Marco Antônio. 1997. *Canudos: O povo da terra*. São Paulo: Editora Ática.

———. 2000. *Vida e morte no sertão: História das secas no Nordeste nos séculos XIX e XX*. São Paulo: Editora Ática.

Wallace, Anthony. 1956. "Revitalization Movements." *American Anthropologist* 58: 264–81.

Weber, Max. 1947. *Theory of Social and Economic Organization*. New York: Free Press.

———. 1963. *The Sociology of Religion*. Boston: Beacon Press.

Wells, Allen, and Gilbert M. Joseph. 1996. *Summer of Discontent, Seasons of Upheaval: Elite Politics and Rural Insurgency in Yucatan, 1876–1915*. Stanford, Calif.: Stanford University Press.

Willems, Emilio. 1961. *Uma vila brasileira*. São Paulo: Difusão Europeia do Livro.

Williams, Raymond. 1977. *Marxism and Literature*. Oxford: Oxford University Press.

Woodward, Kenneth. 1996. *Making Saints: How the Catholic Church Determines Who Becomes a Saint, Who Doesn't, and Why*. New York: Simon and Schuster.

Zaluar, Alba. 1973. "Sobre a lógica do catolicismo popular." *Dados* 11: 173–93.

———. 1983. *Os homens de Deus: Um estudo dos santos e das festas no catolicismo popular*. Rio de Janeiro: Zahar Editores.

INDEX

the academy: cultural rescue and, 188–91; language of social memory and resistance, 197–99; on millenarian religious beliefs, 6; resistance understood by, 229; tourism, 197–98

Afro-Brazilian religion, 39, 56, 140, 145, 182, 244 n.17

agriculture: batalhão (unpaid labor exchange), 120; coronelismo, 26–27; drought, 3, 26, 29–30, 121–22, 202, 240 n.18; Land Law (1850), 24; land redistribution and, 118–21; markets for, 121; slavery, 24; traditional romeiros and, 154. *See also* colônia; labor force; Sá, João (coronel)

Água Branca, 62–63, 65, 79, 80, 81–82, 113

Alves, João Oliveira Manuel, 147, 172–75

Alves, Mariano, 52, 118, 122, 124

apocalypse: Batista's message of, 2, 41–42, 101–2; Antônio Conselheiro and, 30, 31; Day of Judgment, 2, 31, 57, 101–2; Ralph Della Cava, 241 n.23; narratives of, 29–31; natural disasters and, 29–30; rituals, 108–12

Araújo, Maria, 78

Assis, Machado de, 48

Azzi, Riolando, 18, 19, 20

backlanders: bandits and, 71–72; charity distribution and, 21–22, 27; Church reforms and, 20–21; cordel stories, 44–45, 48, 242 n.4; coronelismo and, 26–27; fanaticism of, 33–34; folk healing and, 22–23; hard labor as virtue, 116–17; José Antônio Maria de Ibiapina and, 21–23, 115, 239 n.14, 240 n.15; patronage and, 4, 25, 88–89; "resentment" principle and, 31–32; on salvation, 27–28; santos and, 45–47

Bahia, state of, 3, 69; Bahia singulareplural, 191–92; Canudos movement, 7, 32–34, 73, 146, 194, 227, 230, 235 n.1; celebration of difference in, 199–201; documentaries of, 192–93; folklore and, 197–98, 221–23; ministry of culture and tourism, 196–97; pilgrimage sites of, 21; João Sá and, 70–71; Social Democratic Party (PSD), 71, 75, 137. *See also* backlanders; Brazilian government; cultural rescue; Farias, Antônio; Santa Brígida

Bahia singulareplural, 191–92

banditry, 71–72, 101, 117, 138

Barbosa, Ricardo, 176, 177

Barros, Luitgarde Oliveira Cavalcanti, 45, 46

Caetano, Inácio, 179

Canudos movement, 7, 32–34, 73, 146, 194, 227, 230, 235 n.1

casas de caridade, 21–22, 107, 239 n.14

Castelo Branco, Humberto, 130, 131, 248 n.14

Catholic Church: authority of local religious leaders, 214; Brazilian Catholic Church and, 5, 18–23, 236 n.4, 239 nn.7–10, 239 nn.12–13; charismatic healers and, 22–23, 213, 240 n.17; charitable donations for, 21, 27, 239 n.13; ecclesiastical teachings of, 16–17; excommunication of pilgrims to Juazeiro, 78; on fanaticism, 78–79, 112–14; folk Catholicism, 10, 237 n.9; Padre Cícero, sanctions against, 78; hegemonic rule, 17, 238 nn.3–4; Igreja Católica Apostólica Brasileira (Brazilian Apostolic Catholic Church), 242 n.6; irmandades, 19–20, 239 n.10; Jesuits, 16, 238 nn.2–3, 239 n.11; liberation theology and, 162, 213, 230, 240 n.17; on masonry, 18, 19, 239 nn.8–9; política and, 47, 243 n.9; positivism and, 241 n.22; Protestantism and, 10, 18, 213; Religious Question (1872), 19; sacraments of, 20, 114, 115; sainthood in, 45–46, 242 n.6; salvation, 16–17, 30–31; São Pedro Church controlled by, 214; on spiritism, 18, 23, 213–14; tourism, religious, 219–20; ultramontanism in, 5, 18–23, 236 n.4, 239 n.8, 239 n.10, 239 nn.12–13; unorthodoxy negotiated in, 212–13, 250 n.7. *See also* folk Catholicism; millenarianism; resistance

Chandler, Billy Jaynes, 72

charisma, 10, 37–38, 45–47, 48, 64, 171, 232; Pedro Batista and, 11, 57, 64, 104, 134–35, 140, 151; charismatic Catholicism, 213; charismatic leadership, 10,

49, 52, 149, 220, 228; Antônio Conselheiro and, 49, 52; Dona Dodô and, 149, 151–52; gender and, 149–52; José Antônio Maria de Ibiapina and, 22–23; Velho and, 169

charity: casas de caridade (charity houses), 21–22, 107, 239 n.14; esmolas (distribution of), 52–54, 115–16; José Antônio Maria de Ibiapina and, 21–23, 107, 115, 239 n.14; as imitation of God, 54; pardon from sin and, 51–52, 243 n.14; parishes and, 27, 239 n.13; refusal to give, 51–52, 243 n.15

Chuva, Márcia, 250 n.2

Cícero (padre): Batista as incarnation of, 50–51, 64, 79, 84, 245 n.9; beatas of, 78, 79; charity of, 53; Church sanctions against, 78; death of, 79; Dona Dodô and, 82; fanaticism of, 78–79; kinship of, 195; living museum (*museu-vivo*), 219–20; negotiation, 230–31; patronage of, 53; religião and, 47, 105, 242 n.6, 243 nn.9–10, 243 n.11. *See also* Juazeiro

Collective Pastoral Letter (1915), 23, 27

colônia (agricultural cooperative): Pedro Batista and, 123–29; *A Corner of Hope* (Santana), 131–32; fees in, 127; land distribution in, 126–27, 247 n.13; José Dortas Montargil, 125–26, 129; Geraldo Portela and, 123, 128–29, 131; public works in, 127; traditional romeiros and, 154. *See also* labor force; Sá, João (coronel)

colonialism, Portuguese: ecclesiastical teachings, 17, 238 n.4; folk Catholicism, 10, 237 n.9; hegemonic authority, 17, 238 nn.3–4; Jesuits, 16, 238 nn.2–3; millenarianism and, 8, 16–17, 31–33, 226, 237 n.1, 238 n.3

Conselheiro, Antônio: the academy on, 193–94; on the apocalypse, 30, 31;

Patricia R. Pessar is an associate professor of American Studies; Anthropology; African American Studies; and Ethnicity, Race, and Migration; and is the director of the Global Migration Project at Yale University. She is the author of *A Visa for a Dream: Dominicans in the United States* (1995) and *Between Two Islands: Dominican International Migration* (1991, with Sherri Grasmuck). She is editor of *Caribbean Circuits: New Directions in the Study of Caribbean Migration* (1997) and *When Borders Don't Divide: Labor Migration and Refugee Movements in the Americas* (1988).

Library of Congress Cataloging-in-Publication Data
Pessar, Patricia R.
From fanatics to folk : Brazilian millenarianism and popular
culture / by Patricia R. Pessar.
p. cm.
Includes bibliographical references.
ISBN 0-8223-3275-2 (cloth : alk. paper)
ISBN 0-8223-3264-7 (pbk. : alk. paper)
1. Millennialism—Brazil—History—19th century.   2. Brazil—
History—19th century.   3. Millennialism—Brazil—History—
20th century.   4. Brazil—History—20th century.   I. Title.
BR675.P47   2004
209'.0981—dc22   2003015047